57

January
2009

ECONOMIC POLICY

SENIOR EDITORS
GEORGES DE MÉNIL
RICHARD PORTES
HANS-WERNER SINN

MANAGING EDITORS
GIUSEPPE BERTOLA
TULLIO JAPPELLI
PHILIPPE MARTIN
JAN VAN OURS

Published in association with the European Economic Association

Blackwell Publishing Ltd for Centre for Economic Policy Research,
Center for Economic Studies of the University of Munich, and
Paris School of Economics, in collaboration with the Maison des
Sciences Economiques.

STATEMENT OF PURPOSE

Economic Policy provides timely and authoritative analyses of the choices which confront policy-makers. The subject matter ranges from the study of how individual markets can and should work to the broadest interactions in the world economy.

Economic Policy is a joint activity of the Centre for Economic Policy Research (CEPR), the Center for Economic Studies (CES) and the Paris School of Economics (PSE). The Paris School of Economics replaces the research center, Paris-Jourdan Sciences Economiques, which is now part of the larger school. *Economic Policy* offers an independent, non-partisan, European perspective on issues of worldwide concern. It emphasizes problems of international significance, either because they affect the world economy directly or because the experience of one country contains important lessons for policy-makers elsewhere.

All the articles are specifically commissioned from leading professional economists. Their brief is to demonstrate how live policy issues can be illuminated by the insights of modern economics and by the most recent evidence. The presentation is incisive and written in plain language accessible to the wide audience which participates in the policy debate.

Prior to publication, the contents of each volume are discussed by a Panel of distinguished economists from Europe and elsewhere. The Panel rotates annually. Inclusion in each volume of a summary of the highlights of the Economic Policy Panel discussion provides the reader with alternative interpretations of the evidence and a sense of the liveliness of the current debate.

Economic Policy is owned by the Maison des Sciences Economiques, CEPR and CES. The 47th panel meeting was held in Ljubljana with support from the Bank of Slovenia. We gratefully acknowledge this support, without implicating any of these organizations in the views expressed here, which are the sole responsibility of the authors.

PANEL

57

January 2009

CONTENTS

CONTENTS

Editors' introduction

Earlier drafts of papers in this issue of *Economic Policy* were presented and discussed at the April 2008 Panel Meeting, hosted in Ljubljana by the Bank of Slovenia. In this editorial introduction, we summarize them focusing on their contribution to policy debates.

Everybody agrees that easing trade across national borders is the essential feature of Europe's Economic and Monetary Union (EMU). A vast amount of controversial research deals with assessing the more or less obvious consequences of this fact: easier trade may make macroeconomic policy coordination more important, or may decouple cyclical booms and busts across the participating countries; it may foster convergence, or increase inequality. And nearly as much work and controversy has focused on the apparently simpler quantitative issues of the extent to which EMU has in fact made trade easier, and of the impact of easier trade on the economy's efficiency – which, after all, should be positive and significant for trade integration to be a sensible policy in the first place.

EMU AND COMPETITION

Gianmarco Ottaviano, Daria Taglioni, and Filippo di Mauro assess the link between easier trade and higher productivity in EMU as directly as possible – but not very directly, since the data are not amenable to straightforward measurement. The paper's important premise is that trade does not need to occur in order to improve efficiency: when trade is easier, all producers face stronger competitive pressure, and selection of the producers that are better able to compete will increase average productivity. Of course, many other features of reality matter for productivity. To zero-in on the mechanism of interest, the paper lets the relevant notion of firm-specific 'competitiveness' levels be randomly spread across all potential firms, according to a distribution that is shaped realistically and differently across countries and sectors. Exit of insufficiently productive firms truncates the observed distribution,

Economic Policy January 2009 pp. 1–4
© CEPR, CES, MSH, 2009.

all the more severely when easier trade afforded by economic integration cuts a different slice of the underlying productivity distributions in countries that adopt the euro. The effects detected by the paper's implementation of this mechanism on the basis of real-life information investigation are all insightful, and range from the obvious to the intriguing. It is obvious that easier trade increases productivity, less obvious that this occurs through firm selection, and very intriguing to find that assessing the strength of that mechanism yields vastly different results for different countries. The Panel found that the machinery that generates the results is at this stage not so transparent as to foster complete confidence in the real-life relevance of the proposed modelling strategy and in the results' robustness. The paper, however, does point to a very important direction for further theoretical and, especially, empirical investigation. As more data on firm entry, exit and productivity become available, researchers will need to focus on the relevance of easier trade for firm selection. While quantitative assessment continues to be refined, policy-makers will do well to keep in mind that such channels contribute importantly to shape the impact of economic integration.

Economic integration has many faces. One is the flow of capital across countries' borders, which can foster efficiency both by matching savings with productive investments, and by allowing investors to diversify risk. The next paper we publish focuses on the relationship between EMU and a potentially very important component of this mechanism.

M AND A

Using an original dataset, Nicolas Coeurdacier, Roberto De Santis and Antonin Aviat study cross-border mergers and acquisitions (M&As) between 21 acquiring countries and 31 target countries for a period of 20 years (1985–2004). They distinguish ten service and ten manufacturing industries. All in all, their data cover 70–75% of the world cross-border M&As and cover annual transactions of about €450 billion. The authors find different patterns for manufacturing and services. Overall, EMU had a large effect on M&A activity in manufacturing but no effect in services. The effect in manufacturing was large: an increase of 200% in intra-euro area cross-border horizontal M&As activity. EMU therefore fostered the reallocation of capital across firms. Whereas in manufacturing cross-border M&As in the EMU have been following trade patterns there is no such phenomenon in services. The authors conclude that developments in cross-border M&As in manufacturing have been influenced by European integration and the introduction of the EMU. Cross-border M&As in manufacturing increased much more rapidly in the intra-euro area than it did between euro and non-euro areas. Several mechanisms could be at work: the euro could either decrease financial transaction costs of M&As between two countries of the euro zone or it could increase its profitability because the euro increases trade flows and market size in the euro zone. In the presence of the second mechanism, those sectors for which the euro has had the largest effect on trade flows should be the ones for which the effect of the euro on M&As is the strongest. They find such evidence for manufacturing. The authors conclude that cross-border M&As in services have been deterred by the level of protection and barriers to entry – domestic regulations – in the service sectors. Finally, the authors find a strong effect of corporate taxation, suggesting that changes in corporate taxes would be an efficient tool to attract foreign capital. This of course raises the question of the coordination of tax policies in Europe. The large effects found by the authors surprised the panel and there were several questions on the mechanisms through which the euro could have affected the M&A activities. There was also a lively discussion on the question whether M&As are always beneficial for countries.

In the capital markets, household savings meet firms' investment opportunities. But not all households are in a position to save. Some borrow, and some of these when hit by negative labour market or personal shocks find it difficult to repay their debts. Europe, a relatively prosperous and financially underdeveloped region of the world, has not yet experienced much household debt and repayment problems. But the potential for excessive household indebtedness is an increasingly important policy concern, especially so when worldwide financial markets are in turmoil as a consequence of abundant issuance and securitization of mortgages. This makes it very important to explore empirically the sources and consequences of household debt repayment problems.

HOUSEHOLD DEBT

Burcu Duygan-Bump and Charles Grant present the results of an empirical analysis on household arrears in ten European countries focusing on the influence on institutional arrangements, i.e. judicial and financial institutions. There are two types of institutions. First, institutions related to cost of enforcement of repayment. The higher these costs the more difficult it is for lenders to enforce repayment. Second, institutions related to exposure of the borrower. A borrower who might be exposed to be in arrears is more likely to repay, for example to avoid difficulties in future borrowing. In many countries there is a similar strong relationship between adverse events such as wage earners' unemployment and ill health, and arrears. However, the authors also find that indeed in many circumstances institutions matter. Households in different countries react differently to adverse shocks. In countries where the costs of enforcement to repay (measured as duration of dispute resolution), the number of legal procedures that must be followed in order to legally recover a debt and the direct cost of judicial proceedings are higher, arrears are more likely to occur. In countries where there is public coverage of unpaid debts or outstanding debts, arrears are less likely to occur. Apparently, economic incentives matter. Although in many cases there should be serious concern about households being in arrears there is also an element of strategic behaviour by borrowers that cannot be ruled out. The authors also indicate that there is a trade-off concerning optimal institutions. Making enforcement costs high increases arrears but reduces the probability of bankruptcy, which is not always beneficial to households. Making enforcement costs low increases the probability of arrears but may also discourage lending. In other words governments face a mechanism design problem. Finally, the authors advocate that across the EU 'repayment' institutions should be allowed to differ. Financial problems of households are not only influenced by the 'repayment' institutions but also by other institutions such as unemployment benefits. Since these other institutions differ between countries there is no immediate need to harmonize the 'repayment' institutions. The panel discussion was lively, focusing on many details of the analysis and the interpretation of parameter estimates. Furthermore there was discussion concerning the potential strategic behaviour of households.

Last, but not least, our authors and panellists revisit aspects of recent inflation experience. Inflation is by definition a generalized change of the price level, expressed in a given currency. Across countries with different currencies, monetary policy bears importantly on inflation dynamics. A 'generalized' price level change can also be measured at the level of regions within a country with a single money: that inflation rate, while still a measure of that region's overall price changes, will differ across regions for reasons that pertain to 'relative' prices – those of goods produced or consumed there, in comparison to those produced or consumed in other regions – and therefore reflect the balance of demand and supply of non-tradable goods and immobile factors.

REGIONAL INFLATION

The paper by Guenter Beck, Kirstin Hubrich and Massimiliano Marcellino studies the dynamics of inflation across regions of Europe before and after adoption of the euro. It uncovers a range of facts, and aims at connecting them to the policy-relevant question of whether different regional inflation rates reflect undesirable and potentially avoidable adjustment problems, possibly engendered by lack of monetary policy flexibility, or desirable and natural adjustment of relative prices. The Panel appreciated the importance of the problem, which however proves difficult to study with the available data and proposed techniques. Not all of the theoretical demand, supply and adjustment mechanisms are relevant along the regional dimension in a reality where prices and quantities are shaped by structural and institutional features that vary across sectors or across countries rather than across regions. The data do not detect changes associated with EMU inception. It is difficult to tell whether the facts that the paper does detect – such as the particular regional relevance of certain price index components (such as Energy), or the 'eurozone factor' in a descriptive model of regional price levels – are surprising and precise enough to support a structural interpretation. But the Panellists were intrigued by these findings, and we are sure readers and future researchers will be similarly interested in the paper's approach and results.

EMU and competition

Much attention has been paid to the impact of a single currency on actual trade volumes. Lower trade costs, however, matter over and beyond their effects on trade flows: as less productive firms are forced out of business by the tougher competitive conditions of international markets, economic integration fosters lower prices and higher average productivity. We assess the quantitative relevance of these effects calibrating a general equilibrium model using country, sector and firm-level empirical observations. The euro turns out to have increased the overall competitiveness of Eurozone firms, and the effects differ along interesting dimensions: they tend to be stronger for countries which are smaller or with better access to foreign markets, and for firms which specialize in sectors where international competition is fiercer and barriers to entry lower.

— *Gianmarco I.P. Ottaviano, Daria Taglioni and Filippo di Mauro*

The euro and the competitiveness of European firms

Gianmarco I.P. Ottaviano, Daria Taglioni and Filippo di Mauro

University of Bologna and CEPR; European Central Bank; European Central Bank

1. INTRODUCTION

A decade after the creation of the European Economic and Monetary Union (EMU), Denmark, Sweden and the United Kingdom still show reluctance towards adopting the euro. How much, if anything, are they losing in terms of the economic gains generated by the reductions in trade costs that a monetary union appears to imply?

More generally, has the introduction of the single currency affected – via the trade channel – the intensity of competition across countries while forcing the least efficient firms out of the market? If so, to what extent has this selection process affected unit delivery costs, mark-ups, prices, quantities, revenues and profits in participating and non-participating countries?

While these continue to be very relevant policy questions, there is currently no straightforward approach to deriving a quantitative assessment of the wider benefits

We are grateful to Giordano Mion for valuable advice on data collection and processing as well as to Jonathan Eaton, Katrin Forster, Kevin O'Rourke, Patrizio Pagano, Beatrice Weder di Mauro and Ekaterina Zhuravskaya for comments on earlier drafts. We have benefited from comments by four anonymous referees. The views expressed in this study are those of the authors and do not necessarily reflect those of the European Central Bank.

The Managing Editor in charge of this paper was Giuseppe Bertola.

Economic Policy January 2009 pp. 5–53
© CEPR, CES, MSH, 2009.

of monetary union. Existing studies are very much focused on its impact on trade flows.[1] Trade flows, however, are only an imperfect measure of the gains that the euro may have created through the trade channel, as they fail to capture potential welfare improvements accruing to economic agents through a more efficient and productive economic environment. Such benefits stem from fostering countries' specialization in sectors in which they are more efficient, enabling a richer product variety, weakening the market power of firms, enhancing the exploitation of economies of scale and improving the efficiency of production through the exit of the least efficient firms. The main objective of this paper is to assess the impact of the adoption of the euro on the productivity and international competitiveness of firms belonging to different European countries and industries.

In principle, empirical estimates could be obtained through direct measures of firms' productivity and competitiveness changes, which could be aggregated to perform cross-sector and cross-country comparisons. Unfortunately, firm level data are not detailed and homogenous enough across countries to allow for a consistent estimation (Mayer and Ottaviano, 2007); the analysis then has to be restricted to individual countries (see, for example, work by Berthou and Fontagné, 2008, on France).

This paper opts for an alternative solution. It bypasses the problems related to the lack of data by simulating counterfactual scenarios of euro membership on a general equilibrium multi-country multi-sector model of international trade which we calibrate using macro and micro data. Following the approach of Melitz and Ottaviano (2008), our model accounts for a number of real world features linking trade liberalization and firm productivity. These features include: richer availability of product varieties; tougher competition and weaker market power of firms; better exploitation of economies of scale; and efficiency gains via the selection of the best firms.

The model is calibrated on 12 manufacturing sectors across 12 EU countries for the years 2001–2003 and is used to evaluate the competitiveness of European manufacturing firms in terms of an efficient use of available inputs, given the institutional and market set-up in which they operate. In so doing, we derive a ranking of European countries in terms of the cost effectiveness of the firms located therein – which we use as a measure of the 'overall competitiveness' of the corresponding countries. This indicator is then adopted as a benchmark for a set of experiments, where we simulate three counterfactual scenarios designed to evaluate how alternative (and hypothetical) euro membership set-ups would have affected the baseline overall competitiveness of the European countries considered. The competitiveness effects we estimate range from 1.4% to 3.5% on average across countries, and up to a (negative) 5.8% for France in the scenario where that country abandons the Eurozone.

---

[1] Between 1998 and 2007, the value of exports and imports of goods within the euro area has increased from 26% to 33% of GDP, that of services from 5% to 7% of GDP. Controlling for exogenous effects, the early literature on the trade impacts of monetary unions has come up with an extremely large range of estimates, comprised between nil (Berger and Nitsch, 2005) and almost 1400% (Alesina et al., 2002). The current consensus on the trade impact of the euro is that the single currency had a small, but positive effect on trade flows.

The analysis that yields such estimates establishes a link between trade barriers and industry performance indicators, and highlights fruitful directions for analysis of new statistical data in the future. The proposed approach produces micro-founded measures of countries' competitiveness that are more comprehensive than international comparisons of prices, total factor or labour productivity, trade shares, and other traditional gauges of competitiveness, and can be decomposed in terms of various determinants for every country and sectors. This makes them very useful for policy impact evaluation purposes, not only in the international context but also for a variety of competition and industrial policies.

The structure of the paper is as follows. Section 2 provides some stylized facts and a brief account on how the trade literature has evolved in line with actual changes in the structure of markets and production patterns. This is useful to put in perspective the main characteristics of the model we use. The model itself is described in some detail in Section 3. Its empirical implementation – which consists in circumventing data limitations through the calibration of the model relationships – is presented in Section 4. Section 5 examines how firm competitiveness is affected within three different scenarios of euro membership. Section 6 concludes. Sections 3.2, 3.3, 3.4 are necessarily rather technical. They can be skipped without losing the flow of thought and the main message of the paper.

2. GAINS FROM TRADE: FACTS AND THEORIES

In the last few decades, developments in trade theory have been characterized by constant attempts to include 'real life' complexities in the basic trade models of Ricardo and of Heckscher and Ohlin. This includes a re-definition of (1) what gains have to be expected from trade and (2) what channels are likely to be most relevant for generating such gains. In what follows, we underline some of the most important stylized facts in recent economic history, which have been incorporated in theory, and most notably in the model we use in this paper.

During the 'first wave of globalization' – that is, from the industrial revolution to the First World War – the pattern of international trade was mainly characterized by the exchange of manufactured goods from industrialized countries for imports of raw materials from less developed countries. World trade was mostly 'inter-sectoral', and was explained by international differences in relative factor endowments, and technologies. Countries' specialization in production and in exports was in accordance with their relative costs of production (i.e. having a 'comparative advantage' in relatively 'cheap' sectors): the so-called 'specialization effect' of trade liberalization. The theories of Ricardo and of Heckscher and Ohlin were developed to explain such patterns of international trade.

With the 'second wave' of globalization after the Second World War, the previous paradigm became partly obsolete as a dominant share of international trade was taking place within industries among countries having relatively similar endowments and technological development (Linder, 1961; Grubel and Lloyd, 1975). This led to the appearance of new trade theories, the principal characteristic of which is the attention to the details of market structure. Two distinct strands of literature – both relevant to the model proposed in this paper – underline the different mechanisms at play.

The first strand of literature underlines that horizontal product differentiation within sectors assigns market power to firms even in sectors characterized by a large number of competitors that are free to enter and exit the market (Krugman, 1980). In this set-up of 'monopolistic competition' with increasing returns to scale, the following results apply. First, firms operate at a given minimum scale if they want to break even. Second, within a sector, firms specialize in the production of distinct varieties of their differentiated goods. Third and last, intra-industry trade arises because consumers love variety, but countries can produce only a limited number of varieties, depending on their 'size', i.e. their resource endowment. Hence, trade liberalization has a 'variety effect' insofar as it broadens the range of varieties available for consumption.

A second strand of new trade theory is built on an 'oligopolistic competition' set-up where a few large firms sell homogeneous products and, due to trade barriers, achieve larger market shares at home than abroad (Brander and Krugman, 1983). Whenever they are able to discriminate in terms of prices between domestic and foreign customers, they are willing to accept smaller profit margins abroad than at home, therefore selling additional units of their output abroad. This gives rise to bilateral trade within industries even between identical countries. As firms charge lower margins on foreign than on domestic sales, the resulting exchange is sometimes called 'reciprocal dumping'. In this set-up, trade liberalization reduces the market share of domestic firms with respect to their foreign rivals, thus increasing their perceived elasticity of demand. The result is an average compression of profit margins as prices fall towards marginal costs. This efficiency-enhancing consequence of freer trade is called the 'pro-competitive effect'.

If production faces increasing returns to scale at the firm level, tougher competition due to freer trade has an additional efficiency-enhancing effect. The reason is that, to restore profitability, firms compensate for the decrease in prices resulting from the pro-competitive effect by raising their output. Then, in the presence of increasing returns, rising output leads to a decline in the average cost of production. This efficiency gain is called the 'scale effect' of trade liberalization.

Recent analyses of micro-datasets tracking production and international involvement at the firm and at the plant levels demonstrate that firms vary tremendously along a number of dimensions even within industries and this plays an important role in aggregate outcomes. In particular a hallmark regularity is that firms serving foreign markets are more productive than their purely domestic competitors. In this setting, allowing for heterogeneous firms, tougher competition and scale economies implies also that freer trade causes the most performing firms to expand and grow – both domestically and internationally – and the least performing firms to exit the market altogether. In the ensuing selection process, the scale of surviving firms increases – as this improves their profitability – while their number drops. As a result, technologies are used more efficiently – the so-called 'rationalization effect' of trade liberalization. Average firm productivity also rises, as less productive firms exit – the so-called 'selection effect' of trade liberalization.[2]

3. THEORETICAL FRAMEWORK

Building on the stylized facts and theoretical insights described in Section 2, our model provides an account of the determinants of trade and mechanisms of adjustment to trade liberalization as realistically as possible, as this comprises the existence of intra-industry trade, firms' market power and heterogeneity, existence of scale economies and consumers' love of variety. The main purpose of the model is to provide a solid theoretical underpinning for the construction of broad-based indicators of competitiveness in Europe and to use this framework to study the gains from the introduction of the euro, considering the latter as an 'instrument' of trade liberalization among the countries participating in Stage 3 of EMU, i.e. the adoption of the euro.

The basic logic of the model is rather intuitive. Consider a sector in which firms differ in terms of efficiency in the use of available inputs. With trade liberalization, lower trade costs allow foreign producers to target the domestic markets, therefore lowering the mark-ups and the operating profits of domestic firms. At the same time, however, some domestic firms gain access to foreign markets and generate additional profits from their foreign ventures: these are the firms that are efficient enough to cope with the additional costs of reaching foreign customers (such as those due to transportation, administrative duties, institutional and cultural barriers). In the process, a number of firms – the least productive and those unable to afford access to foreign markets – will be forced to exit. The selection process will eventually increase the average efficiency of surviving firms, and lower average prices and mark-ups.

3.1. Main features

Our model is to be seen in the tradition of the new trade theories briefly surveyed in Section 2. Most notably, it exhibits the following five main features. First, the market structure is one of monopolistic competition. Each firm in a sector produces only one variety of a differentiated good. Consumers have inelastic demand and love to have as many varieties to choose from as possible. Second, in order to enter in a sector and start producing, firms must pay *ex-ante* fixed entry costs, which include for example

---

[2] The above stylized facts have been highlighted by a growing empirical literature. For example, the exit of the least productive firms is reported by Clerides *et al.* (1998), Bernard and Jensen (1999) as well as Aw *et al.* (2000). Market share reallocation towards the most productive firms is reported by Pavcnik (2002) as well as Bernard *et al.* (2003).

the research and development (R&D) costs needed to create and market a new variety. With respect to their nature these costs are therefore 'sunk', i.e. cannot be recovered, should firms exit the market later on. Bringing entry (and exit) to the forefront, our analysis focuses on the medium to long-run effects of trade liberalization. Third, in addition to the entry costs, firms incur production costs and delivery costs, which include not only transportation fees – both within a country and for shipping abroad – but also all tariff and non-tariff costs needed to reach the final consumers. We collapse these costs – which vary by sector and by country – into a single indicator, which we will call the 'freeness of trade'. Fourth, trade flows are driven by technology and demand, and there is no role for international cost differentials arising from different relative resource endowments, which are instead critical in the Heckscher–Ohlin trade theory mentioned in Section 2.[3] Fifth and last, in our model the size of the markets matters. The larger the markets, the tougher the competition in terms of the increased elasticity of demand faced by firms and thus the lower are the mark-ups. In this tougher competitive environment, firms have to achieve a larger scale of operations in order to break even, and this is possible only for the most efficient firms, i.e. those with the lowest marginal costs. Accordingly, the key indicator of industry performance in the model will be the 'cut-off' marginal cost. This is the maximum marginal cost that can be profitably sustained by firms in the market. The inverse of the cut-off cost is the minimum productivity or efficiency of firms that are able to at least break even. Knowing how the cut-off varies following trade liberalization will be enough to evaluate all the ensuing changes in terms of productivity, prices, mark-ups, output and overall welfare.

3.2. A stylized EU economy

With our empirical application and our data constraints in mind, we focus on an economy consisting of 12 countries and 12 manufacturing sectors (more on this in Section 4). Each manufacturing sector (henceforth indexed by the subscript 's') supplies a differentiated good. This good is available in a certain range of varieties which are traded in monopolistic competitive markets. The model assumes that each firm produces one variety only.[4] The rest of the economy is represented by a single residual homogeneous good, which serves as the *numeraire* (i.e. unit of value). The homogeneous good is freely traded in perfectly competitive markets and it is sold at the same price by all firms across the economy. The market for this good will also absorb all labour imbalances in the economy so that nominal wages – but not real ones – will be constant in the model.

---

[3] We consider this as a reasonable assumption for the EU countries that are the object of the empirical analysis in Section 4, given that their relative resource endowments are very similar and bilateral trade flows mostly intra-industry.

[4] Monopolistic competition can be considered as a reasonable macroeconomic representation of the market structure in our manufacturing sectors as long as sectors are fairly aggregated and our model allows for the pro-competitive effect of richer variety presented in Section 2.

3.3. Industry equilibrium

Our model is formally described in Appendix 1. It accommodates several countries and several sectors that differ from each other along several dimensions. While this is important for the empirical application, the intuitive logic of the model can be usefully grasped by concentrating on the simplest case of a single manufacturing sector, labelled 's', that operates in two identical countries, labeled 'h' (mnemonic for 'here') and 't' (mnemonic for 'there'). In the following description we focus on country h with the understanding that everything applies symmetrically to country t.

As already mentioned, to introduce a new variety of a good produced in sector s and country h, a firm incurs a (sector-and-country) specific R&D sunk cost, which we call f_s^h. Typically, due to the uncertain R&D outcome, the entrant does not know in advance what will be the marginal cost connected to the production of the new variety that he wants to launch on the market, i.e. it does not know how efficient it will be in producing its variety relative to the production of all other varieties in the market (and actually whether it will be able to produce it at all, given market conditions). To capture such uncertainty, we assume that the marginal cost of production c is determined randomly upon entry as a draw from a sector and country-specific probability distribution.

The production cost distribution is portrayed in the middle panel of Figure 1 where, for any firm, possible cost draws range from a lower external bound equal to 0 (i.e. where c can approximate 0, but always remaining strictly positive) to a country and sector-specific upper bound equal to $c_{A,s}^h$. The panel shows a realistic situation (see Box 1 for details) in which high cost draws for firms (large c) are much more likely than low cost draws (low c). There are two key parameters in this panel. The first is $c_{A,s}^h$, which identifies the maximum possible cost of producing a variety (i.e. the worst possible return from the investment in R&D) in sector s and country h. The inverse of $c_{A,s}^h$, which we call o_s^h, is an index of 'absolute advantage': the higher it is, the more cost effective country h is in producing good s and the more likely it is for a firm willing to introduce a new variety in sector s of country h to succeed. The second key parameter is represented by the curvature, or 'shape' k_s, of the cost distribution curve. The parameter k_s, is a direct measure of the bias of the distribution of sector s towards high cost outcomes (i.e. inefficient firms). Hence, the larger k_s is, the more likely it is for a new variety in sector s to have high marginal costs of production. Given these parameters – technological in nature – country h has a 'comparative advantage' in sector s with respect to country t and another sector S if $(c_{A,s}^h/c_{A,S}^h) < (c_{A,s}^t/c_{A,S}^t)$. In this case and other things equal, firms entering sector s are more likely to produce at lower cost (i.e. to be more productive) in country h than in country t.

While all firms have identical expectations on their future fortunes, when they enter, some may subsequently end up being luckier than others, giving rise to an *ex-post* distribution of firm efficiency that mirrors the ex-ante distribution of cost draws (provided that, as in our industries, there is a number of entrants large enough).

Box 1. Pareto distribution

Our model is based on the assumption that marginal costs draws c in sector s and country h follow a Pareto distribution with possible outcomes ranging from 0 to $c_{A,s}^{h}$ and shape parameter k_s. Formally, the *ex ante* cumulative density function (i.e. the share of draws below a certain cost level c) and probability density function (i.e. the probability of drawing a certain cost level c) are given by:

$$G(c) = \left(\frac{c}{c_{A,s}^{h}}\right)^{k_s}, 0 \leq c \leq c_{A,s}^{h} \text{ and } g(c) = \frac{k_s(c)^{k_s-1}}{(c_{A,s}^{h})^{k_s}}, 0 \leq c \leq c_{A,s}^{h}, \text{ respectively.}$$

On account of the law of large numbers, these are also the *ex post* cumulative density function and probability density function of entrants across marginal cost levels. The cumulative density function is represented in the middle panel of Figure 1. A useful property of this Pareto distribution is that any truncation thereof also belongs to the Pareto family with the same shape parameter k_s. This is due to the fact that, for any value of c, $d \ln G(c)/d \ln(c) = k_s$, i.e. a 1% increase in c leads to a k_s% increase in $G(c)$. In particular, since firms produce for the domestic market as long as their cost draws fall below c_s^{hh}, the distribution of producers across marginal cost levels is characterized by the following cumulative and probability density functions:

$$G_s^h(c) = \left(\frac{c}{c_s^{hh}}\right)^{k_s}, 0 \leq c \leq c_s^{hh} \text{ and } g_s^h(c) = \frac{k_s(c)^{k_s-1}}{(c_s^{hh})^{k_s}}, 0 \leq c \leq c_s^{hh}.$$

Is this anywhere close to what we observe in the data? This is easily testable, as stated above, under the Pareto assumption $d \ln G(c)/d \ln(c) = k_s$ for any value of c. Then, if the marginal cost c were indeed distributed as Pareto, a simple regression of $\ln G(c)$ on $\ln(c)$ plus a constant would fit the data perfectly ($R^2 = 100\%$) and, by definition, the estimated coefficient of $\ln(c)$ would provide a consistent estimate of k_s as the constant elasticity of $\ln G(c)$ to $\ln(c)$. The results of such regression, run by sector, are reported in the table below. They clearly show that the Pareto distribution provides a very good description of the data. This has the additional useful practical implication that the average marginal cost in sector s and country h is equal to $c_s^{hh} k_s/(k_s + 1)$, which can be used to obtain a consistent estimate of the cut-off cost from sector- and country-specific averages.

Industry	k_s	Std. Error	Adj.R^2
1 Food, Beverages and Tobacco	1.91	0.0027	0.96
2 Textiles, Leather Products and Footwear	1.67	0.0028	0.96
3 Wood Products except Furniture	1.95	0.0044	0.95
4 Paper Products, Printing and Publishing	1.91	0.0015	0.99
5 Rubber and Plastic	2.42	0.0035	0.98
6 Chemicals, including Pharmaceuticals	1.68	0.0028	0.98
7 Non-metallic Mineral Prod., incl. Pottery and Glass	2.11	0.0033	0.98
8 Basic Metals and Fabricated Metal Products	2.55	0.0019	0.98
9 Non-electric Machinery	2.48	0.0021	0.99
10 Electric Machinery, incl. Prof. and Scient. Equip.	2.22	0.0029	0.98
11 Transport Equipment	2.32	0.0042	0.98
12 Other Manufacturing, incl. Furniture	2.02	0.0037	0.96
Average	2.10	0.0030	0.97

Source: AMADEUS, authors' calculations.

Accordingly, after entering, firms observe their own costs, as well as those of their competitors, and realize whether they can produce profitably. Firms that do not manage to make profits, will have to exit the market. This is shown by the Home sales schedule in the top panel of Figure 1, in which downward sloping demand implies that the quantity that firms are able to sell domestically decreases proportionally to the increase in marginal cost of their draw, as a higher marginal cost maps into a higher price. The extent to which a higher price reduces demand depends on product differentiation: the more differentiated products are, the fewer sales are lost on account of a given increase in price. Thus, a flatter slope of the Home sales schedule would portray stronger product differentiation. Henceforth, we will call D_s the index of product differentiation in sector s.

The Export sales schedule is lower than the Home sales schedule because exporters face additional delivery costs than domestic producers and this increases the price they need to charge to final consumers, therefore lowering the latter's demand for their products. The higher these delivery costs are, the further apart are the two lines. Accordingly, decisions to produce and export follow simple cut-off rules: firms with costs (and sales price) above c_s^{hh} realize that they are too inefficient to sell in the domestic market, and thus quit; firms with costs below c_s^{hh} but above c_s^{ht} realize that they are too inefficient to export, and thus serve only the domestic market; firms with costs below c_s^{ht} realize that they are efficient enough to sell both at home and abroad, and thus do both.

The outcome portrayed in the top panel of Figure 1 is anticipated by firms at the entry stage when they have to decide whether to incur the sunk R&D cost f_s^h or not. In addition, the information contained in the middle panel of the same figure allows them to calculate the probability of drawing marginal costs above or below c_s^{hh} and c_s^{ht}. They can, therefore, figure out their overall expected profits and check whether these

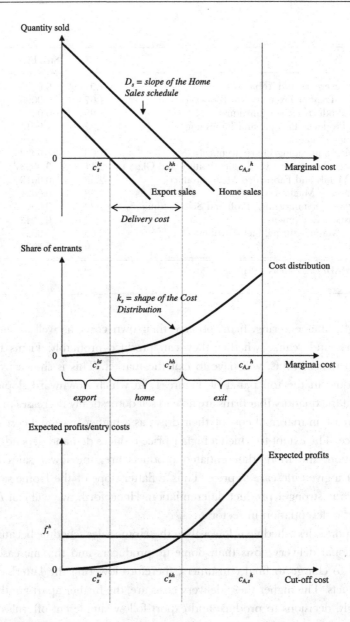

Figure 1. Theoretical framework

cover the sunk entry cost. The bottom panel of Figure 1 provides a graphical representation of the problem set faced by the firm. The upward sloping curve indicates that expected profits are a function of the domestic cut-off cost (threshold beyond which firms are forced to exit the market). As all firms are identical before investing in R&D, they all share the same expected profits. On their part, expected profits are an increasing function of the domestic cut-off cost since a higher cut-off implies that the average efficiency within the sector is lower and, therefore, that incumbents face weaker competition. The horizontal line identifies the sunk entry cost f_s^h It crosses the curve of expected profits only once. The resulting intersection of those two lines identifies the equilibrium domestic cut-off level c_s^{hh}. This is the only equilibrium cut-off compatible with a stable number of firms active in the market: If the domestic cut-off were above c_s^{hh}, expected profits would be higher than the entry cost, thus inducing additional entry. Conversely, if the domestic cut-off were below c_s^{hh}, expected profits would be lower than the entry cost, implying that some incumbent firms would shut down as they would be making losses.

Once c_s^{hh} is determined, the equilibrium export cut-off level can be derived by applying the additional delivery costs. In particular, if we call $d_s^{ht} > 1$ the factor measuring these additional costs of delivering goods from country h to country t (and vice versa), the equilibrium export cut-off level is simply c_s^{hh}/d_s^{ht}, implying that an exporter has to be d_s^{ht} times more efficient than a domestic producer in order to make the same amount of sales in the same country.

3.4. Key parameters

For a given domestic cut-off level, firms expect higher profits under the following conditions: (i) in larger countries as these would support larger firms; (ii) in sectors in which products are less differentiated as these would also support larger firms; (iii) in sectors and countries offering better chances of good cost draws as this would foster firms' expected efficiency; and (iv) when trade is freer as this would allow firms to grow, thanks to easier access to the foreign market.

In all these cases the curve of expected profits in the bottom panel of Figure 1 would shift upwards. A detailed gallery of the corresponding outcomes is portrayed in Figure 2, where cases (i), (ii) and (iii) are presented in the top panel (a) while case (iv) is presented in the middle panel (b). For a given level of the domestic cut-off, a larger country size, weaker product differentiation, better technological opportunities and freer trade all imply higher expected profits. The effects of shocks leading to such structural changes are shown graphically by the upward shift of the Expected profits curve in panels (a) and (b) and the corresponding shift to the left of the intersection point between the curves representing respectively Expected profits and Entry costs. As shown graphically, the new equilibrium domestic cut-off c_s^{hh} will have a lower level. This outcome is due to the following sequence of events: the higher expected profits result in the entry of new firms, which increases competition in the market, thereby causing firms' mark-ups to shrink and making survival harder for the weakest among the incumbents. Tougher competition hits all firms but sinks only some of the least efficient ones, i.e. those firms that had marginal costs just below the cut-off before the shock, and that, as a result of the shock, see their sales disappear thereby failing to break even. As only relatively more efficient firms survive, the average efficiency of the industry rises, thereby leading to a lower level for the domestic cut-off c_s^{hh}, as previously mentioned. This selection effect is accompanied by an increase in average scale of firms as well as by a decrease in the average price and mark-up, revealing

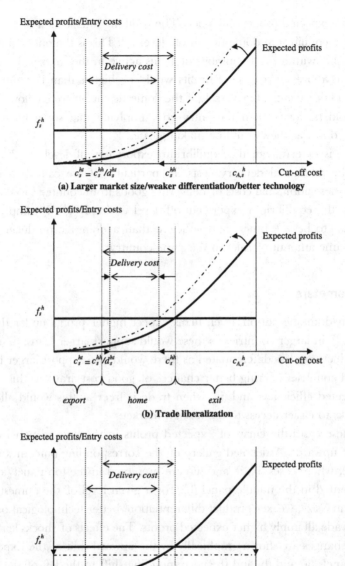

Figure 2. Industry reallocations

that scale and pro-competitive effects are also at work. For a given reduction of the domestic cut-off, the intensity of the selection effects depends on the number of firms that exit the market. What percentage of firms exit when the cut-off falls by a percentage point? Given the discussion in the previous section (see Box 1 for details), the answer is clearly k_s per cent. Hence, we refer to k_s as the 'sensitivity to firm selection', or more technically to the 'elasticity of the extensive margin' of industry adjustment, which is high in sectors characterized by large fractions of high cost firms.

The difference between panels (a) and (b) in Figure 2 stems from the fact that in the former delivery costs are unaffected while they, of course, fall in the latter. This explains why in panel (a) a lower domestic cut-off leads to a lower export cut-off forcing the least efficient exporters in the initial equilibrium to discontinue their foreign operations. In panel (b), by contrast, as delivery costs fall due to trade liberalization, the export cut-off rises since some firms that were not exporting under the initial conditions are now able to serve the foreign market.

Finally, a fifth case is presented in panel (c) of Figure 2. This shows that countries and sectors in which entry costs are lower support lower equilibrium cost cut-offs for both domestic and foreign sales. The reason is that, for given cut-offs, lower entry costs foster the entry of additional firms. This increases competition forcing the least efficient domestic producers to shut down and the least efficient exporters to abandon their foreign operations. Hence, as in the other panels, selection leads to larger average scale of firms as well as to lower average price and mark-up.[5]

Summarizing what we have learned from Figure 1 and Figure 2, the domestic cut-off c_s^{hh} determines the average efficiency, the average scale, the average price and the average mark-up of firms selling the products of sector s to consumers in country h. Therefore, it determines the overall welfare generated by that sector for that country. In turn, the domestic cut-off is determined by six key parameters:

1 the country-specific *market size*, L^h;
2 the sector-specific *product differentiation*, D_s;
3 the sector-and-country specific *absolute advantage*, o_s^h;
4 the sector-specific *elasticity of the extensive margin*, k_s;
5 the sector-and-country specific *entry cost*, f_s^h;
6 the *delivery cost*, d_s^{ht}, which is specific to the sector, the country of origin and the country of destination.

In particular, we have argued that larger L^h and o_s^h as well as smaller D_s, k_s, f_s^h and d_s^{ht} reduce the equilibrium domestic cut-off (see Box 4 for the formal expression of c_s^{hh} as a function of the various parameters and Appendix 1 for its derivation). The delivery cost parameter deserves further attention. First, d_s^{ht} determines the ratio between the number of exporters and the number of firms that sell only to domestic consumers. This ratio is inversely related to d_s^{ht} and can be interpreted as an index of the 'freeness of trade' as it equals zero in autarky and one when trade is perfectly free and exporters face no additional delivery cost with respect to domestic sellers. Second, in the more realistic set-up with several countries we will use for our empirical analysis, there are several export destinations and a reduction in any of the delivery costs to those destinations causes an upward shift of the Expected profit schedule as in the middle panel (b) of Figure 2. Then, if country h is characterized on average by lower

---

[5] In general, the gains in terms of efficiency, scale and prices are associated with ambiguous effects in terms of product variety. Appendix 1 shows that in our model the former always dominate, implying that a lower domestic cut-off is always associated with higher national welfare and that, conversely, a higher domestic cut-off necessarily delivers lower national welfare.

delivery costs than country t to all other countries, it will attract the entry of more firms, thereby leading to a higher average efficiency and average scale, a lower average price and mark-up, as well as to higher welfare.

4. EMPIRICAL IMPLEMENTATION

As mentioned in the introduction, a direct estimation of the gains to be attributed to the euro is at present not feasible because of the unavailability of sufficiently detailed and harmonized cross-country firm-level data. In particular, as shown by Mayer and Ottaviano (2007), existing data face five types of limitations. First, general information on firms is not always available. Second, the available data do not display the same information across countries. Third, important differences in coverage and methodology reduce the comparability of the available data. Fourth, when available, firm-level data collected homogeneously across Europe are not oriented towards international trade. Finally, confidentiality requirements typically prevent a single research team from directly accessing the source data in different countries. Hence, the econometric analysis of the competitiveness effects of the trade changes triggered by the euro is necessarily restricted to investigating individually the outcome for the very few countries for which all relevant data are available (such as Belgium and France).

To circumvent current data limitations, we use the theoretical structure of the model described in Section 3. In this respect, our approach should be seen as a practical second-best solution to overcome concrete – but hopefully temporary – data availability constraints. Specifically, in order to investigate the gains in competitiveness induced by the euro via the trade channel we test how the actual performance of European economies (as measured by our broadly defined indicators of competitiveness) compares with their simulated performances in counterfactual model scenarios in which some of them changes its official currency (i.e. to or from the euro). Adapting the methodology developed by Del Gatto et al. (2006), the analysis is developed in three steps. First, the model is fitted to reality. This is achieved by estimating as many of its parameters as possible and 'calibrating' the values of the remaining ones so that the model is able to reproduce selected patterns of the data. In particular, the calibration of the model allows generating the indicators of competitiveness needed to assess the impacts from the euro. Second, the model is 'validated' by checking its consistency with additional patterns of the data, different from the ones used in its calibration. Finally, the model is used to 'simulate' the counterfactual scenarios relative to the adoption of the euro and provide an assessment on the competitiveness effects of the euro.

Specifically, as we discuss in some technical detail in Appendix 1, in view of producing the above-mentioned indicators of competitiveness, the key objective of the empirical strategy is to compute the cut-offs from the model's prediction (Equation 12 of Appendix 1) by ensuring that these latter fit the actual values observed – or calibrated – from the data (see Box 4 for details). As discussed in Section 3.4 and in Appendix 1, the cut-off cost in sector s and country h is determined by the following six key parameters: the country-specific market size L^h; the sector-specific product differentiation D_s; the sector-and-country specific absolute advantage o_s^h; the sector-specific elasticity of the extensive margin k_s; the sector-and-country specific entry cost f_s^h; and the delivery costs to and from all other countries, with each bilateral delivery cost d_s^{ht} being specific to a sector, a country of origin and a country of destination. Some of these parameters are directly measurable, such as the population, which proxies market size.[6] Other parameters can be estimated. This is the case for the delivery costs and the sensitivity to firm selection (i.e. the elasticity of the extensive margin). The remaining parameters (i.e. product differentiation, entry costs and absolute advantage) are neither directly measurable nor estimable with the available data. This is the case for product differentiation, fixed entry costs and the absolute advantage. However, since we can estimate the cost cut-offs c_s^{hh}, the above unobservable parameters can be attributed values (i.e. 'calibrated') to ensure that the model exactly matches the cost cut-offs, with these latter estimated on the basis of the directly measured or estimated values of all other parameters.

4.1. Estimation

We consider data relative to 12 manufacturing sectors over the period from 2001 to 2003. We focus on 12 European countries. Nine of them belong to the euro area (Austria, Belgium, Finland, France, Germany, Italy, the Netherlands, Portugal and Spain). The remaining three are outsiders (Denmark, Sweden and the United Kingdom).

Notwithstanding the focus on 12 European countries, trade frictions across and within countries are estimated using a far larger panel of bilateral exports and domestic production data (212 countries worldwide), to ensure that our estimated coefficients of trade freeness for the 15 countries in the sample are as accurate as possible. Industry-level trade data and country-level geographical information come from the Centre d'Etudes Prospectives et d'Informations Internationales.[7] Delivery costs within a country are calculated, by subtracting the country's overall exports in a given sector from domestic production in the same sector, a standard procedure in international trade studies. This latter is measured by gross output at current basic prices, taken from the *Industrial Statistics Database* of the United Nations Industrial Development Organisation.

Marginal costs are calculated from sector- and country-specific productivity, measured as value added per hour worked, with data on value added and hour worked at the sectoral level from EU KLEMS.[8] The sensitivity to firm selection is calculated using estimates of firm-level total factor productivity based on balance sheet data from the *Amadeus database* of the Bureau Van Dijk. Finally, population data come from the *World Development Indicators* by the World Bank.

[6] The robustness of our results when using alternative measures is discussed in the Web Appendix available at www.economic-policy.org.

[7] Freely downloadable from www.cepii.fr.

[8] Freely downloadable from www.euklems.net.

4.1.1. Measuring trade frictions. Trade frictions d_s^{ht} comprise the total costs of delivering a product from factory to consumers, irrespective of whether located at home or abroad. They include not only transportation fees, but also tariffs and non-tariff costs, and can be estimated through their negative impact on trade flows embedded in the 'gravity regression' detailed in Box 2.

Box 2. Trade freeness estimation

As shown in Appendix 1, our theoretical framework generates a 'gravity relation' between bilateral trade flows, country characteristics and trade impediments (Anderson and Van Wincoop, 2004). We exploit this relation to estimate bilateral trade freeness compatible with the observed flows between European countries. For trade flows from country h to country t in sector s we have:

$$\ln(EXP_s^{ht}) = EX_h + IM_t + \delta_s \ln(Distance^{ht}) + \beta(Border^{ht}) + \lambda(Language^{ht} Border^{ht}) + \ldots$$
$$\ln\{\exp[\mu(Firmshare^{ht} + Selection^{ht})] - 1\} + \xi(Selection)^{ht} + Dummy^{time} + e^{ht}$$

where EXP_s^{ht} are the exports of sector s from country h to country t, while EX_h and IM_t are dummies specific to the countries of origin and destination. Trade barriers are captured by two variables: the bilateral distance ($distance^{ht}$) and the border effect ($Border^{ht}$). The former measures all distance-related trade frictions, the latter additional frictions due to crossing a border. These differ across importing countries and include a language dummy ($Language^{ht}$) that equals 1 when the two countries share a common language. The variables $Firmshare^{ht}$ and $Selection^{ht}$ control for the unobserved underlying firm-level heterogeneity, which is likely to be correlated with trade flows (Helpman et al., 2008). $Selection^{ht}$ also corrects for biases arising from a possible non-random sample selection of the observations (Heckman, 1979). Finally, $Dummy^{time}$ is a time dummy and e^{ht} is a residual term. We use data for the years from 1999 to 2004 to increase the statistical robustness of the estimated coefficients. Details and robustness checks are provided in Appendix 2 and in the Web Appendix. The interested reader will also find online an Excel spreadsheet providing the country-pair and sector specific values for trade freeness.

Following standard practice in the literature (see Head and Mayer, 2004a), trade freeness from country h to country t is defined as:

$$T_s^{ht} = [\exp(\beta^2 - \lambda Language^{ht})](distance^{ht})^{\delta_s}$$

where crossing a border and speaking different languages induce a drop in bilateral trade beyond that implied by the distance effect. Within country h the above expression reduces to $T_s^{hh} = (distance^{ht})^{\delta_s}$, where the internal distance of h is the weighted average bilateral distance between its biggest cities, with weights reflecting their relative sizes.

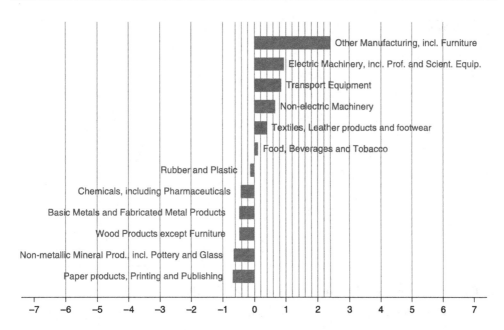

Figure 3. Freeness of trade by sector (difference from the median, 2001–2003)

Note: Industries are ranked by degree of trade freeness, relative to median.

Source: Trade and Production database (DEPII), authors' calculations.

Figure 3 shows the 'freeness of trade' T_s^{ht}, associated with delivery cost d_s^{ht}, as simple sectoral averages plotted relative to the median sector. *Paper products, printing and publishing* is the manufacturing sector with the highest trade frictions and lowest trade freeness, followed by *non-metallic mineral products, metals* and *wood products*. On the other hand, *electrical machinery, including professional and scientific equipment* is the sector with the highest trade freeness along with the residual sector of *other manufacturing*.

The results in Figure 3 are broadly in line with previous estimates of trade barriers and border effects in Europe. For instance, in a sample of 12 countries and 113 NACE industries, Head and Mayer (2000) find that, up to 1995, most industries producing machinery (electric and non-electric), leather goods and textiles were relatively open sectors, while carpentry, wooden containers and wood-sawing recorded the highest estimated trade frictions along with oil refining and forging. Similarly, using a dataset of 7 European countries and 78 industries, Chen (2004) finds that in 1996 the home bias was highest for ready-mix concrete, carpentry, mortars, printing and publishing and metal structures. With respect to existing literature our results are different only for *food, beverages and tobacco*, a sector which – according to our estimates – enjoys good freeness of trade.

Turning to a geographic perspective, the left panel of Figure 4 shows that, unsurprisingly, accessing foreign markets is easier from core European countries than from peripheral

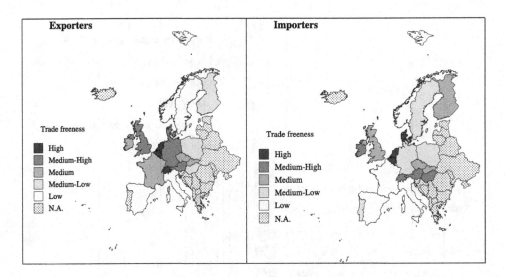

Figure 4. Freeness of trade by country (2001–2003)

Source: CEPII trade data and author's calculations.

ones. On the other hand, the accessibility of a country's markets from abroad is related to its size, as well as to cultural and linguistic factors, though to a smaller extent. In particular, the markets of small countries and of Anglo-Saxon, Germanic and Nordic countries are, on average, more accessible from abroad than those of large and southern countries. These results are in line with Chen (2004), who finds that, in 1996, the reduction in trade flows due to crossing borders (i.e. the 'border effect') was the highest for exports from Finland, Spain and Portugal, followed by Italy and France. By contrast, the preference for domestic goods over imports (i.e. the 'home bias') was the lowest for the United Kingdom and Germany. Overall, the geographical mapping of trade frictions confirms that, while geography is an important determinant of delivery costs, other factors also have a strong influence.

4.1.2. Calculating the sensitivity to firm selection. As mentioned in Section 3.4, the degree at which sectors adjust to the process of firm selection (or the sector-specific elasticity of the extensive margin k_s) is determined by the percentage of firms that exit a sector when the cut-off cost falls by a percentage point. Hence, the larger the elasticity is, the stronger the selection effect of trade liberalization.

We derive such parameter from the distribution of firms across marginal cost levels, as detailed in Box 3. It exploits the fact that, given the same conditions in factor markets, different marginal costs of production across firms stem from their different efficiencies in using capital and labour (i.e. from 'total factor productivity' or simply 'TFP'). In other words, more efficient firms produce more output with the same amounts of inputs, and thus have lower marginal costs. Indeed, the distribution of the inverse of TFP represents the distribution of the marginal costs.

Box 3. Estimation of firms' marginal costs

We recover the marginal cost of firm i as the inverse of its 'total factor productivity' (TFP), which measures its efficiency in the use of available inputs. Our baseline results come from a simple least square (LS) log-linear regression of value added over measures of capital and labour employment. The details of the TFP estimation are reported in Appendix 2. Specifically, we rely on the following log-linear estimation of a Cobb–Douglas production function on firm level data for the years 2001–2003:

$$\ln Y_{it,s} = \ln A_{it,s} + a\ln K_{it,s} + b\ln N_{it,s} + timedummy + u_{it,s}$$

where $Y_{it,s}$ is output (value added) of firm i in sector s at time t, $K_{it,s}$ is capital input (proxied by fixed tangible assets), $N_{it,s}$ is labour input (total employment), $A_{it,s}$ is firm efficiency in the usage of capital and labour (TFP), and $u_{it,s}$ is a white noise. Inputs $K_{it,s}$ and $N_{it,s}$ are recovered from the firm's balance sheet whereas $A_{it,s}$ is estimated from the residual of the regression. LS estimations of productivity are carried out separately for each of the 12 manufacturing sectors. Given the likely presence of extreme outliers bound to bias the estimations, firm-level data for value added, employment and tangible assets are trimmed by eliminating the 1% lowest and 1% highest observations. Moreover, the usual LS estimates are replaced by iteratively reweighed least squares, a procedure designed to reduce the influence of outliers. We do not run separate estimations by country assuming *de facto* that in any given sector countries have the same technology up to a scale factor. While this hypothesis overlooks the possibility of some heterogeneity of technology across countries, it has the important advantage of yielding a more robust estimation of productivity, given that some countries have very few observations in some sectors.

As discussed in Box 1, our data strongly support the idea that, within sectors, marginal costs follow a distribution with a constant elasticity of the extensive margin k_s. Its estimates by sector are reported in Figure 5.[9]

Accordingly, the selection effect is estimated to be the largest in *basic metals and fabricated metal products, non-electric machinery*, as well as *rubber and plastic*. They are estimated to be the smallest in *textiles, leather products and footwear, chemicals*, as well as *food, beverages and tobacco*.

4.1.3. Computing sector- and country-specific cost cut-offs. In principle, we could have used the cost distribution estimated from firm-level data also to calculate the cut-off cost c_s^{hh}. In practice, however, our firm-level data exhibit poor coverage for

---

[9] The robustness of our results when using alternative estimates of k_s is discussed in the Web Appendix available at www.economic-policy.org.

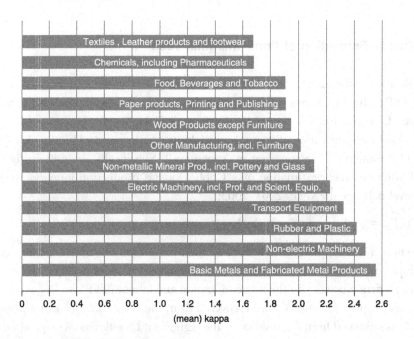

Figure 5. Sensitivity to firm selection

Note: Industries are ranked by skewness factor k.

Source: Amadeus, authors' calculations.

some countries, and especially for Germany. This is not much of a problem for the estimation of k_s as firms in sector s are pooled across countries to obtain good estimates of such a sector but not country specific parameter. It is, instead, more of a problem for the estimation of the cut-off c_s^{hh}, which is sector-and-country specific. While the cut-off estimates based on firm-level data are reported in the Web Appendix, we prefer to rely on the sectoral productivity statistics publicly available on the EUKLEMS website. For each country and sector, such statistics provide yearly levels of labour productivity (value added per hour worked). This is a productivity measure that differs from TFP in that it measures the efficient use of labour without controlling for non-labour inputs. Its advantage is that it is directly measurable. We use it as our measure of sector- and country-specific productivity after averaging across the years from 2001 to 2003, to smooth out business cycle fluctuations. The inverse of such productivity measure gives us an estimate of average marginal costs. These can be used to recover the cut-off cost c_s^{hh}. Indeed, when the elasticity of the extensive margin is constant, as in our case, the cut-off in sector s and country h is obtained simply by multiplying the average cost by a discount factor accounting for the above-mentioned elasticity of the extensive margin (see Box 1 for an explanation of the methodology and Appendix 2 for the country and sector specific coefficients).

After calculating the weighted average of c_s^{hh} across sectors (with weights determined by sectors' shares in manufacturing output), the resulting country-level average

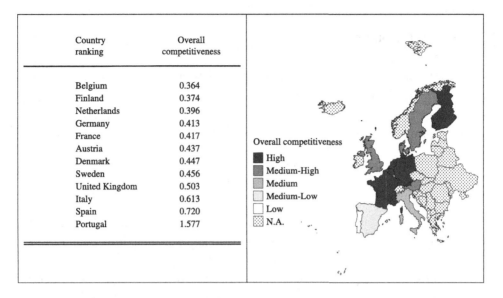

Figure 6. Overall competitiveness

Note: The lower the cut-off, the higher the competitiveness of the country. The darker the colour in the chart, the more competitive the country.

Source: Authors' calculations.

cost cut-off represents a proxy for the country's 'overall competitiveness' in the broad sense identified in our conceptual framework, which includes trade frictions, technology, institutional set-up and demand characteristics, among others. The lower the cut-off cost in a country, the higher its overall competitiveness in the sense of a lower average cost and a higher average productivity of its firms. The geographical pattern of overall competitiveness is portrayed in Figure 6, where competitiveness is higher in countries that are at the heart of Europe – such as Belgium, the Netherlands and Germany – and in Finland. This is consistent with the prediction of the theoretical framework that countries that are large or easily accessible to firms from trading partners should exhibit a tougher competitive environment and stronger selection. Italy, Spain and Portugal are at the bottom of the table because of a less central location and a possible technology disadvantage, which is associated with high entry costs in new sectors.

4.2. Calibrating the remaining parameters of the model and deriving the indicator of producer competitiveness

We are now ready to select values for the unobservable parameters (product differentiation D_s, the absolute advantage o_s^h and the entry cost f_s^h) that make the model exactly match the estimated cost cut-offs c_s^{hh}, given the values of all other directly measured or estimated parameters. See Box 4 for details.

Box 4. Calibration

In Appendix 1 we show that the equilibrium domestic cut-off in country h is determined by the following expression:

$$c_s^{hh} = \left[\frac{2D_s(k_s+1)(k_s+2)\sum_{t=1}^{12}|C_s^{th}|/[f_s^t/(o_s^t)^{k_s}]}{L^h \qquad |T_s|} \right]^{\frac{1}{k_s+2}}$$

where $o_s^t = 1/c_{A,s}^t$ is the index of absolute advantage, $|T_s|$ is the determinant of the matrix whose element T_s^{ht} indexes the freeness of trade from country h to country t, and $|C_s^{th}|$ is the co-factor of that element.

In the above expression market size L^h is directly measurable. The bilateral freeness of trade T_s^{ht} and the elasticity of the extensive margin k_s can be estimated. The remaining parameters – namely the product differentiation D_s, the absolute advantage o_s^h and the entry cost f_s^h – are neither directly measurable nor estimable with the available data. For each sector, however, we can estimate the cost cut-off c_s^{hh} for our 12 countries. This allows us to select values for (i.e. to 'calibrate') the unobservable parameters D_s, o_s^h and f_s^h so that the model exactly matches the estimated cut-offs. In particular, after writing an expression like the one above for each of our 12 countries, we can solve the resulting system of 12 equations for the 12 unknown parameter bundles $D_s/|f_s^t/(o_s^t)^{k_s}|$ that make the model predict the 12 estimated values of the cut-offs. We can then separate the sector specific component D_s from the sector- and country-specific one $|f_s^t/(o_s^t)^{k_s}|$. Details are provided in Appendix 2.

In the simulations presented in Section 5, the above expression is used, in the opposite direction, to predict the impact of changing trade freeness T_s^{ht} on the cost cut-off c_s^{hh}, holding $D_s/[f_s^t/(o_s^t)^{k_s}]$ constant at its calibrated value.

The results of the calibration allow us to obtain separate values for sector specific product differentiation D_s from a sector- and country-specific bundle of technological parameters $[f_s^t/(o_s^t)^{k_s}]$. This value measures the difficulty of country h to generate low-cost firms in sector s due to high entry costs and low absolute advantage in production. Hence, calculating its weighted average across sectors (with weights determined by sectors' manufacturing output shares) yields an index of the ability of country t to generate low cost firms abstracting from its market size and accessibility. We call this index 'producer competitiveness' (see Figure 7) to distinguish this concept from 'overall competitiveness'. It is a measure of competitiveness that depends solely on technology

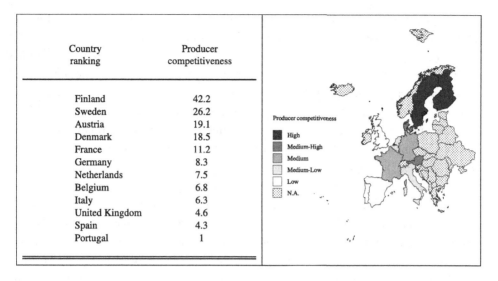

Figure 7. Producer competitiveness

Note: The higher the value, the higher the competitiveness. The darker the colour in the chart, the more competitive the country.

Source: Authors' calculations.

Table 1. Overall versus producer competitiveness (country rankings)

Country ranking	Overall competitiveness	Producer competitiveness
Austria	6	3
Belgium	1	8
Germany	4	6
Denmark	7	4
Spain	11	11
Finland	2	1
France	5	5
United Kingdom	9	10
Italy	10	9
Netherlands	3	7
Portugal	12	12
Sweden	8	2

Source: Authors' calculations.

(i.e. the ability to produce at low cost) and institutional factors (i.e. cost of entry in a sector). As such, the index 'producer competitiveness' can be interpreted as the relative performance of countries in an ideal world in which all firms face the same barriers to international transactions in all countries. The index of 'overall competitiveness', by contrast, quantifies the actual performance of countries in the real world.

According to this second ranking (see Table 1 for a comparison between the two indicators), the following interesting results emerge. First, Sweden becomes the second most competitive country in terms of producer competitiveness. This implies that the country shows a strong technology advantage (large o_s^t) and/or a good institutional environment (low f_s^t), but has a disadvantage in terms of location (since it ranks only eighth in terms of overall competitiveness). Hence, being at the periphery does not per se represent a problem for a country, unless it is compounded by clear relative technological and institutional disadvantages that hamper firm productivity. In this context, it is worth noticing a rather substantial improvement in the ranking of Denmark, in terms of producer competitiveness compared to its ranking in terms of overall competitiveness. The opposite is true for Belgium, Germany and the Netherlands, whose rankings in terms of producer competitiveness are substantially lower than those in terms of overall competitiveness. This signals weak technology advantages and/or a worse institutional environment, only partially offset by their central location. Finally, Portugal and Spain – and, to a lesser extent, Italy and UK – are consistently at the bottom of the competitiveness ranking, no matter how this is measured, suggesting the presence of parallel negative impacts of all the determinants of competitiveness identified in the model, namely geographical location, market access, technological and institutional (dis)advantage.

4.3. Validation

After fitting the model to reality and before using it to simulate counterfactual scenarios, we need to check its consistency with additional features of the data, different from those used in its calibration, i.e. different from the cut-off costs. Obvious targets are some key features at both firm and sector levels.

At the firm level, Table 2 reports several quantitative predictions of the model that could be compared with cross-country data. The second column shows the prediction that exporters are a small subset of the total number of producers. Moreover, the third, fourth and fifth columns respectively show that the model also predicts that exporters are a selected elite, being larger, more productive and more price competitive than non-exporters. The reported numbers are so-called exporters' 'premia' defined as ratios of exporters' values to non-exporters' values.

Unfortunately, the limited availability of firm-level data constrains the number of predictions that can actually be compared with adequate observations. Mayer and Ottaviano (2007) report some information on a subset of countries. According to Table 2 of that study, the actual percentages of exporters in France and Germany are 67% and 59% respectively. These percentages are higher than those predicted in our Table 2 (45% and 36% respectively). Likewise, the predictions of the model for Italy and the United Kingdom (both at 20%) are smaller than the percentages reported in Mayer and Ottaviano (2007), namely 64% for Italy and 28% for the United Kingdom.

Table 4 in Mayer and Ottaviano (2007) also reports exporters' premia. Their size premia for France, Germany, Italy and the United Kingdom are 2.24, 2.99, 2.42 and

Table 2. Predicted shares and premia of exporters

Country	Share of exporting firms	Size advantage exporters	Productivity advantage of exporters	Price advantage of exporters	Perceived productivity advantage of exporters
Austria	26%	3.58	2.40	0.80	1.84
Belgium	27%	2.18	2.27	0.80	1.76
Germany	36%	6.14	2.14	0.83	1.69
Denmark	21%	3.45	2.81	0.78	2.09
Spain	22%	3.17	2.27	0.79	1.76
Finland	25%	2.55	2.56	0.79	1.94
France	45%	7.56	1.67	0.86	1.4
United Kingdom	20%	2.96	2.49	0.78	1.9
Italy	21%	3.01	2.42	0.78	1.85
Netherlands	18%	3.13	2.91	0.76	2.15
Portugal	1%	2.09	8.53	0.65	5.51
Sweden	21%	3.05	2.31	0.78	1.79
Total/Average	24%	3.57	2.90	0.78	2.14

1.01 to be compared with 3.08, 2.53, 2.31 and 2.11 in our Table 2. In the case of Belgium, the size premium reported by Mayer and Ottaviano (2007) is 9.16, which is far larger than the predicted 2.18. This can be explained by the fact that their Belgian sample is exhaustive and, therefore, includes a large number of small firms that are excluded from the Amadeus dataset. Overall, while better – but currently unavailable – firm-level data would be needed to refine both calibration and validation, there seems to exist some remarkable conformity between the actual patterns and those predicted by our stylized theoretical framework.

Turning to the sectoral level, we compare the pattern of competitiveness predicted by the model to check its consistency with aggregate export performance. In particular, our model predicts that, in some industries more than in others, countries generate highly productive and thus internationally competitive firms. As a result, they should be net exporters of the goods supplied by the former sectors and net importers of the goods supplied by the latter sectors. A way to see whether this prediction is consistent with reality is to check the sign of the correlation between an index of relative productivity and an index of export specialization across sectors (see Box 5 for details). If the predictions of the model are consistent with the observation, such a correlation should be positive. Table 3 confirms that this is indeed the case for 11 out of 12 sectors.

5. GAINS FROM THE EURO

Has the introduction of the single currency affected the intensity of competition in the euro area and forced least efficient firms out of the market? If so, to what extent has this selection process affected unit delivery costs, mark-ups, prices, quantities,

Box 5. Relative productivity and export specialization

Following Mayer and Ottaviano (2007), we measure the relative productivity for country h in sector s as the 'estimated comparative advantage' (ECA), which is defined as:

$$ECA_{h,s} = \frac{P_{h,s}/\bar{P}_h}{P_{w,s}/\bar{P}_{w,s}}$$

where $P_{h,s}$ is productivity (the inverse of the cost cut-off c_{hh}^s) of country h in sector s while w is the label for the group of the other countries in our sample. The averages $\bar{P}$'s are defined as:

$$\bar{P}_h = \frac{\sum_{s=1}^{n} P_{h,s}}{n}, \ \bar{P}_w = \frac{\sum_{h=1}^{m}\sum_{s=1}^{n} P_{h,s}}{m \cdot n}$$

where n is the number of sectors (12) and m is the number of countries (also 12). The index is larger (or smaller) than one if country h is relatively more (or less) productive in industry s than the other countries. In this case, country h is said to exhibit an estimated comparative advantage (or disadvantage) in industry s.

We quantify export specialization of country h in sector s by a standard measure, the 'index of revealed comparative advantage' (RCA) which is defined as:

$$RCA_{hs} = \frac{X_{hs}/X_s}{X_{ws}/X_w}$$

where X designates exports. This index is larger (or smaller) than one if the exports of country h are more (or less) specialized in industry s than the exports of the other countries. In this case, country h is said to exhibit a revealed comparative advantage (or disadvantage) in industry s.

The correlations between the two indices in our sample are reported in Table 3.

revenues and profits? Are countries that are eligible to adopt the euro losing anything in terms of economic gains?

To answer these questions, we simulate on our calibrated model three counterfactual scenarios of alternative euro area membership set-ups. The baseline is the actual cross-country pattern of overall competitiveness in 2003, as estimated through the cut-off costs in the previous section: countries with lower cut-off costs are generally more competitive. In the counterfactual scenarios, we let some countries change

Table 3. Relative productivity and export specialization

Industry	Correlation (RCA, ECA)
Food, Beverages and Tobacco	0.45
Textiles, Leather Products and Footwear	0.77
Wood Products except Furniture	0.41
Paper Products, Printing and Publishing	0.36
Rubber and Plastic	0.22
Chemicals, including Pharmaceuticals	−0.32
Non-metallic Mineral Prod., incl. Pottery and Glass	0.70
Basic Metals and Fabricated Metal Products	0.46
Non-electric Machinery	0.50
Electric Machinery, incl. Prof. and Scient. Equip.	0.64
Transport Equipment	0.67
Other Manufacturing, incl. Furniture	0.15

status with respect to their participation in Stage 3 of the European EMU. Since changes in euro area membership affect trade frictions among our countries, the alternative scenarios are generated by altering the trade freeness parameters T_s^{ht} in the appropriate way. Then, holding all other parameters constant, we use our model to simulate the resulting cut-off costs for each scenario (see Box 4), and compare them with the baseline.[10]

5.1 Trade freeness and the euro

In the logic of our framework, abandoning the euro results in trade frictions. Accordingly, we generate our counterfactual scenarios by changing the bilateral trade frictions as follows. When two countries use the euro in the baseline scenario, while they do not do so in the counterfactual scenario, we increase their bilateral trade frictions. When two trading partners do not share the same currency in the baseline scenario, while they do so in the counterfactual scenario, we decrease their bilateral trade frictions.

In order to proxy the impact of the euro on trade frictions, we rely on the findings from the substantial body of empirical research that in the past decade has investigated the trade-enhancing effects of the euro and, in general, of monetary unions. Results are very heterogeneous due to the adoption of different econometric specifications. Nonetheless, economists seem recently to be reaching the consensus view that the euro has had a positive effect on trade, though smaller than previously thought. The single currency appears to have boosted the growth of euro area countries' trade on average by a figure below 5 percentage points of the country's total trade growth.[11]

---

[10] We present here our baseline results. Their robustness to alternative measures of trade freeness and productivity is checked in the Web Appendix available at www. economic-policy.org.

[11] For details on the comparative evaluation of methodologies used to capture the trade impact of the euro, see e.g. Baldwin and Taglioni (2007). On the need to disentangle appropriately the effects of the euro from those of other EU integration measures, see e.g. Baldwin (2006).

Table 4. Trade effects of the euro in the literature (estimated impacts on trade frictions[a]; percentages)

	BT (lower bound)	FN (upper bound)
Intra-euro area	2%***	8.8%***
Exports by non-euro users to the euro area	−1%**	0.8%
Euro area exports to the non-euro area	3%***	7.1%***
Period of analysis	1996–2006	1980–2002

[a] Estimates based on EU-15 sample.
** Statistically significant at 5%.
*** Statistically significant at 1%.

To generate our counterfactuals, we select two studies, by Flam and Nordström (2003) and by Baldwin and Taglioni (2008), as respectively providing the upper and the lower bounds of the estimated impacts of the euro on trade frictions. These are reported in Table 4 where column 'FN' refers to the former and column 'BT' to the latter. We use them to increase/decrease our bilateral measures of the freeness of trade in the various scenarios.

5.2. Three counterfactual scenarios

Three scenarios are particularly revealing when it comes to highlighting the effects of the euro on countries' overall competitiveness. In the first, we see what happens when all euro area countries drop the single currency. In the second, we study the implications of Denmark, Sweden and the United Kingdom adopting the euro. In the third, we assess the impact of France abandoning the euro and reverting to the French franc as its national currency.

5.2.1. Scenario 1. For the first scenario, we increase trade frictions within the euro area by either 2% or 8.8% (see first row of Table 4) and those from the euro area to the non-euro area (Denmark, Sweden and the United Kingdom) by either 3% or 7.1% (see third row of Table 4).

The results, reported in Figure 8, are shown both in terms of new implied cut-off costs for individual countries and – in the chart on the right – as a difference with respect to the previously computed domestic cut-off, used as a baseline. Had all euro area countries reverted to their national currencies in 2003, the average loss in overall competitiveness for Europe as a whole – as measured by higher cut-off costs – would have been substantial. As expected, all euro area countries would have lost, in particular the relatively small euro area countries (most notably Finland, followed by Belgium and Austria). In comparison, gains accrued to non-euro area countries would have been rather minor and limited only to Denmark and Sweden, with the United Kingdom basically remaining unaffected.

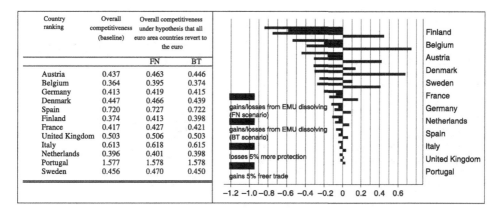

Figure 8. All countries in the euro area revert to national currencies in 2003 (Scenario 1)

Note: Higher values than the baseline cut-off costs indicate losses in competitiveness and are shown in the chart in terms of changes from baseline with a negative sign; the term '5% more protection' indicates the losses arising from a uniform 5% increase in all trade frictions relative to their real value. Conversely the term 'gains 5% freer trade' indicates the gains from a 5% reduction of all bilateral trade frictions.

Source: Authors' calculations.

In order to provide a benchmark for the gains/losses resulting from dropping the euro, Figure 8 also shows ranges resulting from a comparison of the effects of increasing or reducing trade protection by 5% in all countries in the sample. Two comments are in order. First, the extent of the losses in overall competitiveness resulting from a dissolution of the European currency union (Stage 3 of the EMU) are about the same size – or actually slightly larger – than the losses caused by a 5% increase in trade protection. Second, increasing trade protection by 5% has an asymmetric effect with respect to decreasing it by 5% from the same initial situation. For example, Finland appears to be clearly more disadvantaged by an increase in protection than it is favoured by a reduction. The opposite is true for other countries. This is due to the fact that the effects of trade liberalization are non-linear.

Taking a sectoral perspective, Figure 9 reveals that the industry in which firm productivity falls the most is *electric machinery*, followed by *basic metals and fabricated metal products* and *transport equipment*. This is due to a combination of trade freeness and the sensitivity to firm selection. In particular, according to the evidence reported in Figure 3 and Figure 5, *electric machinery* and *transport equipment* are both characterized by a relative dominance of small unproductive firms and a relatively high openness to international competition. For both reasons, selection effects are strong in these sectors, making them more sensitive to frictions related to the existence of different currencies and other trade barriers. While trade freeness is below the median in *basic metals and fabricated metal products*, this sector ranks first in terms of the sensitivity to firm selection (or elasticity of the extensive margin), which explains why it also exhibits a strong selection effect.

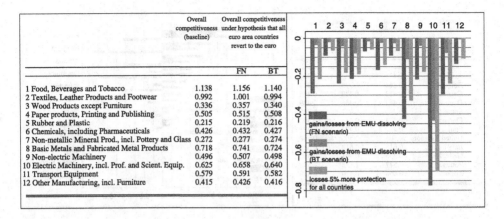

	Overall competitiveness (baseline)	Overall competitiveness under hypothesis that all euro area countries revert to the euro	
		FN	BT
1 Food, Beverages and Tobacco	1.138	1.156	1.140
2 Textiles, Leather Products and Footwear	0.992	1.001	0.994
3 Wood Products except Furniture	0.336	0.357	0.340
4 Paper products, Printing and Publishing	0.505	0.515	0.508
5 Rubber and Plastic	0.215	0.219	0.216
6 Chemicals, including Pharmaceuticals	0.426	0.432	0.427
7 Non-metallic Mineral Prod., incl. Pottery and Glass	0.272	0.277	0.274
8 Basic Metals and Fabricated Metal Products	0.718	0.741	0.724
9 Non-electric Machinery	0.496	0.507	0.498
10 Electric Machinery, incl. Prof. and Scient. Equip.	0.625	0.658	0.640
11 Transport Equipment	0.579	0.591	0.582
12 Other Manufacturing, incl. Furniture	0.415	0.426	0.416

Figure 9. Impact on specific industries when all countries reverted to national currencies in 2003 (Scenario 1)

Note: Higher values than the baseline cut-off costs indicate losses in competitiveness and are shown in the chart in terms of changes from baseline with a negative sign; term '5% more protection' indicates the losses arising from a uniform 5% increase in all trade frictions relative to their real value. Conversely the term 'gains 5% freer trade' indicates the gains from a 5% reduction of all bilateral trade frictions.

Source: Authors' calculations.

To summarize, reverting to national currencies reduces the overall competitiveness of all euro area countries while generating small productivity gains for non-euro area countries. These effects are stronger for smaller countries with better access to European markets and specialized in sectors with higher trade freeness and higher sensitivity to firm selection. The same logic will explain what we find in the following scenarios.

5.2.2. Scenario 2. For the second scenario, we reduce trade frictions between the euro area and Denmark, Sweden, the United Kingdom by either 3% or 7.1% (see third row of Table 4) while obviously leaving unchanged trade frictions within the euro area. The results of the corresponding simulation are reported in Figure 10. The benchmark range is now generated by the effects of increasing/decreasing trade protection between euro area and non-euro area countries by 5%.

Overall, the average impact for Europe as a whole is positive, although rather small. Only two of the three non-euro area countries (namely Denmark and Sweden) would gain in terms of overall competitiveness to an extent similar to an across-the-board reduction of trade frictions by 5%, while the United Kingdom would record an only minor gain.[12] As for the euro area countries, the changes in overall competitiveness are very modest, except in the case of Finland, which sees its competitive position worsening because of proximity to Denmark and Sweden.

---

[12] Figure 10 also shows the rather remarkable gains for Denmark from a 5% decrease in trade frictions. The reason is the critical importance of Sweden as a trading partner for a rather small and nearby country like Denmark.

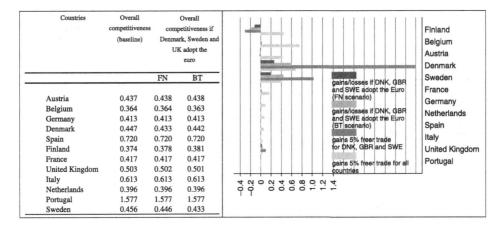

Countries	Overall competitiveness (baseline)	Overall competitiveness if Denmark, Sweden and UK adopt the euro	
		FN	BT
Austria	0.437	0.438	0.438
Belgium	0.364	0.364	0.363
Germany	0.413	0.413	0.413
Denmark	0.447	0.433	0.442
Spain	0.720	0.720	0.720
Finland	0.374	0.378	0.381
France	0.417	0.417	0.417
United Kingdom	0.503	0.502	0.501
Italy	0.613	0.613	0.613
Netherlands	0.396	0.396	0.396
Portugal	1.577	1.577	1.577
Sweden	0.456	0.446	0.433

Figure 10. Denmark, Sweden and the United Kingdom adopt the euro in 2003 (Scenario 2)

Note: Higher values than the baseline cut-off costs indicate losses in competitiveness and are shown in the chart in terms of changes from baseline with a negative sign; the term '5% more protection' indicates the losses arising from a 5% increase in trade frictions for trade involving Denmark, Sweden or the United Kingdom. Conversely the term 'gains 5% freer trade' indicates the gains from a 5% reduction of trade frictions affecting bilateral trade where one of the trade partners is Denmark, Sweden or the United Kingdom.

Source: Authors' calculations.

5.2.3. Scenario 3. Finally, for the third scenario, we change only the trade frictions for French exports to the euro area, increasing them either by 2% or 8.8% (see first row of Table 4). The benchmark range is generated by the effects of increasing/ decreasing trade protection between France and the other euro area countries by 5%.

Figure 11 shows that the loss in overall competitiveness for France is rather notable, ranging from 1.4% to 5.8%. The fact that all other countries are hardly affected is in line with the logic of the model. When market size matters, a departing partner faces a sharp reduction in market access across the board, while remaining members compensate for the negative impact of such departure by strengthening trade among themselves.

To summarize, the introduction of the euro appears to have benefited the overall competitiveness of member countries as defined in our 'holistic' framework that combines the effects on delivery costs, mark-ups, prices, quantities, revenues and profits. The impact appears to be relatively stronger for small central countries specialized in sectors that (i) are relatively tradable, so that euro-related frictions are more relevant for them, and (ii) have large fractions of small inefficient firms, so that selection effects via firm entry and exit are stronger for them.

6. CONCLUSION AND POLICY IMPLICATIONS

In this paper, we have exploited available data to calibrate a state-of-the-art trade model that we have used to quantify the microeconomic benefits of the euro. These

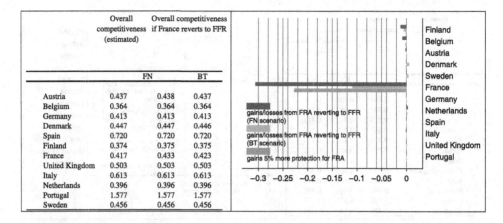

	Overall competitiveness (estimated)	Overall competitiveness if France reverts to FFR	
	FN	BT	
Austria	0.437	0.438	0.437
Belgium	0.364	0.364	0.364
Germany	0.413	0.413	0.413
Denmark	0.447	0.447	0.446
Spain	0.720	0.720	0.720
Finland	0.374	0.375	0.375
France	0.417	0.433	0.423
United Kingdom	0.503	0.503	0.503
Italy	0.613	0.613	0.613
Netherlands	0.396	0.396	0.396
Portugal	1.577	1.577	1.577
Sweden	0.456	0.456	0.456

Figure 11. France reverts to the French Franc in 2003 (Scenario 3)

Note: Higher values than the baseline cut-off costs indicate losses in competitiveness and are shown in the chart in terms of changes from baseline with a negative sign; the term '5% more protection' indicates the losses arising from a 5% increase in trade frictions for trade involving France.
Source: Authors' calculations.

benefits, which are due to an enhanced price transparency and lower transaction costs, arise from a further specialization of countries in sectors in which they are more efficient, from richer product variety, from weakened market power on the part of firms, from a better exploitation of economies of scale and from improved production efficiency through the exit of the least efficient firms.

The model has been calibrated on 12 manufacturing sectors across 12 EU countries for the years from 2001 to 2003 and has been used to evaluate the competitiveness of European manufacturing firms in terms of an efficient usage of available inputs. In so doing, we have derived a ranking of European countries in terms of the cost effectiveness of the firms located therein – which we have taken as an indicator of the 'overall competitiveness' of the corresponding countries. This indicator has then been used as a benchmark for two sets of experiments. First, in order to distinguish the extent to which the ability of a country to generate low-cost firms stems from aspects related to technology, versus market size and accessibility, we have derived another indicator, which we have called 'producer competitiveness'. This indicator gives us the extent to which a country would be competitive in an ideal world in which trade frictions did not matter.

In the second set of experiments, we have simulated three counterfactual scenarios designed to evaluate how alternative (and hypothetical) euro membership set-ups would have affected the baseline overall competitiveness of the European countries considered. In the first scenario, in which all members of the euro area are assumed to have dropped the single currency in 2003, the average loss in their overall competitiveness ranges from 1.4% to 3.3%. In the second scenario, in which Denmark, Sweden and the United Kingdom adopt the euro in 2003, the average gain in overall competitiveness for those countries ranges from 1.5% to 3.4%. In the third and last scenario, in which France reverts to the French franc in 2003, the average loss in French overall competitiveness ranges from 1.4% to 5.8%.

Our findings have several policy implications. First, the impact on trade flows is at best only a first approximation of the possible gains arising from the euro. The reason is that trade creation is not a welfare gain in itself, but rather a channel through which different types of microeconomic gains can materialize. This casts a shadow on the customary obsession with the effects of the euro on trade flows.

Second, market size and accessibility are not the only key drivers of competitiveness. In particular, Mediterranean countries remain at the bottom of the competitiveness league even after controlling for their peripheral location, as shown by the rather insignificant difference between their indicators of overall and producer competitiveness. This suggests that being peripheral does not per se represent the problem with these countries. High entry barriers and poor technological opportunities seem to be more important.

Third, small central countries specialized in tradable sectors – especially if characterized by a relative dominance of small and medium-sized enterprises (SMEs) – experience the strongest reactions to our counterfactual experiments, which suggests that these countries gain most from the euro.

Finally, our methodological approach should be thought of as a practical second-best solution to concrete, but hopefully temporary, constraints on firm-level data availability that prevent a full-fledged econometric investigation. Its main shortcoming is its forced reliance on a complex theoretical structure. In this respect, our results should be interpreted as the 'partial effects' of the euro, holding constant all the features of the economy that the theoretical model keeps constant in the first place, such as nominal wages and aggregate employment in the selected European countries, as well as competitiveness elsewhere in the world.

Discussion

Kevin O'Rourke
Trinity College Dublin

This is an ambitious paper on an important issue. It is notable in its use of very recent developments in trade theory. It shows that these developments are helpful in understanding important policy issues. And the empirical strategy adopted in calibrating the model is extremely ingenious, and represents an astonishing amount of work.

I particularly welcome the close attention paid to calibration in this paper, since in any simulation exercise calibration will matter for the results as much as model structure, but too often little attention is paid to it. I like the fact that since the model is symmetric across countries, differences in the results for different countries will depend crucially on calibration. The question then arises is, do the numbers make sense? I was pleased to see that in this version of the paper the numbers seem to make a lot more sense than in previous drafts, although there remains the question of how representative the Amadeus database is, and in particular the question of whether it is equally representative for all countries, given its focus on large firms. One finding that may strike some readers as strange is the low ranking of United Kingdom in the two competitiveness tables produced by the calibration exercise. This is a reminder, I suppose, that this exercise is limited to the manufacturing sector, and that one might expect the financial services sector to also be influenced by the introduction of the euro. However, one has to start somewhere, and the authors can hardly be accused of a lack of ambition.

The authors are to be commended for the way in which they confront the predictions of their model with reality, where this is possible. I find their predicted share of exporting firms for Portugal (1%) to be worryingly low, and the model seems to underpredict this figure more generally across all countries. I would be interested to find out more about why this is the case.

The results also depend crucially on the experiment conducted with the calibrated model. Drawing on existing gravity studies, the authors model the introduction of the euro as a lowering of trade costs between euro countries, and a lowering of trade costs for Eurozone exports to the non-euro area. There is, however, relatively little impact on the trade costs facing non-Eurozone firms exporting to the euro area. It is disappointing that the realism of these shocks depends crucially on the accuracy of gravity studies, since these have come up with such a wide range of estimates. More seriously, one might ask whether the effect of the euro was really the same as that of an across-the-board decline in trade costs. We typically think of single currencies as eliminating risk, and there may be reasons why such risk reduction would be more valuable in particular sectors than in others. On the other hand, it is hard to think of an alternative empirical strategy which the authors could realistically have pursued.

It is a shame, given the authors' comments regarding gravity studies, and the fact that trade flows are not a measure of welfare, that this exercise has not yielded any welfare measures itself (although clearly the competitiveness results presented here are getting us a lot closer to welfare than results regarding the volume of trade). More generally, I would have liked the authors to discuss how the results of the study might be biased, if at all, by its partial equilibrium nature, and by its neglect of factor endowment differences between countries.

Ekaterina Zhuravskaya
New Economic School and CEFIR

The New Trade Theory paradigm (e.g., Melitz, 2003) implies important microeconomic effects of trade liberalization in addition to the classic Ricardian macroeconomic effect of specialization in sectors with a comparative advantage. Namely, trade liberalization should lead to significant changes within sectors: growth of the most efficient firms, a richer variety of goods, tougher competition (i.e., smaller mark-ups), and, consequently, exit of the least efficient firms. Despite the fact that these changes have (in theory) a first order effect on the competitiveness of trading partner countries, many policy settings do not allow a direct estimation of the microeconomic effects of trade liberalization due to a lack of microdata comparable across countries. Ottaviano, Taglioni and di Mauro suggest an alternative approach: develop a model with a closed-form solution, estimate those parameters of the model which can be directly estimated with the available data, and deduce the rest of the parameters from a calibration exercise in which the verifiable model's predictions fit the actual data patterns. They develop a state-of-the-art New Trade Theory general equilibrium model and calibrate it using country, sector, and firm-level data. The paper is a great and rare example of using cutting-edge theory tools to address policy-relevant questions.

Ottaviano *et al.* apply their methodology to study the effect of changes in the composition of the European Monetary Union (EMU), which are modelled as having a trade liberalization effect through an increase in price transparency and a decrease in transaction costs and exchange-rate risk. The paper addresses a very important policy issue: how the European currency union affects the competitiveness of European firms. To be more precise, the paper quantifies the effects of possible changes in the composition of the EMU on average productivity of manufacturing firms in each of 12 considered EU countries located both within and outside the Eurozone. The authors give definitive answers to these questions: What are the benefits of the Union for member countries? What would happen to the competitiveness of European firms if the UK, Denmark or Sweden were to join, or France were to exit the Eurozone?

The results of the paper constitute a significant contribution that informs the policy debate on the effects of currency unions. Ottaviano *et al.* conduct counterfactual experiments on the effects of changes in the Eurozone. Had all nine members of the EMU reverted to their initial national currencies in 2003 without any change in the national currencies of the UK, Denmark and Sweden, the average competitiveness of European firms would have dropped significantly. Moreover, every member of the EMU would have lost in competitiveness, with the largest losses occurring in Austria, Belgium and Germany; while there would have been hardly any gain in countries initially outside the EMU. Had the UK, Denmark and Sweden entered the Eurozone in 2003, Denmark and Sweden would have had a substantial increase in their competitiveness, the UK would not have gained much, while Finland would have been the only country which would have lost a substantial amount due to increased competition from its immediate neighbours. If France had switched back to the franc from the euro and no other country changed its currency in 2003, France would have had a sizeable decline in its competitiveness and other countries would have experienced practically no change in their competitiveness. These exercises demonstrate that the focus of previous literature on trade flows (see, for instance, Alesina, Barro and Tenreyro, 2007) missed out on important productivity gains from adopting the euro.

If applied to a wider set of countries, the methodology developed by Ottaviano *et al.* would also allow for answering a related question that is high on the European policy agenda after the EU enlargement: What are the costs and benefits of including new member states (such as Poland or the Czech Republic) in the EMU from both the perspective of competitiveness of firms of the old member states and from the perspective of newcomers?

One of the building blocks of the methodology developed in the paper has a direct policy implication of its own. The paper evaluates the relative contribution of two sets of factors to the overall competitiveness of each country: the first group of factors are the standard inputs into the gravity equation, i.e., market size and accessibility; the second group of factors includes institutional quality and the technological possibility set of the country. In particular, the paper demonstrates the role of technological advances and freeness of entry regulation as key drivers of the competitiveness of such relatively peripheral European countries as Spain, Portugal and Finland. Spain and Portugal lose out to the rest of the 12 EU countries in terms of competitiveness even after taking their market size and distance into account; in contrast, Finland ranks very high in terms of overall competitiveness despite its remoteness and relatively small size. This suggests a public policy strategy to improve competitiveness for Spain and Portugal focusing on liberalization of entry regulations and general improvement of the business climate.

It is important to recognize that the authors' approach is based on theory that necessarily implies assumptions leading to the simplification of reality. Some of these assumptions are more innocuous than others. For example, the authors' calculation is valid under the assumption of fixed wages and labour supply, which gives it a short-run partial equilibrium flavour. In addition, throughout the paper, competitiveness of the rest of the world is held constant. Yet, the patterns predicted by the model for the 12 EU countries suggest that many countries outside the EU are also quite likely to be affected by changes in the Eurozone, and this, in turn, should have a spillover effect on EU countries that is not accounted for in the present calculation. Changes in the EMU should have especially pronounced effects in emerging markets which have (or potentially could have) high volumes of trade with European countries. There could be two countervailing effects at work here. On the one hand, the effect of the euro on trade liberalization is similar to that of a preferential trade agreement. Thus, one should expect trade diversion for emerging markets outside the European Union. On the other hand, enlargement of the Eurozone should substantially decrease trans-action costs and foreign exchange risk for emerging markets that use the euro as a reserve currency. This, in turn, may create an important competitive pressure from outside the EU. Therefore, policy analysis should try to take these effects into account.

A key input into the calculation of the size of the effects in the paper are the estimates of the effect of the euro on trade frictions. They are borrowed from the literature, and are used by Ottaviano *et al.* to assess changes in the bilateral freeness of trade in the considered hypothetical scenarios. There is, however, no consensus in the literature about the size of the effect of the euro on trade frictions. This is reflected in a four-fold difference in the size of estimates from two sources, Flam and Nordstrom (2003) and Baldwin and Taglioni (2008) (based on different methodologies and different time periods). These estimates are used by the authors as the upper and lower bounds for the effect. Such a large spread of the input into the calculation, not surprisingly, produces a large spread in the predicted effect of EMU changes on competitiveness in the considered scenarios. Yet, there is a potentially more important concern that further lowers confidence in these estimates. The effect of the euro on trade frictions was estimated based on actual changes in the monetary union that can hardly be considered random; moreover, the decisions of countries to join the EMU surely are related to their expectations about the benefits from the Union. In particular, it is conceivable that countries that expected to have a larger liberalizing effect of euro on trade had already entered the EMU, and the rest of the eligible countries would have had a lower effect had they joined (which may have been the reason not to join in the first place). This creates a problem for applying these estimates when evaluating the counterfactual scenarios in which non-members (such as the UK, Denmark and Sweden) join the Eurozone. This is a serious concern that needs to be taken into account in the policy discussion, but it is worth keeping in mind that it applies to the whole body of literature in this area and not just to this paper. In addition, this concern applies to a lesser extent to the other two counterfactual exercises, as their focus is on the effects of reverting from the euro for those countries which initially joined the EMU. So, under a reasonable assumption of symmetry in the effects of entering and exiting the Eurozone, the predictions of this paper about the effects of reverting from the euro should be valid ones.

Panel discussion

The panellists focused first on the theoretical framework of the paper. Jean Imbs noticed that the Melitz and Ottaviano (2008) framework models both decisions to export and decisions about firm location, and wondered which of these are crucial in this paper's approach. The authors replied that from a long-run perspective the decision is immaterial, but admitted that in the short run firms may be able to relocate production plants without drawing a new competitiveness realization in the new location. Jean Imbs agreed that exit and location effects of a permanent and credible regime change can be similar, however in the long run decisions about relocation are also potentially driven by market-access considerations, and this should be taken into account by the model. Diego Puga noted that while the theoretical model can only be solved with a specific distribution, this paper's calibration exercise could use the actual observed distributions. The authors argued that the results would be similar for more general distributions, including the actual observed one. The panel then questioned the suitability of the paper's framework of analysis. Josef Zweimuller wondered how robust the conclusions were to a general equilibrium experiment, where income effects would perhaps strengthen the effect of the introduction of the euro. Massimiliano Marcellino argued that joining or abandoning the euro would also have implications for taxes and interest rates and wondered which assumptions the authors made with respect to the latter.

Then, the discussion focused on methodological issues. On calibration, Morten Ravn said that a structural model would allow the authors to generate data from the model and see whether the data generating process can be recovered from regressions like those used to calibrate it. Kevin O'Rourke suggested to validate the model on patterns of comparative advantage, too. On the simulation part, Ravn said that he had doubts that all the experiments are interesting ones. Christian Shultz added that Denmark and Sweden do not enter the euro for reasons different from monetary policy independence (Denmark, for instance, is already basically pegged); hence, tradability effects are likely to be different. Jacques Melitz noticed that the various numbers reported are not necessarily coherent, but intriguingly indicate that some countries may gain if a country exits but then lose if all exit.

APPENDIX 1: THE CALIBRATION MODEL

This appendix presents the main equations of the model we calibrate. It is aimed at making the paper self-contained, so that only necessary information is provided. Interested readers should refer to Melitz and Ottaviano (2006) as well as to Del Gatto *et al.* (2006).

The inverse demand of a consumer in country h for the variety of firm i, when a set Ω of alternative varieties are on offer in sector s, is given by:

$$p_s^h(i) = A_s - D_s e_s^h(i) - B_s \int_{i\in\Omega} e_s^h(i)di \tag{1}$$

which shows that, if the firm wants to increase the quantity sold $e_s^h(i)$, it has to lower its price $p_s^h(i)$. For an envisaged increase in quantity, the price drop is the larger, the smaller is D_s, which is thus a measure of product differentiation. The firm is unable to sell any quantity at all if it prices above the 'choke price' $p_{s,max}^h = A_s - B_s \int_{i\in\Omega} e_s^h(i)di$ at which $f_s^h e(i)$ nullifies. This threshold price falls as the total quantity $\int_{i\in\Omega} e_s^h(i)di$ brought to the market by all firms increases. Equivalently, it falls as the average price p_s^h falls and the total number of firms N_s^l increases given that (1) allows us to write

$$p_{s,max}^h = \frac{D_s A_s - B_s N_s^h}{D_s + B_s N_s^h}. \tag{2}$$

Pricing closer to this choke price implies an increase in the elasticity of demand as this evaluates to

$$\varepsilon_s^h(i) = \left(\frac{p_{s,max}^h}{p_s^h(i)} - 1\right)^{-1}. \tag{3}$$

The firm producing variety i for L^h consumers in country h faces a total demand equal to $q_s^h(i) = L^h e_s^h(i)$. If it draws a marginal cost c, the profit-maximizing quantity sold to domestic consumers is

$$q_s^{hh}(c) = \frac{L^h}{2D_s}(c_s^{hh} - c) \tag{4}$$

where $c_s^{hh} = p_{s,\max}^h$ is the maximum cost at which the quantity sold is (marginally) positive. Analogously, the profit maximizing quantity sold to foreign consumers in country t is

$$q_s^{ht}(c) = \frac{L^h}{2D_s}(c_s^{ht} - c) = \frac{d_s^{ht}L^h}{2D_s}(c_s^{tt} - d_s^{ht}c) \tag{5}$$

where $d_s^{ht} > 1$ is the factor measuring the cost increase per unit sold that is linked to international deliveries. Hence, the marginal exporter from country h to country t is necessarily d_s^{ht} times more efficient than the marginal local producer in country t, i.e. $c_s^{ht} = c_s^{tt}/d_s^{ht}$. Quantities (4) and (5) are both decreasing in c, meaning that less efficient firms are able to sell lower quantities and therefore achieve a smaller market share. The case of two identical countries (such that $L^h = L^t$, $d_s^{ht} = d_s^{th}$ and $c_s^{hh} = c_s^{tt}$) is represented in the top panel of Figure 1 in the main text.

If entrants draw their marginal costs from a Pareto distribution with cumulative density function $G_s^h(c) = (c/c_{A,s}^h)^{k_s}$ and probability density function $g_s^h(c) = k_s c^{k_s-1}/(c_{A,s}^h)^{k_s}$ (the latter is portrayed in the middle panel of Figure 1; see Box 1 for details), all average performance measures of the industry in country h are directly determined by the domestic cut-off. In particular, the average marginal cost, the average price and the average markup are respectively:

$$\bar{c}_s^h = \frac{k_s}{k_s + 1}c_s^{hh}, \quad \bar{p}_s^h = \frac{2k_s + 1}{2(k_s + 1)}c_s^{hh}, \text{ and } \bar{m}_s^h = \frac{c_s^{hh}}{2(k_s + 1)}. \tag{6}$$

The average quantity, the average revenue and the average profit are:

$$\bar{q}_s^h = \frac{L^h}{2D_s}\frac{c_s^{hh}}{k_s + 1}, \quad \bar{r}_s^h = \frac{L^h}{2D_s}\frac{(c_s^{hh})^2}{k_s + 2}, \text{ and } \bar{p}_s^h = \frac{L^h}{2D_s}\frac{(c_s^{hh})^2}{(k_s + 1)(k_s + 2)}. \tag{7}$$

The (indirect) utility associated with demand (1), as achieved by a local resident, is

$$U^h = I^h + \frac{1}{2B_s}(A_s - c_s^{hh})\left(A_s - \frac{k_s + 1}{k_s + 2}c_s^{hh}\right) \tag{8}$$

which shows that any decrease in the domestic cut-off c_s^{hh} generates higher welfare.

At the entry stage firms incur the sunk entry cost f_s^h in country h until this is exactly matched by expected profits. Since all firms are identical before drawing their marginal costs, they share the same expected profits. For each possible country of destination t, these consist of two ingredients: the profit of the average seller in the market

$$\bar{p}_s^{lt} = \frac{L^t}{2D_s}\frac{(c_s^{tt})^2}{(k_s + 1)(k_s + 2)}, \tag{9}$$

and the probability of being efficient enough to sell in that market

$$prob_s^{ht} = \left(\frac{c_s^{ht}}{c_{s,A}^h}\right)^{k_s} = \left(\frac{c_s^{tt}}{c_{s,A}^h}\right)^{k_s} T_s^{ht} \tag{10}$$

where the second equality is granted by $c_s^{ht} = c_s^{tt}/d_s^{ht}$ and by the definition of the bilateral trade freeness index $T_s^{ht} = (d_s^{ht})^{-k_s}$. Summing up across all 13 countries of destination, expected profits match the sunk entry cost as long as

$$\sum_{t=1}^{12} prob_s^{ht} \cdot \bar{p}_s^{tt} = \frac{(c_{s,A}^h)^{-k_s}}{2D_s(k_s+1)(k_s+2)} \sum_{t=1}^{12} [T_s^{ht}(c_s^{tt})^{k_s+2} L^t] = f_s^h \tag{11}$$

which is portrayed in the bottom panel of Figure 1 in the case of two identical countries.

Since a free entry condition like (11) holds for each of our 12 EU countries, we have a system of 12 equations in 12 unknown domestic cut-off costs. Its solution gives an equilibrium domestic cut-off cost for each country:

$$c_s^{hh} = \left[\frac{2D_s(k_s+1)(k_s+2)}{L^h} \frac{\sum_{t=1}^{13} |C_s^{th}|/[f_s^t/(o_s^t)^{k_s}]}{|T_s|}\right]^{\frac{1}{k_s+2}} \tag{12}$$

where $o_s^t = 1/c_{A,s}^t$ is the index of absolute advantage, $|T_s|$ is the determinant of the trade freeness matrix, whose element T_s^{ht} indexes the freeness of trade from country h to country t, and $|C_s^{th}|$ is the co-factor of its T_s^{th} element. In the case of two identical countries the cut-off cost corresponds to the intersection between the entry cost and the expected profit curves in Figure 1.

Finally, the model also yields a 'gravity equation' for aggregate bilateral trade flows. A firm operating in sector s with cost c and exporting from country h to country t generates export sales $r_s^{ht}(c) = p_s^{ht}(c)q_s^{ht}(c)$ where the quantity exported $q_s^{ht}(c)$ is given by (5) with the associated price

$$p_s^{ht}(c) = \frac{1}{2s}(c_s^{tt} + d_s^{ht}c). \tag{13}$$

Aggregating these export sales $r_s^{ht}(c)$ over all exporters from country h to country t (with cost c below $c_s^{ht} = c_s^{tt}/d_s^{ht}$) yields the aggregate bilateral exports from country h to country t

$$EXP_s^{ht} = \frac{1}{2D_s(k_s+2)} N_E^h(o_s^h)^{k_s} L^t(c_s^{tt})^{k_s+2}(d_s^{ht})^{-k_s} \tag{14}$$

where N_E^h is the number of entrants in sector s and country h. This is a 'gravity equation' insofar as it determines bilateral exports as a log-linear function of bilateral trade barriers and country characteristics. As in Helpman *et al.* (2008), (14) reflects the joint effects of country size, technology (absolute advantage), and distance on both the extensive (number of traded goods) and intensive (amount traded per good) margins of trade flows. Similarly, (14) highlights how, holding the importing country size L^t fixed, tougher competition in that country, reflected by a lower c_s^{tt}, dampens exports by making it harder for potential exporters to break into that market. The gravity equation (14) is used in Section 4.1.1 to estimate bilateral trade freeness.

APPENDIX 2: EMPIRICAL IMPLEMENTATION AND ROBUSTNESS CHECKS

Trade freeness

On the basis of Helpman *et al.* (2008) and in line with our theoretical model, the gravity estimation discussed in Box 2 consists of two stages. In the first stage, a probit regression is run on a dataset of world trade at the sectoral level. The dataset covers bilateral trade among 212 countries in 27 three-digit NACE manufacturing industries.[13] It also accounts for domestic flows, constructed as the difference between a country's domestic production and its exports. The probit equation specifies the probability that country h exports to country t as a function of observable variables:

$$
\begin{aligned}
pr_{ht} &= \Pr(EXP_s^{ht} = 1 | observed\_variables) \\
&= \phi[\ln(distance^{ht}) + EX_h + IM_h + col + comcol + col45 + smctry]
\end{aligned}
\tag{A.1}
$$

where $\Phi(.)$ is the cumulative density function of the unit-normal distribution, EXP_s^{ht} are the exports of sector s from country h to country t, EX_h and IM_t are dummies specific to the countries of origin and destination. Trade barriers are captured by bilateral distance ($distance^{ht}$) and a range of other accessory geographical controls: *col*, indicating if two countries were ever in a colony-colonizer relationship; *col45*, indicating if the colony-colonizer relationship extended beyond 1945; *smctry* indicating if two countries were ever part of the same nation. The probit estimation allows us to generate additional variables (*Firmshare^{ht}* and *Selection^{ht}*) that can be used to control for the unobserved underlying firm-level heterogeneity, which is likely to be correlated with trade flows (Helpman *et al.*, 2008). *Selection^{ht}* also corrects for biases arising from a possible non-random sample selection of the observations (Heckman, 1979). Predicted components of this equation are then used in the second stage to estimate the gravity equation expressed in log-linear form and reported in Box 2. This second estimation is free from biases arising from the non-random selection of observations as well as from potentially heterogeneous groups of firms selling to different export markets.

TFP and elasticity of the extensive margin

We have estimated the elasticity of the extensive margin in sector s (k_s) from the sectoral distribution of total factor productivity (TFP). Such distribution is generated by estimating TFP at the level of the individual firm by exploiting the balance sheet

---

[13] While we are interested in bilateral trade between the EU-15, these include a very large number of observations (97%) whose characteristics are such that their estimated probability of trade is indistinguishable from 1. This jeopardizes the first step of the approach of Helpman *et al.* (2008). For this reason, we have expanded our sample to include as many trade partners as possible grouping the 27 NACE sectors in our 12 aggregated industries.

information (unconsolidated accounts) information provided by the Amadeus data-base of the Bureau van Dijk. This covers the value added, fixed assets (capital), sales and the cost of materials (intermediate consumption) in thousands of euros, as well as the number of employees from a large cross-section of European manufacturing firms. We have used data from a sample covering our 12 countries and eliminated firms with missing values and extreme observations. These are defined as having either value-added-to-employee or capital-to-employee ratios out of the range identified by the 1st and 99th percentiles. The resulting sample consists of 427,242 firms.

The simplest way to estimate TFP is by means of a log-linear OLS regression of value added over measures of capital and labour employment (see Box 3). This method, however, might lead to biased estimates due to the underlying assumption that TFP is constant over time. To correct for these biases, more sophisticated methods have been proposed by Olley and Pakes (1996) as well as by Levinsohn and Petrin (2003). These approaches are, nonetheless, more data demanding than OLS, as they require information on firms' investment behaviour and intermediate inputs. Since such information is only available for a subset of firms and countries in our sample, we have opted for a standard log-linear OLS regression for our baseline.[14] Summary statistics for the corresponding results are reported in Table A1. Moreover, Table A2 reports the average TFP, by country and sector.

Cost cut-offs

As discussed in Box 1, the cost cut-off in sector s and country h is computed by multiplying the corresponding average cost by the factor $k_s/(k_s+1)$. Results by sector and country are reported in Table A3. In turn, the baseline average cost in sector s and country h is computed as the inverse of the corresponding average labour productivity (value added per hour worked). This is reported in Table A4.

Producer competitiveness

Table A5 reports the values of producer competitiveness by sector and country. These are obtained from the calibrated bundle $D_s/[f_s^t/(o_s^t)^{k_s}]$ reported in Table A6. In particular, since the parameter of product differentiation D_s is sector but not country-specific, we have separated it from $[f_s^t/(o_s^t)^{k_s}]$ by regressing the logarithm of $D_s/[f_s^t/(o_s^t)^{k_s}]$ on a complete set of sectoral dummies ($sdum$). Table A7 presents the estimated coefficients of such regression, which provide an indication of product differentiation across sectors.

WEB APPENDIX

Available at www.economic-policy.org.

[14] A comparison (not reported here) of results using the baseline TFP estimation and the one proposed by Levinsohn and Petrin (2003) for the subset of countries that allow such computation shows, however, that differences are minor.

Table A1. Summary statistics on TFP (sectoral averages), 2001–2003

Sector	Firms	Average TFP	Std. Dev.	Min.	Max	Adj. R^2
1 Food, Beverages and Tobacco	51001	22.11	42.87	2.29	1476.7	0.90
2 Textiles, Leather Products and Footwear	40510	25.04	21.93	3.51	562.02	0.85
3 Wood Products except Furniture	25930	20	17.75	3.39	444.33	0.89
4 Paper Products, Printing and Publishing	49196	33.67	78.45	2.98	3272.43	0.91
5 Rubber and Plastic	19416	32.94	58.51	5.18	943.63	0.92
6 Chemicals, including Pharmaceuticals	15551	42.92	172.99	2.62	3016.16	0.92
7 Non-metallic Mineral Prod., incl. Pottery and Glass	22772	23.06	30.17	3.68	791.1	0.90
8 Basic Metals and Fabricated Metal Products	92139	29.45	90.56	2.67	4738.54	0.91
9 Non-electric Machinery	38314	36.52	46.3	3.54	1216.43	0.93
10 Electric Machinery, incl. Prof. and Scient. Equip.	30095	59.48	249.88	2.33	4187.55	0.92
11 Transport Equipment	12727	29.43	62.81	3.8	1480.83	0.95
12 Other Manufacturing, incl. Furniture	29591	27.85	76.91	2.71	2883.22	0.89

Source: AMADEUS and authors' calculations.

Table A2. TFP (firm-level based estimates), 2001–2003

Country / Sector	Austria	Belgium	Germany	Denmark	Spain	Finland	France	UK	Italy	Netherlands	Portugal	Sweden
1	22.06	29.64	21.72	30.07	13.31	21.17	20.56	19.66	20.54	40.28	11.36	14.96
2	24.10	30.33	28.93	32.50	15.54	24.27	30.67	24.64	24.71	36.24	8.91	19.61
3	17.33	31.48	21.39	26.93	14.71	19.81	22.03	18.05	20.77	18.90	10.26	18.32
4	34.37	43.98	33.15	52.42	21.92	39.12	42.98	32.19	26.30	32.10	16.60	28.96
5	23.83	33.97	83.35	38.44	20.77	40.68	26.59	21.07	24.50	46.79	12.41	22.89
6	25.57	44.02	102.49	44.79	21.11	38.71	33.76	29.44	36.47	102.71	14.04	21.88
7	23.28	26.48	24.50	34.33	16.05	24.64	25.80	22.19	19.84	28.71	13.29	17.61
8	27.49	51.61	42.02	34.95	20.03	27.27	30.43	26.69	24.01	30.98	16.15	21.77
9	43.03	41.52	43.23	45.41	26.60	47.20	36.87	34.69	30.97	46.05	14.22	28.42
10	39.37	44.34	41.79	54.61	25.24	34.58	37.66	34.58	30.32	320.84	22.11	28.26
11	27.95	45.01	32.02	33.94	22.72	30.98	28.89	27.30	36.50	34.00	12.15	21.72
12	24.69	36.90	29.96	42.84	16.03	28.14	36.01	24.04	30.56	36.50	8.37	20.21

Source: AMADEUS and authors' calculations.

Table A3. Country and sector specific cost cut-offs, average 2001–2003

Sector	Austria	Belgium	Germany	Denmark	Spain	Finland	France	UK	Italy	Netherlands	Portugal	Sweden
1	0.078	0.052	0.085	0.059	0.100	0.061	0.071	0.060	0.079	0.044	0.161	0.063
2	0.092	0.081	0.095	0.088	0.193	0.134	0.096	0.121	0.121	0.086	0.377	0.101
3	0.071	0.063	0.086	0.071	0.158	0.071	0.078	0.102	0.114	0.166	0.303	0.080
4	0.043	0.048	0.061	0.064	0.078	0.035	0.059	0.061	0.070	0.054	0.110	0.046
5	0.049	0.043	0.050	0.049	0.071	0.049	0.050	0.067	0.064	0.052	0.132	0.056
6	0.046	0.035	0.042	0.040	0.064	0.045	0.028	0.046	0.052	0.030	0.104	0.028
7	0.051	0.042	0.057	0.054	0.077	0.056	0.050	0.063	0.065	0.069	0.140	0.063
8	0.045	0.045	0.048	0.054	0.074	0.049	0.050	0.069	0.069	0.054	0.171	0.053
9	0.049	0.042	0.041	0.052	0.071	0.052	0.053	0.059	0.061	0.051	0.135	0.051
10	0.046	0.046	0.047	0.046	0.080	0.027	0.050	0.061	0.066	0.068	0.129	0.071
11	0.039	0.045	0.034	0.059	0.070	0.059	0.038	0.054	0.064	0.049	0.112	0.048
12	0.078	0.069	0.074	0.067	0.149	0.092	0.079	0.092	0.102	0.070	0.288	0.122

Table A4. Labour productivity, average 2001–2003

Sector	Austria	Belgium	Germany	Denmark	Spain	Finland	France	UK	Ireland	Italy	Netherlands	Portugal	Sweden
1	26.81	40.69	24.74	35.57	21.09	34.31	29.60	35.32	43.94	26.70	47.79	13.06	33.17
2	26.88	30.73	26.09	28.35	12.86	18.53	25.82	20.51	18.69	20.48	28.73	6.58	24.58
3	28.89	32.44	23.97	29.15	12.98	28.88	26.23	20.08	18.69	17.96	12.36	6.78	25.78
4	48.64	43.58	34.17	32.91	27.02	59.95	35.62	34.65	81.42	30.16	39.05	19.14	45.23
5	34.55	39.79	33.92	35.15	24.16	34.72	34.41	25.66	22.94	26.72	32.69	12.97	30.71
6	54.00	70.41	59.40	62.48	38.41	54.77	87.15	53.62	252.24	47.88	81.44	23.67	87.03
7	37.59	44.79	33.27	35.14	24.72	34.11	38.07	30.33	31.23	29.35	27.38	13.54	29.96
8	36.40	36.54	34.17	30.67	22.15	33.27	31.05	23.85	23.29	23.97	30.42	9.59	30.94
9	34.47	39.94	40.47	32.01	23.74	32.04	34.41	28.57	25.67	27.53	32.83	12.45	32.98
10	39.57	39.83	38.43	39.49	22.84	67.50	36.60	30.02	53.07	27.64	26.56	14.12	25.53
11	45.51	38.74	51.37	30.00	25.19	29.94	46.69	32.82	25.72	27.53	35.64	15.69	36.92
12	25.44	28.81	26.94	29.48	13.34	21.64	25.28	21.52	13.88	19.40	28.35	6.89	16.33

Source: EUKLEMS.

Table A5. Producer competitiveness: sector and country specific coefficients

Sector	Austria	Belgium	Germany	Denmark	Spain	Finland	France	UK	Italy	Netherlands	Portugal	Sweden
1	1.226	1.104	0.298	2.549	0.470	4.569	0.901	0.962	0.738	1.475	0.142	3.374
2	2.390	1.196	1.029	2.764	0.308	2.623	1.293	0.547	0.961	1.246	0.057	3.168
3	2.922	0.321	1.007	2.332	0.621	6.048	1.794	0.766	1.267	0.191	0.095	3.843
4	2.640	0.592	0.455	1.394	0.660	8.440	0.953	0.457	0.641	0.556	0.272	4.285
5	2.336	0.863	0.867	2.507	0.678	4.642	1.339	0.324	0.750	0.778	0.096	2.984
6	1.466	0.872	0.607	2.261	0.439	3.422	2.074	0.435	0.625	1.051	0.130	4.921
7	2.621	0.534	0.716	2.262	0.796	4.763	1.713	0.519	1.043	0.354	0.122	2.900
8	2.799	0.933	1.250	2.389	0.625	4.969	1.297	0.373	0.773	0.836	0.037	3.529
9	2.225	0.938	1.297	2.125	0.556	3.621	1.216	0.481	0.757	0.862	0.077	2.956
10	2.525	0.608	1.040	2.408	0.560	5.052	1.382	0.572	0.797	0.484	0.163	1.844
11	2.683	0.794	1.525	1.525	0.513	2.584	1.731	0.537	0.515	0.760	0.145	2.873
12	2.195	1.339	1.223	2.584	0.331	2.918	1.269	0.738	0.864	1.433	0.059	1.619

Table A6. Calibrated parameter bundles $D_s(f_s^t/(o_s^t)^{k_s}$.

Sector	Austria	Belgium	Germany	Denmark	Spain	Finland	France	UK	Italy	Netherlands	Portugal	Sweden
1	7.707	6.936	1.872	16.021	2.953	28.713	5.662	6.045	4.635	9.272	0.895	21.202
2	0.761	0.381	0.328	0.880	0.098	0.836	0.412	0.174	0.306	0.397	0.018	1.009
3	5.306	0.582	1.829	4.233	1.128	10.981	3.256	1.391	2.300	0.347	0.172	6.978
4	137.001	30.714	23.634	72.336	34.238	437.932	49.475	23.711	33.249	28.828	14.125	222.345
5	228.821	84.554	84.934	245.578	66.405	454.651	131.145	31.686	73.484	76.187	9.403	292.222
6	55.161	32.817	22.838	85.043	16.497	128.741	78.006	16.373	23.501	39.537	4.894	185.133
7	175.343	35.731	47.886	151.349	53.253	318.686	114.605	34.694	69.792	23.666	8.189	194.053
8	498.106	166.091	222.494	425.078	111.301	884.176	230.786	66.397	137.525	148.777	6.649	627.893
9	154.884	65.303	90.250	147.877	38.689	251.987	84.632	33.444	52.703	60.017	5.328	205.739
10	44.567	10.723	18.356	42.502	9.889	89.164	24.396	10.099	14.065	8.548	2.886	32.540
11	130.730	38.680	74.328	74.297	25.019	125.902	84.372	26.192	25.106	37.047	7.084	140.005
12	1.423	0.868	0.793	1.675	0.214	1.892	0.822	0.478	0.560	0.929	0.039	1.050

Table A7. Regression results of OLS estimation of $D_s(f_s^t/(o_s^t)^{\kappa_s}$ over a full set of sectoral dummies

Variable	Coefficient
sdum1	−1.84 ***
sdum2	1.140 ***
sdum3	−0.6 *
sdum4	−3.950 ***
sdum5	−4.580 ***
sdum6	−3.630 ***
sdum7	−4.200 ***
sdum8	−5.180 ***
sdum9	−4.240 ***
sdum10	−2.870 ***
sdum11	−3.890 ***
sdum12	0.430 *
N	144
r2_a	0.91

REFERENCES

Alesina, A., R. Barro and S. Tenreyro (2007). 'Optimal currency areas', in M. Gertler and K. Rogoff (eds.), *NBER Macroeconomic Annual*, MIT Press, Cambridge, MA.

Anderson, J. and E. van Wincoop (2004). 'Trade costs', *Journal of Economic Literature*, 42, 691–751.

Aw, B., S. Chung and M. Roberts (2000). 'Productivity and turnover in the export market: Micro-level evidence from the Republic of Korea and Taiwan (China)', *World Bank Economic Review*, 14, 65–90.

Baldwin, R. (2006). *In or out: does it matter? An evidence-based analysis of the euro's trade effects.* Centre for Economic Policy Research, London.

Baldwin, R. and D. Taglioni (2007). 'Trade effects of the euro: A comparison of estimators', *Journal of Economic Integration*, 22, 780–818.

— (2008) 'The Rose's effect: The euro's impact on aggregate trade flows', in R. Baldwin *et al.* (eds.), *Study on the impact of the euro on trade and foreign direct investment*, European Economy no. 321.

Berger, H. and V. Nitsch (2005). 'Zooming out: The trade effect of the euro in perspective', CESifo Working Paper No. 1435.

Bernard, A., J. Eaton, J. Jensen, and S. Kortum (2003). 'Plants and productivity in international trade', *American Economic Review*, 93, 1268–90.

Bernard, A. and B. Jensen (1999). 'Exceptional exporter performance: Cause, effect, or both?' *Journal of International Economics*, 47, 1–25.

Bernard, A., J. Jensen and P. Schott (2003). 'Falling trade costs, heterogeneous firms and industry dynamics', National Bureau of Economic Research, Working Paper No. 9639.

Berthou, A. and L. Fontagné (2008). 'The euro and the intensive and extensive margins of trade: Evidence from French firm-level data', CEPII Working Paper, No. 2008-06, April.

Brander, J. and K. Krugman (1983). 'A reciprocal dumping model of international trade', *Journal of International Economics*, 15, 313–23.

Chen, N. (2004). 'Intra-national versus international trade in the European Union: Why do national borders matter?', *Journal of International Economics*, 63, 93–118.

Clerides, S., S. Lach and J. Tybout (1998). 'Is learning by exporting important? Micro-dynamic evidence from Colombia, Mexico, and Morocco', *Quarterly Journal of Economics*, 113, 903–48.

Del Gatto, M., G. Mion and G. Ottaviano (2006). 'Trade integration, firm selection and the costs of non-Europe', CEPR Discussion Paper No. 5730.

Flam, H. and H. Nordström (2003). 'Trade volume effects of the euro: Evidence from sectoral data', University of Stockholm, mimeo.

Foster, L., J. Haltiwanger and C. Syverson (2005). 'Reallocation, firm turnover, and efficiency: Selection on productivity or profitability?', mimeo, University of Chicago.

Grubel, H. and P. Lloyd (1975). *Intra-industry Trade: The Theory and Measurement of International Trade in Differentiated Products*, Macmillan, London.

Head, K. and T. Mayer (2000). 'Non Europe: The magnitude and causes of market fragmentation in the EU', *Weltwirtschaftliches Archiv*, 136, 284–314.

— (2004a). 'Market potential and the location of Japanese firms in the European Union', *Review of Economics and Statistics*, 86, 959–72.

— (2004b). 'The empirics of agglomeration and trade', in J. Henderson and J.-F. Thisse (eds.), *Handbook of Regional and Urban Economics*, Vol. 4, Elsevier, Amsterdam.

Heckman, J.J. (1979). 'Sample selection bias as a specification error', *Econometrica*, 47(1), 153–61.

Helpman, E., M. Melitz and Y. Rubinstein (2008). 'Estimating trade flows: Trading partners and trading volumes', *Quarterly Journal of Economics*, 123(2), 441–87.

Krugman, P. (1980). 'Scale economies, product differentiation, and the pattern of trade', *American Economic Review*, 70(5), 950–59.

Levinsohn, J. and A. Petrin (2003). 'Estimating production functions using inputs to control for unobservables', *Review of Economic Studies*, 70, 317–41.

Linder, S. (1961). *An Essay on Trade and Transformation*, Almqvist and Wiksell, Stockholm.

Mayer, T. and G. Ottaviano (2007). *The Happy Few: The Internationalisation of European Firms*, Bruegel Blueprint 3, Brussels.

Melitz, M. (2003). 'The impact of trade on intra-industry reallocation and aggregate industry productivity', *Econometrica*, 71, 1695–725.

Melitz, M. and G. Ottaviano (2008). 'Market size, trade and productivity', *Review of Economic Studies*, 75, 295–316.

Olley, S. and A. Pakes (1996). 'The dynamics of productivity in the telecommunications equipment industry', *Econometrica*, 64, 1263–97.

Pavcnik, N. (2002). 'Trade liberalisation, exit and productivity improvements: Evidence from Chilean plants', *Review of Economic Studies*, 69, 245–76.

M and A

SUMMARY

Cross-border mergers and acquisitions activities (M&As) sharply increased over the last two decades, partly as a result of financial liberalization policies, government policies and regional agreements. In this paper, we identify some of the main forces driving M&As, using a unique database on bilateral cross-border M&As at the sectoral level (in manufacturing and services) over the period 1985–2004. The key empirical findings are: (1) EMU helped the restructuring of capital within the same sector of manufacturing activity among euro area firms; (2) joining the EU favoured both horizontal and vertical mergers; (3) policy-makers can help attract capital by reducing the corporate tax rates and the degree of product market regulations and by improving the country's financial systems; (4) the service industry has not yet fully benefited from European integration because the level of protection and barriers to entry in the services sector act as a strong deterrent to cross-border M&As in services.

— *Nicolas Coeurdacier, Roberto A. De Santis and Antonin Aviat*

Economic Policy January 2009 Printed in Great Britain
© CEPR, CES, MSH, 2009.

Cross-border mergers and acquisitions and European integration

Nicolas Coeurdacier, Roberto A. De Santis and Antonin Aviat

London Business School; European Central Bank; Paris School of Economics

1. INTRODUCTION

Among developed countries, the largest share of foreign direct investment (FDI) takes the form of cross-border mergers and acquisitions (M&As). The latter skyrocketed in the 1990s reaching a peak in 2000, amid booming stock markets and financial liberalization worldwide. They declined sharply in 2001–2003, before rebounding thereafter following closely the cyclical developments in the world economy (see Figure 1).[1] Traditionally, developed countries, and in particular the developed countries of the European Union (EU) and the United States, have been the largest acquirer and target countries of M&As. Over the 2003–2005 period, developed countries accounted for 85% of the US$465 billion cross-border M&As, 47% and 23% of

This paper was presented at the 47th Panel Meeting of Economic Policy in Ljubljana, April 2008. We thank the discussants Gianmarco Ottaviano and Morten Ravn, four referees as well as the panel members and other participants of the Ljubljana meeting for useful comments. We also thank Jean Imbs, Dennis Novy and Daria Taglioni for useful discussions. Moreover we thank A. Gasteuil and R. Pereira for research assistantship. The views expressed in this paper are solely the responsibility of the authors and should not be interpreted as reflecting the views of the ECB.

The Managing Editor in charge of this paper was Jan van Ours.

[1] Capital reallocation across firms occurs either through the sale of property, plant and equipment or through M&As, in which the transfer of financial claims from the acquiring firm brings along that of the underlying assets of the targeted firm. In the case of cross-border M&As, the main activity of the acquirer and target firms are registered in two different countries.

Economic Policy January 2009 pp. 55–106 Printed in Great Britain
© CEPR, CES, MSH, 2009.

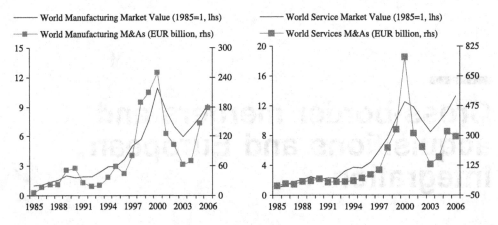

Figure 1. Cross-border M&As in manufacturing and services and stock market developments

Source: Thomson Financial.

which respectively pertain to EU15 and US firms either as acquirer or as target countries (UNCTAD, 2006).

In this paper, we investigate how the process of financial and trade liberalization within the EU and the European Monetary Union (EMU) has fostered cross-border M&As among their members and with the rest of the world.

The theoretical economic arguments of why regional trade agreements (such as EU/EMU) can trigger cross-border merger waves have been recently put forward by Neary (2007a, 2007b). He argues that, by fostering competition, trade liberalization can favour an environment, whereby low-cost firms find it profitable to acquire/merge with high-cost firms. If a monetary union enhanced goods competition across countries (through a reduction in trade costs, the elimination of the exchange rate risk and improved price transparency), then it might also trigger cross-border merger waves.

However, in addition to the 'trade liberalization channel', a monetary union facilitates the movement of equity capital by boosting financial integration, through the reduction of the cost of capital, the elimination of exchange rate risk, the sharing of common trading platforms and integration in post-trading market infrastructure. Moreover, if a monetary union reduces macroeconomic uncertainty by removing exchange rate volatility and stabilizing inflation, then cross-border capital investment would be considered to be less risky. All in all, regional economic and monetary agreements can have an impact on cross-border M&As through (1) an increase in its profitability, as regional agreements increase market size and promote competition, and (2) a reduction in financial transaction costs related to financial integration.

From this perspective, the Single European Market in 1992 and the Third Stage of EMU in 1999 constitute important experiments to evaluate the impact of regional agreements on capital reallocation. We jointly investigate the impact on cross-border

M&As of joining the EU (the EU effect), whose single market formally removes the remaining barriers to free movements of capital, labour, goods and services within the European Economic Community; and the impact of adopting the euro (the EMU effect), whose introduction has eliminated the exchange rate risk and enhanced financial integration.

While the impact of EMU on trade in goods,[2] portfolio flows[3] and FDI[4] has attracted a great deal of attention from policy-makers and scholars, such analysis has not been performed for capital reallocation through cross-border M&As. While there is some anecdotal evidence that trade liberalization and deeper market integration coincide with episodes of cross-border M&As waves (see European Commission, 1996), it remains an important empirical question. Has EU/EMU fostered capital reallocation through M&As across their member states? Has EU/EMU increased their capacity to attract capital from the rest of the world? Which sectors have been mostly affected? These are crucial questions for potential entrants who would like to assess the benefits of joining EU/EMU.

Besides the role played by EU or EMU membership, understanding more broadly the determinants of capital reallocation across countries is key for policy-makers, as most countries try to provide incentives to attract FDI. This study can help by evaluating better their policies. The institutional environment is of a particular interest for cross-border M&As since they are affected by various regulations at the country or regional level, such as competition and trade policy, corporate and capital taxes, various restrictions to capital movements across borders, protection of certain industries. In particular, we also raise the questions of the effectiveness of fiscal policies and of product market regulations in attracting foreign capital. One implication of the processes of financial globalization and European integration is that capital is more mobile internationally, which raises concerns regarding the use of tax and market regulation policies in order to compete across countries. The issue of capital attractiveness leads to several discussions within the EU on possible tax and market regulation harmonization among member states. While one could argue that countries with higher corporate taxes and higher degree of market regulations are less attractive for cross-border M&As, the quantitative impact of these policies on firms' location decisions is essentially an empirical question.

To assess the impact of such policies on cross-border M&As, we construct a unique database for ten acquiring manufacturing sectors and ten acquiring service sectors located in 21 different countries targeting foreign assets in 32 different host countries

---

[2] See Rose (2000), Micco, Stein and Ordonez (2003), Flam and Nordstrom (2003), Baldwin and Taglioni (2006), Baldwin (2006).

[3] See Coeurdacier and Martin (2006), De Santis (2006), De Santis and Gerard (2006), Lane (2006).

[4] Petroulas (2007) estimated the impact of the introduction of the euro on inward FDI flows and finds that the EMU increased FDI flows by approximately 15% within the euro area. See also De Sousa and Lochard (2006a, 2006b), Schiavo (2007) and Brouwer et al. (2008) for related work on the impact of EMU on FDI flows. However, these studies do not control for developments in the stock market and for the general tendency of investing in the euro area from the rest of the world. As a result, their estimates on the impact of EMU may be somewhat upwardly biased ranging between 20% and 30%.

(over the 1985–2004 period). Specifically, an acquiring manufacturing firm (sector) can merge with or acquire foreign firms whose main activity can be classified (1) in the same sector of the acquiring firm ('within mergers'), or (2) in a different manufacturing sector or service sector ('across mergers'). Similarly, an acquiring service firm (sector) can merge with or acquire foreign firms within the same sector, or whose main activity is either in manufacturing or in a different service sector. M&As that occurred within sectors includes mostly horizontal mergers while mergers across sectors can be seen as vertical mergers.[5]

From 1948 to 1994, the General Agreement on Tariffs and Trade (GATT) provided the rules for much of the world goods trade. Moreover, the OECD has been promoting the liberalization of capital account operations among its members since the early 1960s. However, the code of liberalization covering cross-border services has not yet been agreed (OECD, 2002). The General Agreement on Trade in Services (GATS) is the only agreement at the international level that regulates and liberalizes trade in financial services as well as investment of financial services providers.[6] The GATS agreement was negotiated in the Uruguay Round (1986–94). Members (self-)committed to launch successive rounds of services negotiations with a view to achieving a progressively higher level of liberalization. The first such round was to begin no later than 5 years from the date of entry into force of the Agreement and, accordingly, started in 2000. Within the time frame of the overall negotiating deadline of 1 January 2005, the Doha Development Agenda establishes that 'participants shall submit initial requests for specific commitments by 30 June 2002 and initial offers by 31 March 2003'. Needless to say, that large restrictions in trade in services are still in place and their elimination is under policy discussion.

Therefore, we assess the determinants of cross-border M&As in such activities separately, as pooling them in regression analysis would be inappropriate, given different developments on the process of liberalization of trade and investment in manufacturing and services. This is especially important when we test the impact of product market regulations on cross-border M&As.

The key empirical findings can be summarized as follows: (1) EMU helped the restructuring of capital within the same sector of manufacturing activity, particularly among euro area firms; (2) joining the EU implies adopting the Single European Market Act, which favoured both horizontal and vertical mergers; (3) policy-makers can help attract capital by reducing the corporate tax rates and the degree of product market regulations and by improving the country's financial systems. As expected, the degree of market regulations plays a key-role for M&As in the service sector (but not for manufacturing).

---

[5] We must be cautious with this interpretation since cross-border M&As are aggregated at the 2-digit level and some M&As within the same sector might be of vertical nature.

[6] According to the GATS agreement, trade in services can take different forms: cross-border trade, consumption abroad, commercial presence, and presence of natural persons. Commercial presence implies that a service supplier of one member establishes a territorial presence, including through ownership or lease of premises, in another member's territory to provide a service (e.g. domestic subsidiaries of foreign insurance companies or hotel chains).

Overall, we shed light on the major role played by European integration to foster cross-border M&As between EMU countries in the manufacturing sector (preferential financial liberalization). We find that cross-border M&As inside the euro area has increased in those sectors which also registered an increase in goods trade owing to EMU; this result suggests that the 'trade liberalization channel' emphasized by Neary (2007a, 2007b) has been operating within EMU. On top of this reallocation inside EMU, we also find that manufacturing sectors of both EU and EMU have attracted equity capital from the rest of developed countries (unilateral financial liberalization). As this increase in acquisitions of European firms from the rest of the world is not linked to trade patterns across sectors, we believe it is mostly driven by a fall in financial transaction costs to acquire European assets. The European integration effects are not found in the service industry. We provide evidence that the high degree of product market regulations in services hindered entry of foreign firms in national markets. Hence, goods trade barriers in the service industry also hamper the reallocation of cross-border equity capital.

The industrial organization literature classifies the various motives to merge in the following main groups (see e.g. Perry and Porter, 1985; Andrade et al., 2001; Nocke and Yeaple, 2007; Long et al., 2007; Neary, 2007a):[7] (1) high-Tobin's q firms are those with the best technology and seek to expand their capital stock;[8] (2) efficiency gains arise because takeovers increase economies of scale or scope or other synergies, such as tax considerations or acquisition of funds; (3) strategic gains arise if M&As change the market structure and thus a company's competitive position and profit level by forming monopolies or oligopolies; (4) building empires allow to diversify and hedge against sectoral shocks; (5) managers might be motivated by managerial compensation or pure ego. It is very difficult to empirically disentangle these different elements. We focus on the value-enhancing motives, which broadly encompass the first three main groups. M&As can help satisfy future goods demand, can reduce costs, and might change the market structure and the market power, thereby affecting future profits captured by the market valuation of the acquiring firm. We also attempt to look at the building empire motives by looking at M&As within a given sector (horizontal) or across different sectors (vertical).

We analyze the determinants of cross-border M&As in a gravity framework. We use Poisson maximum likelihood method, which allows for a tractable approach

---

[7] See Nocke and Yeaple (2007) and Head and Ries (2007) for additional references on theoretical industrial organization issues.

[8] Q theory suggests that if the market value of a firm over its book value is greater than one – implying the existence of intangibles such as brands, reputation and knowledge or growth potential that business analysts and shareholders value – then the firm should increase its capital stock as investing is profitable. Jovanovic and Rousseau (2002), for example, show that the q-theory of investment can be used to explain domestic investment via M&As and find that M&As respond to stock market developments by more than direct investment. Eisfeldt and Rampini (2005) used Tobin's q to show that capital reallocation between firms is procyclical. De Santis et al. (2004) and Baker et al. (2008) argue that the q-theory of investment can also translate in higher FDI outflows and find that a rise in the domestic stock market led to an increase in outward FDI to the United States. Similarly, De Santis and Ehling (2007) – looking at the interlinkages between FDI and foreign portfolio investment among Germany, the other G7 economies and Switzerland over the quarterly period 1980–2006 – find that German FDI outflows and inflows are both function of Tobin's q.

regarding firms' location decision problems (Guimarães *et al.*, 2003; Head and Ries, 2007). We are aware of the following papers investigating the determinants of cross-border M&As using gravity:[9] (1) Di Giovanni (2005) and Head and Ries (2007), who, using respectively Tobit and the Poisson maximum likelihood method, find financial depth, cultural and geographical proximity to be important determinants of aggregate M&As; (2) Berger *et al.* (2004), who, using Tobit, look at determinants of cross-border transaction values in the financial sector; (3) Hijzen *et al.* (2008) and Focarelli and Pozzolo (2008), who focus on the number of cross-border deals using the negative binomial regression model, respectively for M&As in manufacturing sectors and those in banking and insurance. We use the key determinants of M&As identified in these papers as controls in our regressions.

The remaining sections of the paper are structured as follows: Section 2 describes the estimation strategy following the literature on gravity and FDI and presents the data. Sections 3 and 4 discuss the main empirical results for manufacturing and services, respectively. Section 5 investigates the role of trade and trade barriers (product market regulations). Section 6 presents some additional results and robustness checks regarding the roles of corporate taxation, EMU, financial depth and distance. Section 7 concludes.

2. ESTIMATION STRATEGY TO MODEL CROSS-BORDER M&As

2.1. Theoretical motivation

We follow Head and Ries (2005, 2007) to model the location decision of multinational firms through M&As.[10] For simplicity, we abstract from time and sectoral subscripts.

Denote with p_{ij} the probability that a randomly drawn company from country i acquires a randomly drawn target in country j. Using the total stock of targets in country j (k_j) and the total number of potential acquiring company in country i (m_i), the expected value of mergers and acquisitions between country i and j (M&A$_{ij}$) is:

$$E(M\&A_{ij}) = m_i p_{ij} k_j.$$

Assume also that net profits from an acquiring company s_i in country i for an investment in country j are $(\pi_i - \sigma t_{ij} + \varepsilon_{s_{ij}})$, where π_i is the discounted value of the gross profits due to the profitability of the M&A, t_{ij} denotes transaction costs between markets i and j (note that t_{ij} can be a multi-dimensional vector) and $\varepsilon_{s_{ij}}$ is a random term of unobserved firm level characteristics independently distributed with Type I Extreme value cumulative distribution $(CDF(\varepsilon_{s_{ij}}) = \exp(-\exp(-\varepsilon_{s_{ij}})))$.

Using discrete choice theory (see MacFadden, 1974), one can show that under such assumptions:

---

[9] A review of the literature in management science can be found in Shimizu *et al.* (2004).

[10] See also Guimãraes *et al.* (2003).

$$p_{ij} = \exp(\pi_i - \sigma t_{ij})B_j^{-1},$$

where the probability to win the bid for a firm in country i is positively related to the discounted value of its expected profits and negatively related to transaction costs; but it also depends on the position of all the potential competitors, $B_j = \Sigma_l m_l \exp(\pi_l - \sigma t_{lj})$, with respect to market j. Using the latter expression, we get:

$$E(M\&A_{ij}) = m_i \exp(\pi_i - \sigma t_{ij})k_j B_j^{-1}$$

where B_j is a measure of the 'financial remoteness' of market j. The interpretation of this term is clear-cut: (1) the higher the discounted value of the expected profits of all other potential buyers or (2) the easier it is for all potential acquiring firms to buy a target firm in country j, the more difficult it is for a firm in country i to compete on such an asset. Given the analogy with the 'multilateral resistance factor' developed in the trade literature (Anderson and Van Wincoop, 2003), B_j is like the 'market potential' (or 'supplier access'). We can rewrite the last equation as follows:

$$E(M\&A_{ij}) = \exp\{\log(m_i) + \log(k_j) - \log(B_j) + \pi_i - \sigma t_{ij}\}$$

where m_i and k_j are related to market sizes, π_i is related to the profitability of investments in country i and t_{ij} is related to transaction costs between markets.

We can therefore use the gravity equations framework to estimate the impact of various determinants of cross-border M&A in a given sector s, which takes the following form.

$$M\&A_{ij,s,t} = e^{\alpha_i + \alpha_j + \alpha_t + \alpha_s}(GDP_{j,s,t}GDP_{i,s,t})^\beta Z_{ij,s,t}^\theta \eta_{ij,s,t}$$

where $M\&A_{ij,s,t}$ denote M&As between source country i (acquirer) and host country j (target) at time t in sector s; $GDP_{i,s,t}$ (resp. $GDP_{j,s,t}$) stands for the market size of sector s in country i (resp. j); $Z_{ij,s,t}$ is a set of control variables (linked to expected profitability of firms, transactions costs and other barriers) that might affect cross-border M&As and α_i, α_j, α_t and α_s are the source and host country fixed effects, a time-fixed effect and a sectoral fixed-effect, respectively. $\eta_{ij,s,t}$ is an error term assumed to be statistically independent of the regressors.[11]

The use of acquirer/target fixed-effects is necessary to control for unobservable countries' characteristics in order to limit potential biases due to omitted variables in the estimation. In particular, it allows controlling for the 'financial remoteness' B_j of some host markets (assumed to be constant over time). We also control for time fixed-effects since cross-border M&As have been strongly increasing over time due to increasing financial integration across countries. As for $Z_{ij,s,t}$, we assume that they are a function of geography, institutions and financial variables capturing expected profitability of firms. Variables are described in detail in the following subsections.

---

[11] For other theoretical foundations of gravity models for FDI, see also Bergstrand and Egger (2007) and Ramondo (2007).

2.2. Description of the data on cross-border M&As

We construct an annual panel of cross-border M&As of completed transactions in the manufacturing sector and services at SITC2 classification for a sample of 21 'source' (acquiring) countries and 31 'host' (target) countries using Thomson Financial (SDC Platinum) over the 1985–2004 period. Countries and sectors (ten manufacturing sectors and ten service sectors) are described in Table A1 of the Appendix.

The panel covers the largest industrialized markets, which accounts for a very large share of cross-border M&As. For example, over the 1999–2004 period, the panel covers 74% of the world cross-border M&As (72% in manufacturing and 75% in services). Over this period, the total annual transactions covered by the panel amount to €458 billion, of which services accounted for about two-thirds. At the end of the 1980s, cross-border M&As accounted for about one-tenth the amount of transactions recorded at the turn of the new century (see Tables A2 and A3 of the Appendix).

The most important acquiring manufacturing sectors in terms of size accounting for almost three-quarters of global M&As in manufacturing are (1) chemicals, petroleum, coal, rubber and plastic products, (2) machinery and equipment, and (3) food, beverages and tobacco. For services, one-third of world M&A in services involved electric, gas and water supply as acquiring sectors, with Japan being very active. The second most important sector is financial intermediation excluding banking and insurance, with the United States playing a prominent role.

We divide the 20 years' sectoral observations in two main groups:

1 M&As occurring within the same sector ('within sectors'): acquirer and target firms belong to the same sector.
2 M&As occurring across sectors ('across sectors'): the acquirer firm is targeting a firm whose main activity does not belong to the sector of the acquirer (according to the 2-digit level of disaggregation).

Broadly speaking, this decomposition allows us to indirectly disentangle the determinants of M&As driven to allocate efficiently production across the globe from M&As that are intended to build conglomerates (and essentially driven by risk diversification motives or 'empire building' motives). In the sample, around two-thirds of M&A transactions have occurred within the same sector.

2.3. Description of the regressors

We study M&As by assessing the roles of market size, transaction costs and firms' expected profitability. The first key variable is sectoral GDP in the source and the host country. We restrict the elasticity to be the same for country i and country j by using the log of the product of the two GDPs at date t ($\log(GDP_{i,s,t}GDP_{j,s,t})$, but none of the results depend on this restriction.

As for transaction costs, the empirical literature on trade and FDI flows suggests to control for geography and cultural proximity. Accordingly, we use the bilateral geographical distance between the main cities of country i and country j denoted by $Distance_{ij}$ and a dummy $Border_{ij}$, which equals one when the two countries share a common border.[12] We also use the dummy $Common\ Language_{ij}$, which equals one if the two countries share a common language.

We assess the role of European integration using dummy variables as in the trade literature (see Baldwin, 2006, for a survey). To test a structural change due to EMU, we use two additive dummies constructed as follows: $EMU_{i,t}EMU_{j,t}$ is equal to one if both countries belong to EMU at time t and zero otherwise; $nonEMU_{i,t}EMU_{j,t}$ is equal to one when the host country j belongs to the euro area, but not the source country. Using two different dummies allow us to quantify the impact of EMU on cross-border M&A both within the euro area (preferential financial liberalization) and between non-euro area and euro area countries (unilateral financial liberalization) and to test the existence of a structural break. One could also add a dummy equal to 1 when the source country belongs to EMU but not the target. Indeed, one could potentially expect some diversion effects similar to the trade literature. However, this dummy was never significant and we decided not to consider it in the analysis. A similar set of dummies is used to study the effect of EU: $EU_{i,t}EU_{j,t}$ is equal to one if both countries belong to the EU at time t and zero otherwise; $nonEU_{i,t}EU_{j,t}$ is equal to one when the target belongs to the EU but not the acquirer.

We control for the expected profitability of the acquiring firm by using the average market capitalization over GDP of the acquirer country i in a given sector s at time t: $\log(MarketCapitalization_{i,s,t}/GDP_{i,s,t})$. A neoclassical model of investment predicts that countries/sectors with higher Tobin's q increase their capital stock also through M&As (see Jovanovic and Rousseau, 2008). One could argue that Tobin's q should be better measured by the market-to-book ratio, but unfortunately such a variable is not available for a wide cross-section of countries over the period considered. For the countries/sectors for which data is available, the market-to-book ratio is highly correlated with market-to-GDP ratio: the correlation coefficient is as high as 0.9.[13]

We also control for the market value-GDP ratio of the target country j, as M&As might be more likely when foreign capital is more economical (Baker $et\ al.$, 2008), $\log(MarketCapitalization_{j,s,t}/GDP_{j,s,t})$. The use of the market capitalization to GDP ratio of acquirer and target sectors can also help controlling for equity bubbles, which ex $post$ was particularly evident at the turn of the century. Data on market capitalization is the yearly average market value of the sector from Thomson Datastream and data on sectoral GDPs are obtained from OECD (Stan database). Summary statistics are reported in Table A4 of the Appendix.

---

[12] Geographical distance is taken from the data set on manufacturing trade of the World Bank (Nicita and Olarreaga, 2007).

[13] Note that this correlation should be unity if the capital-output ratio were constant.

Following Rossi and Volpin (2004), Di Giovanni (2005) and Alfaro *et al.* (2007, 2008), we also control for the quality of institutions in the source (resp. host) country by means of an indicator of civil liberties, *Civil Liberties*$_{i,t}$ (resp. *Civil Liberties*$_{j,t}$) at time *t*, which measures over time and across countries the freedom of expression and belief, the association and organization rights, the rule of law and human rights, personal autonomy and economic rights. The Civil Liberties index is taken from Freedom House and ranges between one (the best country) and seven (the worst country). It quantifies the expansion of political democracy, personal liberties, and good government practices, which has been remarkable over the years, also because the abuse of power by governments and their interference with the lives of their citizens have generally been on the declining trend. We expect that an improvement in countries' civil liberties reduces the cost of capital and encourages investment in these economies, because reliable institutions enhance transparency, and sound legal and political systems offer a less uncertain environment to investors. We choose this indicator rather than an indicator of institutional quality more related to economic concepts mostly because of its wide cross-country coverage over the sample. This indicator is nevertheless highly correlated to other institutional variables, such as corruption indices from Transparency International or variables from La Porta *et al.* (2006).

Moreover, we study the role played by trade and trade barriers (product market regulations). Using the world database of international trade at the product level (BACI) provided by CEPII, we study whether comparative advantage revealed by goods trade activity has promoted cross-border M&As. We also look at the sectoral impact of the European integration on goods trade and compare the results with those obtained for sectoral M&As.

As for the trade barriers, the OECD has constructed a comprehensive and internationally comparable set of indicators that measure the degree to which policies promote or inhibit competition in areas of the product market where competition is viable. Specifically, the indicators cover formal regulations in the following areas: state control of business enterprises, legal and administrative barriers to entrepreneurship, and barriers to international trade and investment.[14]

Two different types of product market indicators exist that are consistent across time and countries: (1) economy-wide indicators and (2) sectoral indicators for a given country.

(1) The economy-wide indicator is an index that summarizes a large set of rules and regulations that have the potential to reduce the strength of competition (regulations to entry, public ownership and degree of competition). This indicator has been constructed for the economy as a whole only at two points in time – 1998 and 2003 – and for the service industry for the annual period between 1975 and 2003. Given that the correlation between the aggregate indicators for services and the

---

[14] Data on product regulations are available only for OECD countries (see Indicator of Product Market Regulations on the OECD website for data source). For additional and detailed information on such indicators see also ECB (2006).

whole economy for the two years 1998 and 2003 is very high (around 0.8), the indicator on the regulation for services is used as a proxy for the degree of product market regulation also in manufacturing to cover the time dimension of the sample. Moreover, the OECD disaggregates the product market regulation indicator in three different dimensions: an index of regulation excluding public ownership (based on entry barriers and degree of competition), an index of entry barriers and an index of public ownership. We make use of these disaggregated components, as they can provide valuable information about which dimension of regulations matters most for cross-border M&As. The descriptive statistics indicate that services are strongly regulated particularly in Greece, France and Austria and less so in New Zealand, the UK and the US (see Table A5 of the Appendix). Though by a far lower degree, similar results are valid also in manufacturing. On average, euro area countries are relatively more regulated.

(2) The sectoral indicators in OECD countries between 1975 and 2003 are computed assessing the degree of regulations in some key service industries, such as airline, rail and road transport, electricity and gas, post and telecommunications and retail distribution (see Conway et al., 2005; Conway and Nicoletti, 2006). They measure the potential costs of anti-competitive regulation in a given sector of the economy. Conversely, the indicators for manufacturing are imputed from those in services using input-output tables. The indicators suggest that electricity, gas and water supply, wholesale and retail trade, transport and storage are the most regulated service sectors, while hotels and restaurant are highly deregulated.

Finally, we study the role played by some other potential barriers to cross-border M&As such as corporate taxation and country's financial systems. We assess the role of corporate taxation using annual effective corporate tax rates constructed by Devereux and Griffith (2003) for a wide range of OECD countries.[15] As for the countries' financial depth, we use the ratio of domestic credit to GDP in the target and acquiring country at a given date provided by the World Development Indicators of the World Bank.

2.4. Specification and methodology

Cross-border M&As ($M\&A_{ij,s,t}$) are the total value of assets purchased through M&As in the target country j by firms in sector s resident in country i at year t. The determinants of such variable are obtained estimating the following regression:

$$\log(M\&A_{ij,s,t}) = \alpha_i + \alpha_j + \alpha_s + \alpha_t + \beta_1 \log(GDP_{j,s,t} GDP_{i,s,t}) + \beta_2 \log(Distance_{ij})$$
$$+ \beta_3 Border_{ij} + \beta_4 CommonLanguage_{ij} + \beta_5 CivilLiberty_{i,t}$$
$$+ \beta_6 CivilLiberty_{j,t} + \beta_7 \log(MarketCapitalization_{i,s,t} / GDP_{i,s,t})$$
$$+ \beta_8 \log(MarketCapitalization_{j,s,t} / GDP_{j,s,t}) + \theta' z_{ij,s,t} + \gamma_1 EMU_{i,t} EMU_{j,t}$$
$$+ \gamma_2 NonEMU_{i,t} EMU_{j,t} + \delta_1 EU_{i,t} EU_{j,t} + \delta_2 NonEU_{i,t} EU_{j,t},$$

[15] Data on corporate taxation among OECD countries over the period 1984–2004 are taken from M.P. Devereux's website. See Devereux and Griffith (2003) and Devereux et al. (2002).

where the alphas are the fixed-effects, which control for unobservable country/sector characteristics, and $z_{ij,s,t}$ is a set of additional controls variables, such as corporate taxation, product market regulations and credit. Moreover, we jointly investigate the impact on cross-border M&As of joining the EU, whose single market formally removes the remaining barriers to free movements of capital, labour, goods and services within the EEC; and the impact of adopting the euro, whose introduction should have facilitated the movement of capital by not only enhancing competition among firms via the direct impact on goods trade, but also by boosting financial integration in the euro area, through the reduction of the cost of capital, the elimination of exchange rate risk, the sharing of common trading platforms (e.g. the creation of Euronext through the cross-border merger of the Amsterdam, Brussels, Lisbon and Paris exchanges).

Once we have taken into account data attrition caused by the control variables, we are left with about 8000 observations in each manufacturing and service sectors. Given that we consider ten sectors in manufacturing (resp. ten in services), approximately 80 000 observations, are used in the main specifications, of which only about 5% are non-zero.

As explained by Razin and Sadka (2007a, 2007b), Tobit estimators are consistent if the presence of zeros is due to measurement errors. While M&As data are certainly subject to some measurement errors (i.e. some M&As might not be recorded by Thomson Financial), most of the zeroes are 'true zeros' in the sense that no M&As occurred that year for a given sector s and a given country-pair $\{i,j\}$. In this case, Tobit estimators are biased. Therefore, we use Poisson Maximum-Likelihood estimators throughout the analysis (see Guimarães et al., 2003; Santos Silva and Tenreyro, 2006; and Head and Ries, 2007).[16]

Being concerned with the large amount of zeros, we also ran regressions on bilateral cross-border M&As at the aggregate level (where non-zero observations account for more than 20%): the estimates are fully consistent with the results obtained using sectoral data. Therefore, we mostly focus the analysis showing regression at the sectoral level (except for some robustness checks on the role of EMU in Sections 6.2–6.3 of the paper).

3. CROSS-BORDER M&As IN MANUFACTURING SECTORS

The results of the benchmark specification for manufacturing obtained using Poisson quasi-MLE are shown in column 1 of Table 1. Common language and border dummies are significant. The estimates of the common language dummy are fully in line with previous estimates of Head and Ries (2007).[17] The border dummy has a positive sign

---

[16] Razin and Sadka (2007a, 2007b) also show the bias in OLS or Tobit estimations and correct it using an alternative method based on a Heckman-selection model.

[17] We also tested a dummy variable for a common legal system following La Porta et al. (1998 and 2006), but this variable was not significant.

Table 1. Cross-border M&As in manufacturing and services: The role of institutions and Tobin's q

	Manufacturing			Services		
	All	Within sectors	Across sectors	All	Within sectors	Across sectors
$Log(GDP_{i,t}\,GDP_{j,s,t})$	0.812***	0.883***	0.690***	0.155	0.142	0.052
	(0.177)	(0.228)	(0.248)	(0.217)	(0.298)	(0.223)
$Log(distance_{ij})$	−0.056	−0.059	−0.101	−0.075	−0.218	−0.096
	(0.125)	(0.156)	(0.244)	(0.177)	(0.201)	(0.187)
$Border_{ij}$	0.392*	0.646**	−0.152	1.303***	1.413***	1.101***
	(0.226)	(0.299)	(0.383)	(0.348)	(0.391)	(0.375)
$Common\ language_{ij}$	0.580***	0.226	1.192***	0.648***	1.100***	0.256
	(0.164)	(0.233)	(0.233)	(0.239)	(0.300)	(0.343)
$EMU_{i,t}\,EMU_{j,t}$	0.940***	1.090**	0.377	−0.399	−0.569	−0.167
	(0.336)	(0.430)	(0.368)	(0.280)	(0.410)	(0.355)
$NonEMU_{i,t}\,EMU_{j,t}$	0.599**	0.519	0.882**	0.448	0.827	−0.305
	(0.249)	(0.331)	(0.364)	(0.540)	(0.697)	(0.369)
$EU_{i,t}\,EU_{j,t}$	1.132**	1.091	1.410***	0.598	0.470	0.585
	(0.564)	(0.691)	(0.525)	(0.382)	(0.375)	(0.531)
$NonEU_{i,t}\,EU_{j,t}$	0.868*	0.967*	0.876	−0.295	−1.006	0.678
	(0.451)	(0.517)	(0.544)	(0.575)	(0.624)	(0.593)
$Civil\ Liberties_{i,t}$	−0.096	−0.284	0.200	0.238	0.167	0.295
	(0.208)	(0.273)	(0.285)	(0.314)	(0.408)	(0.306)
$Civil\ Liberties_{j,t}$	−0.714***	−0.355	−1.44***	0.150	0.349	−0.136
	(0.238)	(0.271)	(0.361)	(0.260)	(0.391)	(0.214)
$Log(MarketCapitalization_{i,s,t}/GDP_{i,s,t})$	0.557***	0.413***	0.811***	0.535***	0.648**	0.407**
	(0.097)	(0.105)	(0.202)	(0.174)	(0.286)	(0.198)
$Log(MarketCapitalization_{j,s,t}/GDP_{j,s,t})$	−0.120	−0.100	−0.180	0.110	0.181**	−0.016
	(0.085)	(0.100)	(0.119)	(0.073)	(0.084)	(0.093)

Notes: Gravity models on bilateral cross-border M&As at sectoral level. Estimation using Poisson-QMLE estimators. Country dummies of acquiring countries and target countries, sectoral dummies, and time-dummies are included but not reported. Standard errors in parentheses. Statistical significance at the 10% (resp. 5% and 1%) level are denoted by * (resp. ** and ***). Estimation with robust standard errors. The number of observations is 76 642 in manufacturing and 83 034 in services. Observations are clustered within country pairs.

contrary to the large negative effect discussed in the trade literature (McCallum, 1995; Anderson and van Wincoop, 2003; Balistreri and Hillberry, 2007). This means that it is not capturing a trade cost, but a positive adjacency effect. Surprisingly, the impact of geographical distance is close to zero and non-significant, while in previous papers it has been shown to be a major determinant for M&A transactions (Di Giovanni, 2005; Head and Ries, 2007, Hijzen *et al.*, 2008). We attribute this finding to the combination of three factors. First, as shown by Head and Ries (2007) and Santos Silva and Tenreyro (2006), estimates tend to be strongly biased upwards in standard OLS or Tobit estimations, which have been widely used in past literature.[18] Second, the majority of countries in the sample are developed markets. If distance proxies for information costs (Portes and Rey, 2005) or monitoring costs (Head and Ries, 2007), it is very likely that such costs are much smaller among developed markets. Finally, the specification includes a border dummy and common language dummies which are partly collinear with distance.[19] We investigate further the role of distance in Section 6.5.

The quality of institutions in the host country is found to be an important determinant of cross-border M&As in manufacturing: countries with poor civil liberties might have a higher cost of capital and therefore are relatively less attractive. The effect is quantitatively important since, *ceteris paribus*, an improvement of the indicator of civil liberties in the host country from 5 (the level in Turkey) to 1 (in the US) doubles inward cross-border M&As.

The interpretation of the EMU effects is relatively straightforward: the adoption of the single currency has increased both cross-border M&As between euro area countries (preferential financial liberalization, $\gamma_1 = 0.94$) and M&As from non-euro area countries towards euro area countries (unilateral financial liberalization, $\gamma_2 = 0.6$). The magnitude of these effects is large since the single currency has raised respectively intra-euro area cross-border M&As by 155% and M&As from non-euro area countries towards euro area countries by 80%. In other words, EMU has increased cross-border M&As towards the euro area from all over the globe (including the individual euro area countries) by 80% with an additional increase between euro area countries of about 40%.[20]

The EMU effects on cross-border M&As are of the same order of magnitude than those found for the reallocation of bond portfolios and larger than those found for equity portfolios (see Lane, 2006; Coeurdacier and Martin, 2006; De Santis and Gerard, 2006).

Similarly to the criticisms against the common currency effect on trade, it could be argued that the EMU effects are too large because the gravity equations are not

---

[18] In a non-reported regression, we find that Tobit estimations give a large impact of distance on M&A transactions. Other variables of interest were essentially unaffected.

[19] Without border and common language, the elasticity of distance is significant, yet much lower than previous estimates: −0.255 (s.e.: 0.103).

[20] Given the functional form and the definition of the two EMU dummies, the additional EMU effect between euro area countries is computed as follows $e^{\gamma_1 - \gamma_2} - 1$.

well performed. First, we control for the common preferential trade agreement (i.e. EU), geography as well as institution quality. Second, the EMU effects are neither driven by unobservable characteristics of euro area countries (controlled by source/ host countries fixed effects), nor by an increasing number of M&As through time due to financial liberalization (controlled by the time fixed-effects), nor by some cyclical properties of stock prices in euro countries around the beginning of the EMU (controlled by both the acquirer and the target sector's market capitalization). Still, it can be argued that EMU dummies are capturing the impact of some omitted variables. In the next sections, we will try a number of potential candidates (taxation and product market regulations).[21]

Moreover, we run some additional robustness checks in Section 6.2, focusing on the impact of EMU over time by controlling for unobservable factors among euro area countries that have been constant over time. Results hardly change.

The results concerning the EU effects are similar to those described for EMU. $\delta_1 = 1.13$ and $\delta_2 = 0.87$ are of similar magnitude; everything else equal, the EU Single Market has mostly increased M&As towards the EU from all countries in the world.

These results are indirect evidence of Neary (2007a, 2007b) who argues that trade liberalizations should trigger M&A waves. In particular, it can explain the initial quantitatively enormous impact of EMU/EU that we find: the acquisition of one firm increases the incentive for another to be acquired due to the endogenous fall in competition and thus until 'all the small and relatively inefficient firms in the sector have been acquired' (see Neary, 2007a and 2007b). This suggests that the effect should be hump-shaped, which will be confirmed in Section 6.2. In the next section, we will investigate further the channel through which EU/EMU affected cross-border M&As.

Finally, sectoral M&As strongly react to movements in the market capitalization to GDP ratio of the acquiring sector. Sectors experiencing a stock market boom tend to expand by investing abroad through M&As. This is consistent with standard q-theory of investment. The estimates are both significant and large in magnitude. One could have expected that firms tend to buy assets in countries experiencing a drop in asset prices. This would be consistent with an efficient reallocation of capital from high q countries towards low q countries (see Jovanovic and Rousseau, 2008). This does not seem to be the case, since the estimate is not significant (even though the sign is negative).

Bris *et al.* (2007) show that the euro has increased Tobin's q-ratios among 11 euro area member states relative to the other 5 European countries. Part of the increase in corporate valuations is explained by the decrease in interest rates and by the decrease in the cost of equity. This result is very interesting in the light of this study because the impact of EMU via the stock market capitalization to GDP ratio would capture the effect of the reduction of the cost of capital, while the binary variables would capture other channels linked to trade liberalization or financial integration.

---

[21] We also control for bilateral nominal exchange rate volatility. Results remain invariant and this additional control was not significant (non-reported).

How do results change when considering horizontal and vertical cross-border M&As separately? Results with such decomposition are shown in columns 2 and 3 of Table 1. EMU increased intra-euro area horizontal cross-border M&As in manufacturing by about 200%. The estimated effect on euro area M&As from non-euro to euro area countries amounts to about 70%, but it is statistically significant at the 15% level. The impact of the euro on vertical M&As between euro area countries is not statistically significant, while non-euro area countries seem to have diversified their investment risk purchasing euro area assets. Therefore, the euro has facilitated cross-border M&As within the euro area, which aimed at restructuring capital within the same sector of activity, rather then boosting the formation of conglomerate activities between euro area sectors.

Overall, we have weak evidence that the EU fostered M&As between EU countries in addition to the unilateral financial liberalization effect. Both EU binary variables are very similar in magnitude in both horizontal and vertical mergers of the manufacturing sector. However, reducing the number of completed transactions, by cutting the sample in two, increases the standard errors of the variables capturing the EU effects associated with (1) intra-EU horizontal activity and (2) extra-EU vertical mergers targeting EU firms; thereby making some of the coefficients statistically significant only at 10–15% confidence interval.

A 1% increase in the stock market capitalization to GDP ratio in a given sector is associated with a 0.4% increase in horizontal M&As outflows, while the response of M&As across sectors (vertical) is twice as large (0.8%). We interpret this as a confirmation that stock market developments and profitability are important drivers of M&As regardless of their nature.

4. CROSS-BORDER M&As IN SERVICES

Using the same country sample, the same sample period and the same methodology, we also study the determinants of cross-border M&As in services and report the first set of results in the last three columns of Table 1.

One could argue that we do not control for market sizes properly, given that the impact of GDPs is small and not statistically significant. We can show that most of the impact of market sizes is through the source and host country/sector fixed-effects.[22] GDP changes in the service sector are very smooth making it harder to identify their impact over time.

Unlike in manufacturing, European integration (captured by EU and EMU dummies) has not fostered cross-border reallocation of capital in the service industry. The service industry in Europe is far less liberalized than manufacturing (see Appendix Table A5): large trade costs and barriers to foreign entry remain in service sectors, which could explain why we find no impact of EU/EMU of cross-border M&As in services. We will investigate further this hypothesis in Section 5.

---

[22] We obtain coefficients on $\log(GDP_{i,s,t} \, GDP_{j,s,t})$ equal to 0.733 (s.e.: 0.068) when excluding fixed effects.

Although distance is not significant,[23] physical and cultural proximity affect cross-border M&As in services given the large and highly significant estimates of the impacts of border and common language. This confirms the positive 'adjacency' effect obtained for manufacturing, but the elasticities for services are much larger. Indeed, there is considerable anecdotal evidence to suggest that top management decisions are affected by national culture. Strategic decisions and actions, for example, may be influenced by differences of opportunism and trust in other societies (Angwin, 2001). Cultural differences do play an important role in affecting acquirers' perceptions of target companies and this may have important consequences for the negotiation of cross-border M&As deals, particularly in the service sector.

We also find that cross-border M&As in services are fostered by stock market expansions of the acquiring sector. This result is robust across all specifications aiming at capturing horizontal and vertical M&As. The response to an increase in the acquiring sector's stock market over GDP ratio is very similar to that obtained in the case of manufacturing. This evidence confirms the major role played by waves in stock markets developments in triggering cross-border reallocation of capital across the globe.

5. TRADE LIBERALIZATION AND CROSS-BORDER M&As

While the previous section identifies large effects of EMU and EU on cross-border M&As in manufacturing, the channel through which this happened remains unclear. In this section, we provide evidence that the 'trade liberalization channel' emphasized theoretically by Neary (2007a, 2007b) has been operating within European countries. Neary (2007a, 2007b) argues that trade liberalization can trigger cross-border M&As, whereby low-cost firms acquire high-cost enterprises. Hence, the impact of EMU and EU on cross-border M&As in both manufacturing and services can be partly rationalized if we deepen our understanding on the effect of regional integration on trade flows and on the role of product trade barriers on cross-border M&As.

The link between trade liberalization, European integration, comparative advantage and cross-border M&As is based on general equilibrium principles, which cannot be easily tested empirically, given the lack of instruments and the need for a multiregional empirical model. Therefore, we study the trade liberalization argument indirectly using the gravity approach. First, we look at the role of comparative advantage revealed by manufacturing trade to validate the mechanisms highlighted by Neary. Second, we study the trade mechanism associated with European integration by investigating whether the trade sectors positively affected by EMU are the same sectors that are more engaged in cross-border M&As (see Section 5.1). We cannot

---

[23] When excluding the border and common language dummies, which are partly collinear with geographical distance, the elasticity measuring the impact of distance on cross-border M&As becomes significant and equal to -0.487 (s.e.: 0.160). When also excluding the EU dummies, this elasticity is equal to -0.540 (s.e.: 0.133).

look at trade in services due to lack of data. Finally, we assess whether trade barriers measured by the degree of product market regulation indicators in the target countries have been influencing cross-border M&As in both manufacturing and services (see Section 5.2).

5.1. The 'trade liberalization channel' in manufacturing

Firms seek to merge with their rivals in order to reduce competition in the market and increase their profit margins. The theoretical model by Neary (2007a) predicts that international differences in technology generate incentives for bilateral mergers in which low cost firms absorb high-cost firms located in another country. As a result, cross-border M&As facilitate more specialization in the direction of comparative advantage, moving production and trade patterns close to what would prevail in a competitive Ricardian world. However, relative autarchic prices are not observable. Therefore, empirical trade literature relies on revealed comparative advantage (RCA) measures to assess specialization patterns of countries. The most widely used RCA measure is the Balassa index (BI), which is a sectoral relative export measure in terms of world exports: $BI_{i,s,t} = (X_{i,s,t}/\Sigma_i X_{i,s,t})/(\Sigma_s X_{i,s,t}/\Sigma_i\Sigma_s X_{i,s,t})$, where $X_{i,s,t}$ denotes sectoral exports s of country i at time t. Based on Neary's (2007a) model, acquiring (target) firms operate in sectors with a high (low) revealed comparative advantage, as measured by the Balassa index (see Neary, 2007b and Brakman, Garretsen and van Marrewijk, 2008).

We are aware that bilateral goods trade and cross-border M&A flows should be simultaneously determined, but we cannot provide useful instruments to goods trade that are independent from cross-border M&As. Having said that, the endogeneity is more an issue for multinational firms' sales and less for investment, as the latter requires an adjustment period before it is translated into production. Moreover, the Balassa index is a relative measure based on sectoral exports, thereby further reducing the problem of the simultaneity bias. Thus, we can run the previous regression and control for the Balassa index of the acquirer and target sectors at date t. The results for manufacturing are shown in Table 2.

While we could find a strong positive relationship between cross-border M&As and the Balassa index of the acquiring firm, the relationship between cross-border M&As and revealed comparative advantage of the target firm is not negative as suggested by Neary (2007a).[24] Specifically, the Balassa index of the acquiring firm is strongly statistically significant and robust across the various specifications ranging between 0.34 and 0.40. According to the findings, a competitive firm in the international markets aims to become a global player by merging or acquiring foreign firms, thereby

---

[24] Brakman *et al.* (2008), who tested the implications of Neary's model using the number of completed cross-border M&As deals among the USA, UK, the Netherlands, Australia and France at the 2-digit level (about 12 000 observations), even found that target firms are operative in sectors with a strong comparative advantage.

Table 2. Cross-border M&As in manufacturing and the Balassa index

	All M&As			Within sectors M&As		
$Log(GDP_{i,t}\,GDP_{j,s,t})$	0.816***	0.562***	0.672***	0.920***	0.700***	0.837***
	(0.183)	(0.201)	(0.203)	(0.237)	(0.267)	(0.249)
$Log(distance_{ij})$	−0.059	−0.058	−0.072	−0.067	−0.065	−0.078
	(0.128)	(0.128)	(0.129)	(0.159)	(0.161)	(0.161)
$Border_{ij}$	0.429*	0.430*	0.395*	0.696**	0.698**	0.650**
	(0.232)	(0.233)	(0.236)	(0.308)	(0.311)	(0.311)
$Common\ language_{ij}$	0.555***	0.550***	0.526***	0.191	0.190	0.159
	(0.167)	(0.167)	(0.168)	(0.240)	(0.240)	(0.242)
$EMU_{i,t}\,EMU_{j,t}$	0.912**	0.884**	0.887**	1.052**	1.024**	1.038**
	(0.343)	(0.344)	(0.354)	(0.447)	(0.446)	(0.464)
$NonEMU_{i,t}\,EMU_{j,t}$	0.546**	0.502**	0.506**	0.452	0.417	0.429
	(0.250)	(0.249)	(0.250)	(0.342)	(0.345)	(0.350)
$EU_{i,t}\,EU_{j,t}$	0.846	0.834	0.795	0.763	0.751	0.717
	(0.567)	(0.565)	(0.561)	(0.684)	(0.682)	(0.676)
$NonEU_{i,t}\,EU_{j,t}$	0.652	0.636	0.617	0.695	0.679	0.672
	(0.454)	(0.453)	(0.445)	(0.509)	(0.509)	(0.500)
$Civil\ Liberties_{i,t}$	0.067	0.034	0.062	−0.121	−0.146	−0.109
	(0.232)	(0.231)	(0.233)	(0.291)	(0.292)	(0.296)
$Civil\ Liberties_{j,t}$	−0.719***	−0.735***	−0.767***	−0.358	−0.371	−0.413
	(0.238)	(0.236)	(0.235)	(0.284)	(0.281)	(0.282)
$Log(MarketCapitalization_{i,s,t}/GDP_{i,t})$	0.572***	0.480***	0.489***	0.434***	0.365***	0.374***
	(0.096)	(0.098)	(0.097)	(0.108)	(0.109)	(0.117)
$Log(MarketCapitalization_{j,s,t}/GDP_{j,t})$	−0.142	−0.142	−0.102	−0.116	−0.115	−0.076
	(0.091)	(0.088)	(0.083)	(0.105)	(0.103)	(0.097)
$Balassa\ index_{i,s,t}$		0.403***	0.376***		0.375***	0.336**
		(0.099)	(0.100)		(0.131)	(0.133)
$Balassa\ index_{j,s,t}$			−0.193			0.005
			(0.285)			(0.373)

Notes: Gravity models on bilateral cross-border M&As at sectoral level. Estimation using Poisson-QMLE estimators. Country dummies of acquiring countries and target countries, sectoral dummies, and time-dummies are included but not reported. Standard errors in parentheses. Statistical significance at the 10% (resp. 5% and 1%) level are denoted by * (resp. ** and ***). Estimation with robust standard errors. The number of observations is 63 848 when excluding the Balassa indices or when using the Balassa index of the acquiring sector and 61 132 when using the Balassa indices of both the acquiring and target sectors. Observations are clustered within country pairs.

implicitly reducing the fiercer competition. The results also indicate that the coefficients on all other variables remain robust compared to the benchmark regressions in Table 1 and replicated in Table 2 given that the number of observation declines by one-fifth. This result suggests that M&As are partly driven by comparative advantage as advocated by Neary (2007a).

If EMU and EU dummies are implicitly capturing the impact of trade liberalization, this can be investigated by comparing the impact of EMU on the individual manu-facturing sectors in both bilateral goods trade and cross-border M&As. One should expect that sectors in which trade has increased the most following EMU/EU are those where M&As have also increased the most. In other words, mergers should occur in sectors where competition became fiercer due to a larger fall of trade costs following EMU/EU. We split the sample in half according to the effect of EMU on trade activities. The five sectors, whose trade has been strongly positively affected by EMU, are: 1 – Food, beverages and tobacco; 2 – Textile, wearing apparel and leather industries; 4 – Paper and paper products, printing and publishing; 5 – Chemicals and chemical, petroleum, coal, rubber; 7 – Basic metal industries and fabricated metal products. These sectors recorded an average increase in bilateral trade flows of 22% due to EMU and are also those which recorded a strong positive increase in cross-border M&As after EMU, particularly of horizontal nature (see Panel A in Table 3).[25] The other five sectors have on average recorded a decline in trade flows after EMU of a similar magnitude, but the impact on cross-border M&As within the euro area in these sectors has been negligible. This result suggests that a large part of the increase of M&As among EMU members is due to a strengthening of competition following trade integration within the EMU. Indeed, if EMU had made M&As more profitable through a fall in financial transaction costs inside the euro area, one should not expect such a differential impact across sectors.

Similar conclusions can be drawn when splitting the EU effect between sectors whose bilateral trade has been positively affected after joining the EU from those not affected. Interestingly, the sectors recording an increase in goods trade after joining the EU are those also positively affected by EMU (see Panel B in Table 3). Moreover, the sectors and countries that recorded a boost in trade due to the EU also registered a sharp increase in cross-border M&As among EU firms.

Finally, it is worth pointing out the sizeable goods trade diversion effect of European integration on some specific sectors: 3 – Wood and wood products, including furniture; 6 – Non-metallic mineral products, except petroleum and coal; 8 – Machinery and equipment; 9 – Transport equipment; 10 – Other manufacturing industries. The manufacturing exports of these sectors from non-EU firms to EU countries have declined on average by 88.5% due to the EU over the period 1999–2004. Moreover, exports of these manufacturing goods from non-euro area firms to

---

[25] We are aware that bilateral goods trade and cross-border M&A flows should be simultaneously determined, but we cannot provide useful instruments to goods trade that are independent from cross-border M&As.

Table 3. Cross-border M&As and trade flows in manufacturing

	Goods trade flows	All M&As	Within sectors M&As	Across sectors M&As
	Panel A			
$EMU_{i,t}\,EMU_{j,t}$ if impact on trade flows is positive	0.261***	1.359***	1.561***	0.561
	(0.076)	(0.439)	(0.557)	(0.397)
$EMU_{i,t}\,EMU_{j,t}$ if impact on trade flows is not positive	−0.153***	0.172	0.182	0.120
	(0.053)	(0.358)	(0.464)	(0.419)
$NonEMU_{i,t}\,EMU_{j,t}$	−0.139***	0.605**	0.529	0.883**
	(0.050)	(0.249)	(0.332)	(0.364)
$EU_{i,t}\,EU_{j,t}$	0.186	1.144**	1.107	1.413***
	(0.120)	(0.565)	(0.692)	(0.525)
$NonEU_{i,t}\,EU_{j,t}$	−0.642***	0.866*	0.962*	0.876
	(0.150)	(0.453)	(0.520)	(0.544)
	Panel B			
$EMU_{i,t}\,EMU_{j,t}$ if impact on trade flows is positive	0.096**	1.147***	1.256**	0.529
	(0.047)	(0.440)	(0.540)	(0.448)
$EMU_{i,t}\,EMU_{j,t}$ if impact on trade flows is not positive	−0.015	0.522	0.712	0.167
	(0.052)	(0.396)	(0.519)	(0.398)
$NonEMU_{i,t}\,EMU_{j,t}$	−0.143***	0.610**	0.533	0.884**
	(0.050)	(0.247)	(0.329)	(0.363)
$EU_{i,t}\,EU_{j,t}$ if impact on trade flows is positive	0.481***	1.464**	1.593**	1.458**
	(0.165)	(0.594)	(0.728)	(0.570)
$EU_{i,t}\,EU_{j,t}$ if impact on trade flows is not positive	−0.025	0.742	0.500	1.358**
	(0.114)	(0.550)	(0.636)	(0.543)
$NonEU_{i,t}\,EU_{j,t}$	−0.632***	0.872*	0.976*	0.876
	(0.148)	(0.448)	(0.514)	(0.543)

Notes: Gravity models on bilateral trade flows. Controls of Table 1 excluding market capitalization to GDP ratios are included, but not reported. Gravity models on bilateral cross-border M&As at sectoral level. Controls of Table 1 are included, but not reported. Country dummies of acquiring countries and target countries, sectoral dummies, and time-dummies are included but not reported. Estimation using Poisson-QMLE estimators. Standard errors in parentheses. Statistical significance at the 10% (resp. 5% and 1%) level are denoted by * (resp. ** and ***). Estimation with robust standard errors. The number of observations is 59 632 for goods trade and 76 642 for cross-border M&As. The trade sectors positively affected by EMU are: 1 – Food, beverages and tobacco; 2 – Textile, wearing apparel and leather industries; 4 – Paper and paper products, printing and publishing; 5 – Chemicals and chemical, petroleum, coal, rubber; 7 – Basic metal industries and fabricated metal products.

the euro area have further declined by 15.6% due to EMU. Such a negative effect has not materialized in asset trade diversion. On the contrary, European integration has also promoted equity capital inflows from the rest of the world.

Overall, our results suggest that the increase of M&As in manufacturing between EMU/EU members (preferential liberalization) has been driven by a deeper product market competition and trade integration within the zone, in line with the arguments put forward by Neary (2007a). However, the increase in M&As towards EU/EMU from all over the word (unilateral liberalization) does not seem to be related with trade patterns. We argue that this is due to a deeper financial integration of Europe with the rest of the world (through the reduction of the cost of capital, the elimination of exchange rate risk, the sharing of common trading platforms), although we cannot identify the channel more precisely. In the service sector, EMU/EU had no effect on cross-border M&As. We think that this is due to large remaining trade barriers in these sectors (see below for some evidence) and thus even among European countries. Unfortunately we cannot directly link M&As to trade in services as we did for manufacturing due to lack of data.

5.2. The role of product market regulations in services

A complementary approach to study the links between trade and M&As is to investigate the role of trade barriers and product market regulations on cross-border M&As. Therefore, we make use of product market regulation indicators. The latter consist of 16 indicators grouped in three main categories: state control, barriers to entrepreneurship and barriers to trade and investment. These three main indicators are in turn further aggregated to obtain an overall indicator of product market regulation. These indicators are a synthesis of regulations that have the potential to reduce or increase the intensity of product market competition and therefore they are useful to assess their impact on cross-border M&As.

The key results are shown in Table 4, which includes (but it does not report) the control variable of Table 1. Despite the fact that the number of observations decline by almost one-quarter, the estimates of the control variables are not affected.

The impact of product market regulations on M&As in the manufacturing sector is generally very weak. The sectoral variable $\log(sectoral\ regulation_{j,s,t})$ that measures the potential costs of service regulations on a given manufacturing sector is not significant (not even correctly signed, see Panel A). The economy-wide indicator of regulation $\log(aggregate\ regulation_{j,t})$ is correctly signed but not significant (see Panel B). Only regulations excluding public ownership, a variable mainly capturing the degree of oligopoly in a country, is somewhat statistically significant (see Panel C).

These results capture the impact of services regulations (for which institutional information is available) on the manufacturing sectors using input-output tables. To a certain extent, therefore, their impact on cross-border M&As in manufacturing might be downward biased due to measurement errors. However, we believe that

Table 4. Cross-border M&As in manufacturing and services: The role of product market regulations

	Manufacturing			Services		
	All	Within sectors	Across sectors	All	Within sectors	Across sectors
$\text{Log}(sectoral\ regulation_{j,s,t})$	Panel A					
	0.237	0.366	0.289	−1.27***	−1.47***	−1.25***
	(0.692)	(0.932)	(0.893)	(0.295)	(0.456)	(0.314)
$\text{Log}(aggregate\ regulation_{j,t})$	Panel B					
	−0.569	−0.904	−0.116	−1.14**	−1.74***	−0.570
	(0.693)	(0.878)	(0.954)	(0.564)	(0.621)	(0.592)
$\text{Log}(aggr.\ Reg.\ exc.\ Pub.Own._{j,t})$	Panel C					
	−0.975*	−1.093	−0.983	−1.58**	−2.01***	−0.908
	(0.521)	(0.675)	(0.858)	(0.656)	(0.766)	(0.597)
$\text{Log}(entry\ barriers_{j,t})$	Panel D					
	−0.474	−0.600	−0.359	−1.19***	−1.23**	−0.987**
	(0.349)	(0.454)	(0.526)	(0.434)	(0.550)	(0.420)
$\text{Log}(public\ ownership_{j,t})$	Panel E					
	0.389	0.183	0.704**	−0.116	−0.282	0.015
	(0.310)	(0.350)	(0.349)	(0.346)	(0.343)	(0.334)

Notes: Gravity models on bilateral cross-border M&As at sectoral level. Estimation using Poisson-QMLE estimators. Controls of Table 1 are included, but not reported. Country dummies of acquiring countries and target countries, sectoral dummies, and time-dummies are included but not reported. Standard errors in parentheses. Statistical significance at the 10% (resp. 5% and 1%) level are denoted by * (resp. ** and ***). Estimation with robust standard errors. The number of observations is 60,506 in manufacturing and 68 02 in services. Observations are clustered within country pairs.

regulations play a lower role in manufacturing; as such activities have been strongly liberalized, particularly since the beginning of the 1990s.

Conversely, we expect the role of product market regulations to be a key determinant in services, as most sectors are strongly protected. This is confirmed by the data (see last three columns of Table 2): the impact of product market regulations on cross-border M&As in services is strong, statistically significant and robust across the various alternative measures. Quantitative estimates are also very similar, regardless whether using the sectoral (see Panel A) or the aggregate (see Panel B) indicators. Interestingly, the percentage of shares owned by the government is not an impediment for cross-border M&As in services (see Panel E), while lower competition in the domestic economy (see Panel C) and/or tougher entry regulations (see Panel D) reduce the degree of foreign investment.

Services account for around 70% of value-added in most OECD countries and, depending on the country, account for between one-third and one-half of total intermediate inputs (e.g. business services, transport, telecommunications and electricity) of manufacturing activities. Therefore, policies aiming at liberalizing the service sector can have a quantitatively large impact on cross-border M&As: according to the estimate on total cross-border M&As (and using the aggregate index; see Table 4, column (4), panel (3)), *ceteris paribus*, reducing the degree of regulations from the level of the most regulated countries over the period 1998–2003 (France and Greece) to the level of the least regulated (US and UK) could increase inward investment towards these countries by about 70%, an economically large impact.

Services regulations fall within the competence of individual EU member states and the EU internal market for services remains to date very fragmented. Only in December 2006, the European Parliament and Council have adopted the Directive on services in the internal market (commonly referred to as the Bolkestein Directive), an initiative of the European Commission aimed at creating a single market for services within EU, similar to the single market for goods.[26] If this directive helps liberalizing trade in services, it might trigger a new wave of cross-border M&As.

We interpret the large impact of product market regulation in the service industry as suggestive of the key role played by competition and trade policies in shaping cross-border M&As (in line with the results regarding EMU/EU in the manufacturing sectors). However, one might be cautious with such an interpretation since product market regulation indicators might be correlated with some other unobservable variables that might also affect cross-border M&As (such as the level of financial development, labour market institutions, etc.).

We focus the analysis on cross-border M&As. It would be very interesting assessing whether other forms of foreign entry (through trade or greenfield investment) are

---

[26] This Directive is seen as an important kick-start to the Lisbon Agenda which, launched in 2000, is an agreed strategy to make the EU 'the world's most dynamic and competitive economy' by 2010. With the proposed legislation, the Commission wants to reduce the barriers to cross-border trade in services, objectively justified on the grounds of public interest.

affected negatively in a similar way by product market regulations or, to the contrary, whether such alternative modes are used as a substitute for cross-border M&As to enter in highly regulated economies. Indeed, anecdotal evidence shows that European governments are more active in restricting foreign acquisitions than in limiting greenfield FDI.

6. ROBUSTNESS CHECKS

6.1. The role of corporate taxation

We assess the role of corporate taxation for two reasons. First, the results might have clear policy recommendation, as it is generally argued that multinational firms tend to expand in countries where tax rates are on average lower. Second, the convergence in corporate taxes among EU and EMU countries over time might bias the estimates on the EU/EMU binary variables. Therefore, we control for the difference in effective average corporate tax rates (in percentage points) between host country j and source country i at date t.

The impact of the difference in corporate tax rates has the expected sign and is strongly significant only for manufacturing; the semi-elasticity with respect to differences in corporate taxation is found to be equal to -4.6. This estimate is broadly in line with estimates by Razin and Sadka (2007a), who found elasticities ranging from -3 to -5 for FDI flows among OECD countries (see also Devereux and Griffith, 1998; Benassy et al., 2005; and Razin et al., 2005). M&As within the same sector are those mostly affected by corporate taxation with an elasticity equal to -6.8, suggesting that increasing by 10 percentage points the corporate tax in the host country (while keeping the taxes in the source country constant) reduces horizontal cross-border M&A in manufacturing by 68%. This result points towards a substitution effect of corporate taxation on firms' investment decisions. The estimates on all other variables are essentially unaffected, even though the sample is now halved.

6.2. The EMU effects in manufacturing

One common criticism in the literature on the role of common currencies on trade is that the usual regression does not control for some unobservable characteristics (constant over time) in the bilateral dimension; if such a variable increases both the probability of joining the same currency union and the intensity of transactions between the two countries, the coefficient related to the impact of the common currency would be biased upwardly (see Glick and Rose, 2002; Baldwin and Taglioni, 2006).

Following this literature, the robustness checks require the use of additional dummy variables and are carried out keeping all the controls of the regressions used in Table 1.

First, we identify the impact of EMU in the time-dimension, by adding a dummy variable which is equal to one over the 1985–2004 period for country pairs inside

EMU in 2004 and run the same regression as before. Such a strategy allows us to identify the impact of EMU across time by comparing cross-border M&As within EMU countries after the date of the introduction of the euro with cross-border M&As within EMU countries before the introduction of EMU. We report the results in Panel A of Table 5. They are almost identical to the results of the previous regressions. This additional dummy (not reported) is not significant while the impact of EMU, now fully estimated in the time dimension, is of the same magnitude as reported in Table 1.[27]

Second, in order to assess how the EMU effects have evolved over time, we interact $EMU_{i,t}$ $EMU_{j,t}$ with three time dummies starting in 1999: one for the years 1999–2000, one for 2001–2002 and one for 2003–2004. As shown in Panel B of Table 5, the increase in cross-border M&As within the euro area is not restricted to a specific period though it has not been constant through time. This regression shows that the impact of EMU has been much less pronounced in 2003–2004. Moreover, as expected, the same interaction dummy is no different from zero in 1997–98 (not reported). We conduct the same exercise using aggregate data (data aggregated across sectors), in order to limit the number of zeros. The results reported in the last three columns of Table 3 confirm the large EMU effects over the period 1999–2002 and a smaller impact at the end of the sample. This result suggests that the huge increase of cross-border M&As within the euro area due to EMU is temporary; at the same time, the time series information available after 1999 is too short to estimate with precision the permanent steady-state increase. This result is in line with Neary (2007a), according to which following trade liberalizations cross-border M&As are likely to come in waves, with an initially large impact.

6.3. EMU effects: Extensive versus the intensive margins

We also investigate whether EMU has affected the probability of engaging in M&As with an EMU country ('extensive margin') or affected the volume of M&As among member states ('intensive margin'). Implicitly, the former would capture the effect of EMU on the fixed costs in undertaking M&As, while the latter would capture the effect of EMU on transaction costs. To identify the two margins, we use aggregate data (data aggregated across sectors) of bilateral cross-border M&As, as they have a lower number of zeros.

To assess whether EMU has influenced the decision to engage in M&As for a given country ('extensive margin'), we compute a dummy which is set equal to one if there is at least one transaction between country i and country j at date t ($1_{(M\&Aij,t>0)}$) and we run a logit estimation adding such dummy to the specification reported in Table 1 (see Table 6, column 2).

---

[27] Another standard solution to deal with this problem is to estimate the regression with fixed-effects per country pairs, α_{ij}. We run this regression (non-reported) using aggregate data and find very similar estimates.

Table 5. Cross-border M&As in manufacturing: The role of EMU in the time dimension

	Sectoral			Aggregate		
	All	Within sectors	Across sectors	All	Within sectors	Across sectors
Panel A						
$EMU_{i,t}\,EMU_{j,t}$	0.839**	0.914**	0.603	1.000***	1.216**	0.366
	(0.377)	(0.464)	(0.393)	(0.435)	(0.521)	(0.399)
$NonEMU_{i,t}\,EMU_{j,t}$	0.650**	0.615*	0.789**	0.771(***)	0.890**	0.603**
	(0.256)	(0.332)	(0.359)	(0.238)	(0.312)	(0.305)
Panel B						
$EMU_{i,t}\,EMU_{j,t}\,X\,I_{t=1999,2000}$	1.002*	1.039*	0.450	1.190**	1.391**	0.188
	(0.519)	(0.607)	(0.393)	(0.568)	(0.669)	(0.409)
$EMU_{i,t}\,EMU_{j,t}\,X\,I_{t=2001,2002}$	1.117***	1.788***	0.407	1.414***	2.203***	0.460
	(0.369)	(0.476)	(0.510)	(0.394)	(0.493)	(0.517)
$EMU_{i,t}\,EMU_{j,t}\,X\,I_{t=2003,2004}$	0.190	0.225	−0.026	0.645	0.854*	−0.285
	(0.479)	(0.585)	(0.771)	(0.407)	(0.496)	(0.690)

Notes: Gravity models on bilateral cross-border M&As at sectoral level. Estimation using Poisson–QMLE estimators. Controls of Table 1 are included, but not reported. Country dummies of acquiring countries and target countries, sectoral dummies, and time-dummies are included but not reported. Standard errors in parentheses. Statistical significance at the 10% (resp. 5% and 1%) level are denoted by * (resp. ** and ***). Estimation with robust standard errors. Number of observations is 76 642 for sectoral manufacturing and 10 046 for aggregate manufacturing. Observations are clustered within country pairs.

Table 6. Aggregate cross-border M&As in manufacturing: The role of EMU, intensive versus extensive margins

	OLS-non zero	Logit
	$\text{Log}(M\&A_{ij,t})$ (1)	$1_{(M\&A_{ij},t>0)}$ (2)
$EMU_{i,t}\ EMU_{j,t}$	0.293	0.364***
	(0.198)	(0.160)
$NonEMU_{i,t}\ EMU_{j,t}$	0.480***	−0.240
	(0.186)	(0.154)

Notes: Gravity models on bilateral cross-border M&As at aggregate level. The OLS-non zero estimation is a standard OLS regression dropping all zero observation. The logit estimation is a logistic regression on a dummy variable which equals one when at least one M&A is observed for a given year and a given country-pair. Controls of Table 1 at aggregate level are included, but not reported. Country dummies of acquiring countries and target countries, and time-dummies are included but not reported. Standard errors in parentheses. Statistical significance at the 10% (resp. 5% and 1%) level are denoted by * (resp. ** and ***). Estimation with robust standard errors.

To assess whether EMU affected the volume of M&As for a given country ('intensive margin'), we run a standard OLS gravity regression, which excludes the zero transactions (see Table 6, column 1), as it gives the impact of EMU on the size of M&As conditionally on observed transactions.

The comparison of the two columns provides a decomposition of the overall effect already measured with the Poisson estimations. We can argue that EMU acted as 'preferential liberalization' mostly by increasing the probability of M&As between two euro area countries (Table 6, column 2). The 'extensive margin' effect is large since the probability of M&As between two euro area countries has increased by about 45% after EMU, while the probability of a M&A between non-euro area countries and euro area countries has not been affected by the introduction of the euro.

The single currency has also increased the size of M&As towards the euro area from all countries in the world including euro area countries.[28] The 'intensive margin' effect is around 35% (Table 6, column 1). This decomposition confirms the previous results. If we add the two margins, cross-border M&As (in value) have doubled between euro area countries ($e^{0.293+0.364} = 1.93$), while non-euro area M&As targeting the euro area have risen by about one-quarter ($e^{0.480-0.240} = 1.27$). Namely, the EMU effect between euro area countries in addition to the general tendency to invest in the euro area would amount to about 52% (= 1.93/1.27 − 1).

These results suggest that EMU acted through a decrease in fixed-costs within EMU countries ('extensive margin') and a decrease in proportional transaction costs for every single country in the world ('intensive margin'). With lower transactions costs, the euro area has become more like one bigger economy, and this encouraged M&As also from non-euro area countries.

---

[28] The estimate of the dummy $EMU_{i,t}\ EMU_{j,t}$ is smaller than the one of the dummy $nonEMU_{i,t}\ EMU_{j,t}$, but they are not statistically different.

6.4. The role of financial depth and Tobin's *q*

The various experiments carried out in the previous sections (manufacturing versus services, horizontal versus vertical mergers, controlling for various variables) indicate the importance of the acquiring sector's stock market capitalization to GDP ratio as a key variable explaining cross-border M&As. Di Giovanni (2005), looking at aggregate cross-border M&As, finds them to be a function of aggregate stock market capitalization. He also controls for credit to GDP ratio of the acquirer, but the latter variable is less significant in his regressions. He interprets his results as the consequence of financial depth and puts forward financial deepening as a key driver for M&As on the basis that deep liquid markets provide firms with access to capital necessary to undertake investment projects, which they might otherwise have to forego.

We can show that (1) the fixed-effects control for the degree of financial development across countries and (2) the changes over time of the acquiring sector's market capitalization to GDP ratio is more related to changes in the profitability of investments of the acquiring sector (as in a standard q-theory of investment).

We investigate this hypothesis by running the same regressions with and without fixed-effects at a 2-digit disaggregation and add two additional controls for financial depth: domestic credit over GDP of source and target countries. While Di Giovanni (2005) does not consider the impact of the depth of financial markets of the target country, one could argue that more developed financial markets should also attract M&As.

Regressions in Table 7 (see columns 1 to 3) indicate that countries with deeper financial markets have a more intense M&A activity, both as acquirer and target of financial assets. This holds for both measures of financial depth as market capitalization and domestic credit of the host and source countries are all statistically significant for manufacturing as well as services. However, when controlling for country fixed effects, the only variable which remains statistically significant is the acquiring sector's market capitalization to GDP ratio (Table 7; columns 4 to 6).

This evidence suggests that financial deepening is an important driver of cross-border M&As (both for source and host countries), but this effect cannot be identified across time, as countries' financial depth changes smoothly across time. Across time, only changes in expected profitability of the acquiring sector affect significantly cross-border M&As, supporting the Tobin's q theory of investment.

6.5. The role of geography

The impact of distance on cross-border M&As is found to be very small, which contradicts some previous work where geography has usually been found to play a major role in shaping international financial transactions (Portes and Rey, 2005; Head and Ries, 2007; Hijzen *et al.*, 2008). We test two competitive explanations for this result: first, as already argued, the sample is mostly restricted to developed

Table 7. Cross-border M&As in manufacturing and services: The role of financial deepening and Tobin's q

	Without country fixed effects			With country fixed effects		
	(1)	(2)	(3)	(4)	(5)	(6)
Manufacturing						
$Log(MarketCapitalization_{i,s,t}/GDP_{i,s,t})$	0.506***		0.470***	0.557***		0.563***
	(0.051)		(0.049)	(0.097)		(0.099)
$Log(MarketCapitalization_{j,s,t}/GDP_{j,s,t})$	0.229***		0.244***	−0.120		−0.130
	(0.048)		(0.048)	(0.085)		(0.083)
$Log(DomesticCredit_{i,t}/GDP_{i,t})$		0.469***	0.185*		0.157	0.090
		(0.100)	(0.108)		(0.183)	(0.169)
$Log(DomesticCredit_{j,t}/GDP_{j,t})$		0.729***	0.682***		0.269	0.237
		(0.094)	(0.090)		(0.271)	(0.280)
Services						
$Log(MarketCapitalization_{i,s,t}/GDP_{i,s,t})$	0.562***		0.533***	0.535***		0.530***
	(0.068)		(0.066)	(0.174)		(0.176)
$Log(MarketCapitalization_{j,s,t}/GDP_{j,s,t})$	0.515***		0.487***	0.110		0.098
	(0.052)		(0.053)	(0.073)		(0.071)
$Log(DomesticCredit_{i,t}/GDP_{i,t})$		0.330***	0.154		0.181	0.248
		(0.092)	(0.104)		(0.292)	(0.260)
$Log(DomesticCredit_{j,t}/GDP_{j,t})$		0.532***	0.279**		−0.057	−0.053
		(0.090)	(0.113)		(0.201)	(0.200)

Notes: Gravity models on bilateral cross-border M&As at sectoral level. Estimation using Poisson-QMLE estimators. Controls of Table 1 excluding country dummies in columns (1) to (3) are included, but not reported. Sectoral dummies and time-dummies are always included but not reported. Standard errors in parentheses. Statistical significance at the 10% (resp. 5% and 1%) level are denoted by * (resp. ** and ***). Estimation with robust standard errors. Number of observations is 74 283 for manufacturing and 80 654 for services. Observations are clustered within country pairs.

countries and if distance proxies some information asymmetries, it is likely that information costs are less related to distance for those markets. Second, a large share of M&As occurs from 1995 onwards and it is possible that the improvement of information technologies worldwide reduced information costs dramatically, making distance statistically insignificant.

We investigate the first explanation by estimating whether geographical distance is a larger barrier for M&As towards developing countries compared to M&As towards developed markets (see Appendix Table A1 for the classification) by simply interacting the variable log($Distance_{ij}$) with a dummy which is equal to one when the target country is a developed country. As shown in Table 8 (column 1 in the case of manufacturing and column 3 in the case of services), distance matters more when the target country is a developing country (the elasticity is around −0.5 for both manufacturing and services and highly significant), while the effect of distance is negligible when the target country is a developed market. This evidence supports the hypothesis that distance is essentially related to monitoring and information costs.

We also investigate the second explanation by estimating the effect of distance over time for both developed and developing markets, by dividing the sample in two periods, before and after 1995. While for developed markets, geography played no role over the whole period, the impact of distance has decreased over time only

Table 8. Cross-border M&As in manufacturing and services: The role of geography

	Manufacturing		Services	
	(1)	(2)	(1)	(2)
	Panel A			
Developing countries	−0.452***		−0.518***	
	(0.126)		(0.156)	
Before 1995		−0.521***		−0.527***
		(0.148)		(0.183)
After 1995		−0.459***		−0.518***
		(0.126)		(0.156)
	Panel B			
Developed countries	−0.026		0.008	
	(0.131)		(0.198)	
Before 1995		−0.015		0.024
		(0.137)		(0.212)
After 1995		−0.030		0.006
		(0.138)		(0.199)

Notes: Gravity models on bilateral cross-border M&As at sectoral level. Estimation using Poisson-QMLE estimators. Controls of Table 1 excluding distance are included, but not reported. Country dummies of acquiring countries and target countries, sectoral dummies, and time-dummies are included but not reported. Standard errors in parentheses. Statistical significance at the 10% (resp. 5% and 1%) level are denoted by * (resp. ** and ***). Estimation with robust standard errors. Number of observations is 76 642 for manufacturing and 83 034 for services. Observations are clustered within country pairs.

slightly when the target is a developing country and the acquiring sector belongs to manufacturing (see Table 8, column 2 and 4). This implies that monitoring or information costs remain a predominant obstacle to cross-border M&As towards emerging markets.

7. CONCLUSIONS

We study the determinants of cross-border mergers and acquisition activities (M&As) over the 1985–2004 period in ten manufacturing and ten service sectors among the major economies of the world. This exercise has been carried out by compiling a unique database using Thomson Financial. It includes about three-quarters of observations around the world and covers a broad spectrum of M&As. Following the theoretical and empirical literature on the volume of M&As and FDI transactions and using the gravity modelling approach, we study the role of trade and financial liberalization in Europe in triggering cross-border M&As.

The empirical results suggest that European integration have positively influenced the world developments of cross-border M&As of the manufacturing sector. We can safely argue that institutional changes such as the EU single market and the EMU acted as trigger factors of capital reallocation of manufacturing across the globe. The impact of the euro is very strong for M&As within the same sector (horizontal) in manufacturing. Over the average period 1999–2004, EMU increased intra-euro area cross-border horizontal M&As activity in manufacturing by 200%. The estimated effect on euro area M&As from non-euro to euro area countries amounts to a 70% increase. The impact of the euro on vertical mergers in manufacturing sectors from non-euro to euro area countries is also important (about 140%). Therefore, EMU had the effect typical of unilateral financial liberalization and fostered the reallocation of capital across firms by reducing marginal and fixed costs to undertake such transactions. The euro facilitated cross-border M&As within the euro area, which aimed at restructuring capital within the same sector of activity, rather than boosting the formation of conglomerate activities between sectors. We find that this increase in 'horizontal' cross-border M&As within the euro area occurred in sectors where the EMU had the largest effect on trade. In line with Neary (2007a), this suggests that cross-border M&As in the EMU have been following trade patterns. We have also found that the large average effects rather hide a hump-shape development with an initial jump in transactions. As suggested by Neary (2007a), as a result of trade liberalization, low-cost firms merge with or acquire high-cost firms, thus generating waves in M&As. These results are very indicative particularly for countries which have recently joined the EU and EMU or might join in the near future. They might attract sizeable foreign equity capital and gain from a more efficient reallocation of manufacturing capital.

Conversely, the impact on cross-border M&As in services of EU, EMU and institutions is not statistically significant pointing out that such activities may be affected by the significant barriers to cross-border trade in services, which could have undermined M&A decisions of entrepreneurs. We find support for this hypothesis when testing the impact of various measures of product market regulation indicators on cross-border M&As. The level of protection and barriers to entry in the service sector act as a strong deterrent to cross-border M&As in services across countries. Domestic regulations are relevant for foreign investors, because the implied fixed costs to enter the domestic market are potentially larger than the economies of scale and scope resulting from the M&As. The results suggest that, by deregulating product markets in services, governments can act and be successful to attract foreign equity capital in such sector. This implies that large structural changes will most likely occur as cross-border barriers are dismantled in the service industry, raising the question of the coordination of such policies within regional agreements. Needless to say that M&As may lead to more oligopolistic market structures, which can ultimately affect consumer welfare, and therefore deserves (and receives) regulatory scrutiny.

In this context, the Bolkenstein directive on services in the EU adopted in December 2006 can help breaking such barriers allowing firms to find the most efficient location for their investment in Europe, thereby triggering a new wave of cross border M&As within the EU. Obviously, it is premature to assess the degree of accomplishment of the Bolkenstein directive as well as to disentangle the potential effect of such directive on cross-border M&As. However, it might be worth noting that in 2007 cross-border intra-euro area M&As in services almost tripled with respect to both the average period 2000–2006 and the previous year, respectively from €40–50 billion to €140 billion. At the same time, cross-border intra manufacturing activities contracted.

We also obtain interesting results on the role of corporate taxation, which are informative for government policies. A 10 percentage point decrease in the differential in effective average corporate taxes between target and acquiring countries would increase the outflows of manufacturing equity investment in the same sector by 68%. This large effect suggests that changes in corporate taxes are an efficient tool to attract foreign capital and raise the question of the coordination of fiscal policies in Europe. Finally, the empirical results of this paper suggest that profitability is a key driver of M&As, as the acquiring sector's stock market capitalization is an important explanatory variable of cross-border M&As within the same sector as well as across sectors for both firm type in manufacturing and services.

Discussion

Gianmarco Ottaviano
University of Bologna

The deepening of European integration and the creation of the EMU have been associated with a surge in M&As across participating countries. This paper checks the statistical significance and robustness of such association using very detailed data on cross-border M&As. It also tries to identify the channels through which the relation may have worked.

Two channels are investigated: the straightforward 'financial liberalization channel' due to the reduction in transaction costs and the 'trade liberalization channel' due to the reduction in the barriers to international trade. The authors' conclusion is that the latter channel has been the most important one as M&As have increased the most in those sectors where also international trade has increased the most. I have two comments. The first is that the logic underpinning the trade liberalization channel deserves further empirical scrutiny. This logic is derived from a recent theoretical contribution by Peter Neary (2007a) proposing an analytical framework that shows how changes in market structure accompany the process of trade and capital market liberalization when these lead to tougher competition. Introducing strategic interactions in an otherwise standard model of comparative advantage, Neary concludes that trade liberalization can trigger international merger waves, in the process encouraging countries to specialize and trade more in accordance with comparative advantage. This happens because in his framework M&As are assumed to be the only way industries can restructure. If new players were allowed to enter the restructuring industry, Neary's argument would unfold. This caveat generates interesting implications in terms of the sectoral pattern of industry restructuring that could be exploited for further empirical analysis. From a policy perspective, such analysis would shed light on the relative importance of domestic and international competition in driving industrial restructuring. The second comment concerns the sharp dichotomy that the paper seems to imply between the financial liberalization channel and the trade liberalization channel. In Neary's argument these are not really antithetic. As financial liberalization allows M&As to act as instruments of comparative advantage, there is no role for the trade channel if the financial one is shut down. Accordingly, the conclusions of the paper on the relative importance of the two channels should be handled with care.

Morten Ravn
European University Institute

Coeurdacier, De Santis and Aviat have written an interesting paper on the determinants of cross-border M&A flows. Cross-border M&As constitute a subset of FDI flows and are the dominating component of such cross-border investments among OECD economies. The authors pay particular attention to the impact of integration of European goods markets and of financial markets on the cross-border M&A flows. They examine a very interesting dataset on cross-border M&As and show that European integration has worked as a phenomenal catalyst of M&A activity in the EU, especially among firms in the manufacturing sector. Not only does the single market appear to have significantly promoted M&A activity, but they also find a large impact of the single currency. These results are important for economic policy and the paper adds significantly to the list of empirical findings regarding the economic impact of European integration.

International capital flows

International capital markets allow investors to spread their investments across locations in order to maximize the return on their savings and facilitate the smoothing of consumption over time and across states of nature. During the development process, countries open to inflows of foreign capital can expand their stock of productive capital faster than countries that must entirely rely on domestic resources.

FDI flows appear particularly important. An FDI inflow not only expands the domestic capital stock, but may also bring along with it other benefits such as access to new technologies, improved management techniques, training of workers, etc. The expansion of the capital stock should benefit the host country (since most of the value added ends up paying for labour services) and added benefits (technology spill-overs and so on) should simply make these gains for the home economy even higher.

The simplest of theories would have it that capital flows from capital-rich countries to capital-poor countries in response to return differentials driven by cross-country differences in capital stocks (capital-labour ratios). This simple story, however, does not fare well empirically since cross-country (North-South) capital flows should be much bigger than observed in the data if capital-labour ratios were the only determinants of such cross-border movements of capital (see Lucas, 1990).

For that reason macroeconomists have for some time turned their attention to identifying factors that either affect the return on capital (and therefore the size and direction of capital flows over and above the influence of capital-labour ratios themselves), or factors that limit the flows of capital despite differences in the return on capital. Figure 2 illustrates a simple way of understanding this dichotomy. Suppose there are two countries in the world economy, home and foreign. The total world capital stock is fixed and given by the number K^W. We measure the home economy's capital stock, K^h, on the horizontal axis as the distance from the origin. The foreign capital stock is then measured as the distance from K^W to K^h. On the vertical axis we indicate the return on capital in the two countries. Assuming declining marginal returns implies that the domestic return is declining in K^h while the foreign return is increasing in K^F. Assume first that the two countries are symmetric in terms of returns (indicated by r_h and r_f) and that the home economy is capital-poor (its initial capital stock is given by K^h_0). Since foreigners can increase their returns on capital by investing in the domestic economy rather than in their own, there should therefore be an FDI inflow to the domestic economy.

What might hinder such an inflow of capital to the domestic economy? The first group of factors are those that are associated with return differences not due to differences in capital-labour. If the foreign economy is more productive than the domestic economy, there might be little reason for foreigners to divert capital to the

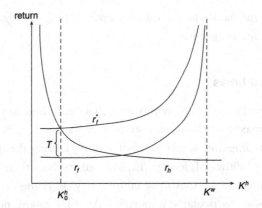

Figure 2. The determinants of international capital flows

domestic economy. We indicate this possibility by the return schedule r_f^* which is drawn in such a way that the productivity difference exactly makes up for the capital intensity difference between home and abroad. What might lead to such productivity differences? The obvious candidates are aspects such as human capital, technology, goods market structures, government policies (regulation, trade policies etc.), and political and economic institutions.

 The other possibility is the existence of impediments to the free flow of capital. We can think of such impediments giving rise to a wedge – an implicit tax – so that capital flows occur only when return differentials exceed this wedge. This is indicated in the figure by the vertical distance T, which is drawn so that it makes up exactly for the return difference even when the two countries are symmetric. This wedge puts sand in the wheel of the international allocation of capital preventing an efficient outcome (at least in terms of the allocation of capital). This wedge consists of aspects such as impediments to financial flows, sovereign debt issues, or informational issues. Some of these aspects may, however, simply slow down capital movements rather than limit the long-run impact of return differentials. Informational issues, for example, may dissolve over time thus simply slowing down the speed of adjustment of capital flows. This distinction may suggest that one takes dynamics serious.

 This dichotomy is useful because it suggests an approach to estimating the determinants of capital flows. The reduced form approach in the current paper can indeed be thought of as determining these factors.

Mergers and acquisitions

The current paper focuses upon the determinants of a subset of FDI flows: M&As. Cross-border M&As occur when a foreign company either purchases a domestic company or when the foreign and the domestic companies jointly agree to merge into one single company. Therefore, M&As involve the change of ownership of two existing companies (rather than a foreign economy directly setting up a new activity in the domestic economy as in the case of greenfield FDI). This does not prevent an expansion of the capital stock as in the simple example above. For that reason, it might be useful to think about broader motives for capital flows than the simple return on investment considerations that I went through above.

In particular, it demands some considerations related to the theory of the firm and industrial organization. It would take me too long to cover all the ground here, but given the authors' analysis, it is useful to highlight Neary's (2007) industrial organization (IO) trade analysis of M&As. Neary shows how M&As may occur in oligopolistic markets in response to trade liberalization (or other cross-country changes in cost structures). He examines a model with Cournot competition in which firms are homogeneous within a country sector but possibly heterogeneous across countries and sectors.

Heterogeneity is important since it is well known that M&As are unprofitable in the homogeneous oligopoly model unless this activity creates a monopoly. In Neary's model, trade impediments allow high cost firms to survive, but when removed, low cost firms have an incentive to take over foreign high cost firms. This M&A activity increases prices but roots out inefficient high cost firms (which are subsequently closed down in Neary's model) and leads to a downward pressure on wages. A testable prediction is that M&A flows should be positively correlated with trade flows as exporting low cost firms are also the firms that have an incentive to purchase foreign high cost firms.

This paper

In considering the authors' analysis, it is worthwhile to keep in mind the dichotomy discussed above together with the special features of M&A flows just highlighted. Coeurdacier *et al.* adopt a gravity approach which can be thought of as a reduced form approach to the estimation (and identification) of the impact of the two sets of factors discussed above on cross-border M&A flows. Their primary controls are measures of market size, 'geography', measures of Tobin's (average) q, and institutional controls for the quality of institutions, for EU membership, and for EMU membership, respectively. We may think of Tobin's q, the quality of institutions and EU membership as being factors that control for return differences (and in the latter case, a direct catalyst of M&As). Distance, border and language indicators may be thought of as affecting returns directly (due to transportation costs etc.), but are probably also related to institutions, and perhaps to informational issues.

EMU membership appears most likely as a component of the wedge. For example, currency matching rules used to prevent pension funds from freely allocating their portfolios; this restriction has now less bite within the euro area. It is less clear how the single currency should directly affect *M&A activity* apart from lowering marginally transactions costs and perhaps improving the extent of price transparency across borders (which in turn may improve goods market competition).

The authors later extend the list of controls to include the Balassa index which measures the direction of trade and therefore is related to Neary's theory of mergers, product market regulation measures, and financial market development indicators. Each of these measures may be thought of as return difference indicators.

In their estimations they distinguish between cross-border M&A flows in manufacturing and in services, and between horizontal and vertical transactions (within or between 2-digit sectors). The sector level aspect of the analysis is clearly a valuable aspect of the analysis since it allows one to take into account issues related to comparative advantage (although one might wonder if a 2-digit analysis is sufficiently refined). Given that the dataset includes a large number of 'zeros' (no M&A flows between two particular sector-country pairs), the authors adopt a (quasi) Poisson maximum likelihood estimator (QPML estimator). I will consider this estimation approach below.

Trade and M&A flows: the evidence

The authors find strong support for a positive impact of EU membership on cross-border M&A transactions but only within the manufacturing sector. Moreover, EU membership appears to be a pull-factor: What matters is whether the host country is a member of the internal market. One interpretation of this result is that it lines up with Neary's theory of mergers: EU membership means lower trade barriers and this stimulates M&As. Indeed, the authors provide further evidence of this line of reasoning. When they introduce the Balassa index, the direction of trade is a strong predictor of cross-border M&As while the EU membership dummy decreases in size and loses statistical significance. Moreover, while EU membership appears to matter only for the manufacturing sector, the direction of trade indicator matters for cross-border M&As in both manufacturing and in services. This might be interpreted as indicating that sectors in countries with comparative advantage engage in M&A purchases in countries with comparative disadvantages.

One worry about these results is endogeneity but the authors back up the analysis with a comparison between the impact of trade integration on bilateral trade flows and the impact of trade integration on M&A flows. Although the results are not entirely clear, it suggests at least some mild evidence in favour of the idea that M&A activities are related to trade and comparative advantage. I think that this is nice and a convincing part of the paper, which also has supporting evidence in other recent work (see e.g. Brakman, Garretsen and van Marrewijk, 2005).

Manufacturing versus services

Another result that deserves highlighting, is the contrasting results for the cross-border M&A flows in the manufacturing sector and in the service sector. To take a few examples, EU membership is a pull factor as far as cross-border M&A flows is concerned in the manufacturing sector but not in services, political institutions matter in the manufacturing sector but not in services, and various measures of the lack of product market deregulation are important determinants of cross-border M&A flows in services but not in manufacturing. These results indicate that although M&A flows in services are large, they are still severely hampered by the lack of international trade and competition in this sector. This result, in my view, is important for economic policy and it might indicate that services still have a way to go before it allows for an efficient cross-country allocation of capital.

The lack of gravity and the strong impact of EMU

Two other results, however, are less convincing in my view. First, the authors find that EMU membership is a strong catalyst of M&A inflows in the manufacturing sector (but not in services). This is the case even after controlling for the Balassa index. Quantitatively, the EMU effect is large. M&A flows between two EMU flows are 155% higher than between non-EMU members, and as a pull factor itself, EMU membership is associated with an 80% increase in M&A inflows. Secondly, in contrast to earlier studies in the trade literature and in the M&A literature, they find no significant 'gravity' effects (in the sense that the distance indicator is insignificant).

The first of these results is, in my view, puzzling because it is unclear exactly why the single currency should have a large impact on M&A flows. After all, we are talking about a monetary phenomenon. It would come as no surprise to find a large impact of EMU membership on portfolio flows (due to exchange rate risk considerations, currency matching regulation of pension funds etc.), but it is not really straightforward to see why the single currency should have a large impact on firms' incentives to buy (or merge with) foreign competitors. It would have been more credible to find that EMU speeds up adjustments to return differentials (as I return to below), but this cannot be investigated using the pooled estimator adopted by NRA. The second result, the lack of gravity, is puzzling mainly because it stands in contrast to much of the literature. One might add to this that if there is no gravity, why estimate a gravity equation, but I will not go that far.

I will suggest a unified answer to these two puzzles. I admit that the answer leaves open other questions, but I think it at least indicates that one might have to be a bit careful with drawing too strong conclusions about the EMU effects and the lack of gravity. The answer I will suggest is motivated by Razin et al. (2005) and in order to get to it, I need to return to the estimation procedure. The authors follow the suggestion of Santos Silva and Tenreyro (2006) and use the QPML estimator. This estimator, as argued by Santos Silva and Tenreyro (2006), addresses the inconsistency of standard estimates of the parameters of constant elasticity models when log-linearized in the face of heteroscedasticity (as usually adopted in the gravity literature). Moreover, this estimation approach allows one to deal with the fact that there are many zeros in the dataset.

Table 9. Gravity and EMU reconsidered

Variable	Estimator	
	QPML	Heckman
Distance	−0.015	−0.430***
EMUi,tEMUj,t	1.101***	0.559
NonEMUi,tEMUj,t	0.696***	0.473

Nevertheless, this estimator, as traditional approaches in this literature, treats the zero observations as exogenous. I am not sure that this is a reasonable assumption. It is likely that zero observations arise due to endogenous selection into potential targets. Such a phenomenon arises if, for example, M&A is associated with fixed costs (see Razin *et al.*, 2005). Of course, it is possible that such considerations have little empirical relevance, but one cannot *a priori* conclude against the possibility of endogenous selection.

Table 9 reports the estimates of key parameters when estimating, in turn, the impact of distance and EMU using either the authors' estimator or the Heckman two-step estimator. The data I used for this are not as good as those studied by Coeurdacier *et al.* since I was able to obtain only aggregate M&A flows. Nevertheless, the results are sufficiently suggestive that they command reporting. Column 1 reports the estimates of the distance indicator and of the EMU variables while column 2 reports the results for the Heckman estimator of the coefficients on these variables. These estimates are amazingly different. The coefficient on distance is zero (both in terms of its point estimate and in terms of statistical significance) when estimated with the QPML estimator but negative and highly statistically significant when estimated with the Heckman estimator. Thus, endogenous selection does seem to be an issue as far as the conclusion regarding the lack of gravity is concerned.[29]

The results are – once again – starkly different across estimators when we examine the impact of the EMU indicators. The QPML estimator indicates a large and significant impact of EMU membership regardless of whether only the host country is an EMU member or whether both the host and the source countries are EMU members. Thus the aggregate data supports the sector level results. However, when we control for selection effects, the EMU effects decline (significantly) in size and become statistically insignificant. The quantitative impact of adopting the Heckman estimator is, thus, economically and statistically very significant.

Admittedly the data studied in Table 9 are of a lower quality than those studied by Coeurdacier *et al.*, and it is also well known that identification might be problematic in the case of the Heckman estimator. However, the results are sufficiently strong that

---

[29] Both estimators include fixed effects and controls for GDP, common border, common language, EU membership and political institutions.

it seems on its own to draw some attention to the fact that the authors' results may be very sensitive to selection issues. I conclude from this that more research is needed before we can firmly conclude in favour of EMU's catalytic role and against the idea that gravity matters for M&A flows.

Dynamics

Let me finish by highlighting a possible extension of the analysis. Given the time-series aspect of the dataset, I think that it might have been interesting to examine the results coming from dynamic panel estimators. There are many reasons why dynamics might be important. First, it is likely that there are serious adjustment costs associated with the flow of capital across countries. Such adjustment costs imply that firms will spread their cross-border investments over time in response to changes in investment opportunities. Moreover, it is well known that mergers often occur in 'waves'. For that reason, it is highly likely that the errors of the pooled regressor are autocorrelated and that proper estimation of the M&A process requires the introduction of a partial adjustment mechanism.[30]

I have no exact guess on how the introduction of dynamics might affect the estimates, but I am quite sure that taking such an approach would bring further insights. In particular, introducing dynamics may potentially shed further light on the return and wedge factors that I discussed earlier. In particular, some of the wedges may act more as short-run factors that lower the speed of adjustment of M&A flows to return difference than long-run factors and the dynamic panel estimator might potentially allow one to estimate these factors. To take one example, the single currency may potentially have acted as such a short-run factor since it probably has improved the transparency of goods and capital markets and therefore has increased the speed of adjustment of cross-border capital flows to return differentials.

Conclusion

The authors have written a very interesting piece on international capital flows. The results have important implications for economic policy for they suggest that trade integration is key for an efficient cross-country allocation of capital. The authors also show quite forcefully that there is a long way to go before service sectors become as integrated as manufacturing sectors. As made clear, I am more sceptical about the results concerning the impact of European monetary integration and the lack of gravity. I think it is likely that the single currency may simply have increased the elasticity of international (EMU) capital flows to cross-country differences in returns (and in the determinants of merger flows according to, e.g., IO theories). That is, the EMU impact may simply have had a short-run impact on cross-border M&A flows

---

[30] Brakman *et al.* (2005) note that the errors are serially correlated.

(rather than a long-run increase in these flows). The rather bleak outlook for the economy at the moment may help shed further light on this issue; if the elasticity story is correct, we should see a large correction of M&A flows in case the EMU area enters a recessionary period.

Panel discussion

Following the discussants, several panel members wondered whether M&As are actually beneficial for countries. Clemens Fuest urged the authors to discuss FDI motives and consequences, as countries are not always eager to attract acquisitions, fearing employment losses. Hans-Werner Sinn agreed that M&As might not be beneficial and that some countries, for example Poland, do not like foreign ownership of firms. On the role of corporate taxation on cross-border investments, Fuest also noticed that while tax incentives are relevant for Greenfield FDI, in the case of M&As they really matter only as far as double taxation is an issue. Jacques Melitz noticed that very few determinants are significant for services (i.e. common border and language). This could mean that information issues are extraordinarily important in the case of services, a point which would deserve more attention, maybe by including more precise explanatory variables than the common language one. Diego Puga noticed that exports and outsourcing could be alternatives to M&As, and that as M&As they are affected by economic integration and institutions. Hans-Werner Sinn closed the panel round with a comment on the possible sources of the results by noticing that EMU could affect M&As because it eliminates currency exchange rate risk: indeed, the establishment of a European capital market and the equalization of interest rates are major achievements of EMU, and apply to all sorts of investments.

APPENDIX

Table A1. Countries and sectors

Countries

Source Countries (21)

Austria, Belgium, Canada, Denmark, Finland, France, Germany, Greece, Ireland, Italy, Japan, Luxemburg, Netherlands, Norway, Poland, Portugal, Spain, Sweden, South Korea, UK, US

Target Countries (32)

Developed Countries (21)

Austria, Belgium, Canada, Denmark, Finland, France, Germany, Greece, Ireland, Italy, Japan, Luxemburg, Netherlands, Norway, Portugal, Slovenia, Spain, Sweden, Switzerland, UK, US

Developing Countries (11)

Bulgaria, Czech Republic, Estonia, Hungary, Latvia, Lithuania, Poland, Romania Slovak Republic, South Korea, Turkey

Sectors

Manufacturing (10)
1 – Food, beverages and tobacco
2 – Textile, wearing apparel and leather industries
3 – Wood and wood products, including furniture
4 – Paper and paper products, printing and publishing
5 – Chemicals and chemical, petroleum, coal, rubber and plastic products
6 – Non-metallic mineral products, except petroleum and coal
7 – Basic metal industries and fabricated metal products
8 – Machinery and equipment
9 – Transport equipment
10 – Other manufacturing industries

Services (10)
1 – Transport and storage
2 – Communication
3 – Electric, gas and water supply
4 – Education, health, social and personal service activities
5 – Hotels and restaurant
6 – Wholesale trade
7 – Retail trade
8 – Banking
9 – Insurance
10 – Other financial intermediation

Table A2. Cross-border in M&As in manufacturing: sectoral and geographical breakdown (1987–2004, %, €billion)

Sectors	1	2	3	4	5	6	7	8	9	10	Annual average €billion
					Percentage share						
World											
1987–1992	18.2	1.7	1.0	5.9	26.5	6.9	5.3	25.9	7.8	0.9	32 020
1993–1998	12.1	1.2	0.6	5.1	36.8	5.8	4.8	19.8	12.9	0.9	71 363
1999–2004	19.3	0.6	1.1	3.5	26.9	5.0	6.9	26.9	9.5	0.2	129 835
Intra plus extra euro area											
1987–1992	11.7	1.0	0.4	2.9	38.1	8.8	3.0	26.5	7.6	0.0	10 755
1993–1998	8.2	1.9	0.7	5.7	31.0	9.7	3.4	14.4	24.7	0.4	25 764
1999–2004	17.2	0.8	1.7	2.8	27.9	9.7	6.7	21.1	11.7	0.1	46 158
Denmark, Sweden, United Kingdom											
1987–1992	29.4	2.5	0.7	5.4	23.7	7.9	5.7	15.3	7.6	1.9	10 265
1993–1998	10.1	0.5	0.0	2.7	59.2	4.1	4.0	11.6	5.9	1.8	22 424
1999–2004	35.2	0.2	0.3	3.2	37.6	3.0	4.4	13.1	2.5	0.3	36 446
United States											
1987–1992	24.3	0.8	1.8	16.7	16.5	2.4	4.6	19.2	12.8	0.8	4862
1993–1998	15.0	0.7	0.5	6.9	26.6	3.8	7.3	30.9	7.6	0.8	16 705
1999–2004	7.0	0.6	0.6	2.3	21.7	2.0	6.0	45.0	14.8	0.1	32 460
Canada											
1987–1992	4.2	7.0	9.8	3.9	4.7	0.0	3.4	58.1	8.7	0.3	1138
1993–1998	35.4	0.4	3.5	7.9	8.0	1.3	4.2	35.4	3.8	0.0	4322
1999–2004	8.1	0.0	3.8	6.4	5.6	0.1	24.6	47.5	3.6	0.4	8317
Japan											
1987–1992	5.6	0.9	0.0	3.4	21.9	6.5	10.3	47.7	3.0	0.8	4759
1993–1998	9.2	3.4	0.0	0.7	5.4	1.8	15.0	55.5	8.4	0.6	1301
1999–2004	28.1	1.0	0.0	2.9	3.0	6.3	5.3	34.5	18.8	0.1	4780
Norway											
1987–1992	27.5	9.4	0.0	0.2	36.9	0.0	1.0	5.8	18.6	0.6	169
1993–1998	7.2	20.0	0.0	23.0	26.8	0.1	5.9	7.5	3.1	6.5	374
1999–2004	2.7	0.9	0.0	43.7	39.8	0.4	0.0	12.2	0.3	0.0	1558

Notes: 1 – Manufacture of Food, Beverages and Tabacco; 2 – Textile, Wearing Apparel and Leather Industries; 3 – Manufacture of Wood and Wood Products, Including Furniture; 4 – Manufacture of Paper and Paper Products, Printing and Publishing; 5 – Manufacture of Chemicals and Petroleum, Coal, Rubber and Plastic Products; 6 – Manufacture of Non-Metallic Mineral Products, except Products of Petroleum and Coal; 7 – Basic Metal Industries and Fabricated Metal Products; 8 – Machinery and Equipment; 9 – Transport Equipment; 10 – Other Manufacturing Industries.

Source: Thomson Financial (SDC Platinum).

Table A3. Cross-border in M&As in services: sectoral and geographical breakdown (1987–2004, %, €billion)

Sectors	1	2	3	4	5	6	7	8	9	10	Annual average €billion
					Percentage share						
World											
1987–1992	3.7	12.2	1.8	3.8	8.3	4.1	4.9	11.2	14.3	35.8	29 514
1993–1998	4.3	18.0	10.6	1.6	6.5	5.7	5.3	9.3	11.6	27.3	85 280
1999–2004	1.9	36.6	10.3	0.6	8.0	2.0	2.6	12.2	6.6	19.1	328 239
Intra plus extra euro area											
1987–1992	2.3	10.4	1.6	3.9	3.1	4.6	3.9	16.9	25.0	28.3	10 345
1993–1998	2.1	12.7	9.5	0.8	2.3	5.3	5.2	12.0	23.4	26.8	32 462
1999–2004	1.7	30.5	14.1	0.8	9.5	1.3	3.4	14.9	9.5	14.4	149 820
Denmark, Sweden, United Kingdom											
1987–1992	5.3	21.8	4.3	3.6	17.9	3.6	5.1	6.3	7.4	24.8	8241
1993–1998	5.7	30.8	3.0	1.1	6.5	4.8	11.4	7.9	3.9	24.8	19 313
1999–2004	1.4	56.4	5.9	0.5	4.7	2.1	1.6	8.2	2.3	16.7	108 546
United States											
1987–1992	3.0	8.2	0.0	3.5	9.5	2.8	1.7	4.9	8.3	58.1	5542
1993–1998	4.4	15.1	19.2	2.7	11.2	4.6	2.0	6.7	4.3	29.8	26 512
1999–2004	2.6	13.2	10.4	0.5	9.6	3.4	2.6	13.8	4.2	39.7	52 450
Canada											
1987–1992	1.9	15.0	0.0	1.0	2.6	1.7	0.6	5.2	1.5	70.6	1723
1993–1998	13.1	23.1	3.4	3.0	10.4	1.0	0.4	12.4	7.6	25.7	4781
1999–2004	5.7	10.6	9.3	1.5	15.3	1.2	2.6	14.3	30.0	9.5	9332
Japan											
1987–1992	5.0	0.6	0.0	6.4	2.2	7.1	15.0	19.5	13.3	30.7	3472
1993–1998	0.0	6.8	0.0	0.2	4.7	57.6	1.1	7.7	2.8	18.9	1524
1999–2004	0.0	71.3	0.3	0.0	3.8	9.5	1.6	0.7	0.4	12.3	6011
Norway											
1987–1992	27.6	0.0	0.0	0.0	0.0	0.5	0.0	0.1	37.9	33.8	179
1993–1998	24.6	9.3	26.3	0.0	14.0	9.2	4.4	0.0	0.2	12.0	315
1999–2004	6.0	55.8	0.1	0.5	2.2	2.1	1.3	3.8	1.0	27.3	1688

Notes: 1 – Transport and Storage; 2 – Communication; 3 – Electric, Gas and Water Supply; 4 – Education, Health, Social and Personal Service Activities; 5 – Hotels and Restaurant; 6 – Wholesale Trade; 7 – Retail Trade; 8 – Banking; 9 – Insurance; 10 – Other Financial Intermediation.

Source: Thomson Financial (SDC Platinum).

Table A4. Descriptive statistics

	Mean	Std dev.	Min	Max	Number observ.	Non zeros
Manufacturing						
$M\&A_{ij,s,t}$ (€millions)	11.249	293.754	0	54 223	121 200	4188
$M\&A_{ij,s,t}$ 'within sectors' (€mil.)	7.158	218.142	0	32 875	121 200	2645
$M\&A_{ij,s,t}$ 'across sectors' (€mil.)	2.630	179.813	0	53 450	121 200	1319
$Log(GDP_i \, GDP_{j,s,t})$	11.848	4.375	-4.071	23.791	78 490	78 490
$Log(MarketCapitalization_{i,s,t}/GDP_{i,s,t})$	1.678	2.286	0	9.572	92 820	66 761
$Log(MarketCapitalization_{j,s,t}/GDP_{j,s,t})$	1.943	2.514	0	10.686	79 008	58 939
$Log(Exp_{ij,s,t}/GDP_i \, GDP_{j,s,t})$	-22.251	3.166	-35.472	-12.491	72 207	72 207
$Log(distance_{ij})$	7.602	0.989	4.190	9.325	121 200	121 200
$Border_{ij}$	0.0621	0.241	0	1	121 200	7530
$Common \, language_{ij}$	0.0358	0.185	0	1	121 200	4340
$Civil \, Liberties_{i,t}$	1.456	0.689	1	5	121 200	121 200
$Civil \, Liberties_{j,t}$	1.888	1.196	1	7	112 800	112 800
$EATR_{j,t} - EATR_{i,t}$	-0.005	0.104	-0.4314	0.4314	51 560	51 500
Services						
$M\&A_{ij,s,t}$ (€millions)	21.839	759.002	0	206 354	105 000	5043
$M\&A_{ij,s,t}$ 'within sectors' (€mil.)	12.953	722.265	0	206 354	105 000	2840
$M\&A_{ij,s,t}$ 'across sectors' (€mil.)	3.092	89.268	0	11 705	105 000	1600
$Log(GDP_i \, GDP_{j,s,t})$	14.648	4.403	1.386	27.660	85 312	85 312
$Log(MarketCapitalization_{i,s,t}/GDP_{i,s,t})$	1.367	2.099	0	9.568	96 950	72 550
$Log(MarketCapitalization_{j,s,t}/GDP_{j,s,t})$	1.263	2.032	0	9.568	85 330	63 752
$Log(distance_{ij})$	7.634	1.026	4.190	9.325	105 000	105 000
$Border_{ij}$	0.0686	0.253	0	1	105 000	7200
$Common \, language_{ij}$	0.0458	0.209	0	1	105 000	4800
$Civil \, Liberties_{i,t}$	1.464	0.715	1	5	105 000	105 000
$Civil \, Liberties_{j,t}$	1.646	0.955	1	5	101 640	10 640
$EATR_{j,t} - EATR_{i,t}$	-0.002	0.105	-0.4314	0.4314	57 720	57 720

Table A5. Descriptive statistics on product market regulation, 1998–2003

Sectoral disaggregation

	Mean	Std dev.	Min	Max
1 – Food, beverages and tobacco	0.11	0.03	0.07	0.18
2 – Textile, wearing apparel and leather industries	0.10	0.03	0.05	0.17
3 – Wood and wood products, including furniture	0.11	0.03	0.06	0.17
4 – Paper and paper products, printing and publishing	0.10	0.03	0.06	0.17
5 – Chemicals and chemical, petroleum, coal, rubber and plastic products	0.12	0.03	0.06	0.18
6 – Non-metallic mineral products, except petroleum and coal	0.11	0.03	0.07	0.19
7 – Basic metal industries and fabricated metal products	0.11	0.04	0.06	0.22
8 – Machinery and equipment	0.10	0.03	0.06	0.17
9 – Transport equipment	0.10	0.03	0.06	0.18
Manufacturing	0.11	0.03	0.05	0.22
1 – Transport and storage	0.36	0.14	0.16	0.70
2 – Communication	0.33	0.08	0.22	0.57
3 – Electric, gas and water supply	0.40	0.17	0.17	0.90
5 – Hotels and restaurant	0.08	0.02	0.05	0.14
6,7 – Wholesale and retail trade	0.38	0.12	0.19	0.59
8,9,10 – Financial services	0.31	0.07	0.17	0.45
Services	0.31	0.15	0.05	0.90

Country disaggregation

	Manufacturing and services				Manufacturing		Services	
	Mean	Std dev.	Min	Max	Mean	Std dev.	Mean	Std dev.
1 – Austria	0.25	0.15	0.12	0.62	0.15	0.02	0.39	0.14
2 – Belgium	0.21	0.14	0.08	0.51	0.12	0.01	0.34	0.13
3 – Finland	0.18	0.13	0.07	0.49	0.09	0.01	0.31	0.13
4 – France	0.25	0.18	0.09	0.74	0.14	0.01	0.41	0.19
5 – Germany	0.19	0.10	0.10	0.45	0.12	0.01	0.29	0.10
6 – Greece	0.25	0.19	0.07	0.69	0.14	0.04	0.43	0.20
7 – Ireland	0.21	0.20	0.07	0.90	0.10	0.01	0.37	0.24
8 – Italy	0.24	0.16	0.10	0.70	0.14	0.02	0.38	0.16
9 – Netherlands	0.15	0.11	0.07	0.70	0.08	0.01	0.25	0.12
10 – Portugal	0.23	0.14	0.08	0.61	0.14	0.01	0.36	0.14
11 – Spain	0.20	0.12	0.07	0.59	0.13	0.01	0.30	0.14
12 – Denmark	0.15	0.11	0.06	0.53	0.08	0.01	0.26	0.11
13 – Sweden	0.14	0.10	0.05	0.40	0.07	0.01	0.24	0.09
14 – United Kingdom	0.14	0.10	0.06	0.42	0.08	0.01	0.23	0.11
15 – Canada	0.15	0.11	0.07	0.38	0.08	0.01	0.26	0.10
16 – Japan	0.20	0.14	0.09	0.59	0.11	0.01	0.34	0.14
17 – New Zealand	0.14	0.08	0.07	0.36	0.09	0.01	0.21	0.07
18 – Norway	0.23	0.13	0.12	0.56	0.14	0.01	0.35	0.13
19 – Switzerland	0.19	0.14	0.07	0.60	0.10	0.01	0.31	0.16
20 – United States	0.14	0.10	0.06	0.35	0.08	0.01	0.23	0.09

REFERENCES

Alfaro, L., S. Kalemli-Ozcan and V. Volosovych (2007), 'Capital flows in a globalised world: The role of policies and institutions', in S. Edwards (ed.), *Capital Controls and Capital Flows in Emerging Economies: Policies, Practices and Consequences*, University of Chicago Press, Chicago, pp. 19–68.

— (2008), 'Why doesn't capital flow from rich to poor countries? An empirical investigation', *Review of Economics and Statistics*, forthcoming.

Anderson, J. and E. van Wincoop (2003), 'Gravity with gravitas: A solution to the border puzzle', *American Economic Review*, 93, 170–92.

Andrade, G., M. Mitchell and E. Stafford (2001), 'New evidence and perspectives on mergers', *Journal of Economic Perspectives*, 15, 103–20.

Angwin, D. (2001), 'Mergers and acquisitions across European borders: National perspectives on pre-acquisition perspectives, due diligence and the use of professional advisers', *Journal of World Business*, 36, 32–57.

Baker, M., C.F. Foley and J. Wurgler (2008), 'Multinational as arbitrageurs? The stock market and investment: Evidence from FDI flows', *Review of Financial Studies*, forthcoming.

Baldwin, R.E. (2006), 'The euro's trade effects', *ECB Working Paper Series*, No. 594.

Baldwin, A. and D. Taglioni (2006), 'Gravity dummies and dummies for gravity equations', NBER Working Paper Series, No. 12516.

Balistreri, E.J. and R.H. Hillberry (2007), 'Structural estimation of the border puzzle', *Journal of International Economics*, 39, 247–65.

Benassy, A., L. Fontagne and A. Lahreche-Revil (2005), 'How does FDI react to corporate taxation?', *International Tax and Public Finance*, 12, 583–603.

Berger, A.N., C.M. Buch, G. DeLong and R. DeYoung (2004), 'Exporting financial institutions management via foreign direct investment mergers and acquisitions', *Journal of International Money and Finance*, 23, 333–66.

Bergstrand, J.H. and P. Egger (2007), 'A knowledge-and-physical-capital model of international trade flows, foreign direct investment, and multinational enterprises', *Journal of International Economics*, 73, 278–308.

Brakman, S., H. Garretsen and C. van Marrewijk (2005), 'Cross-border mergers and acquisitions: On revealed comparative advantage and merger waves', mimeo, Groningen.

— (2008), 'Cross-border mergers and acquisitions', Tinbergen Institute Discussion Paper, 013/2.

Bris, A., Y. Koskinen and M. Nilsson (2007), 'The euro and corporate valuations', mimeo.

Brouwer, J., R. Paap and J.-M. Viaene (2008), 'The trade and FDI effects of EMU enlargement', *Journal of International Money and Finance*, 27, 188–208.

Coeurdacier, N. and P. Martin (2006), 'The geography of asset trade and the euro: Insiders and outsiders', CEPR Discussion Paper, No. 6032.

Conway, P., V. Janod and G. Nicoletti (2005), 'Product market regulation in OECD countries: 1998 to 2003', OECD Economics Department Working Papers, No. 419.

Conway, P. and G. Nicoletti (2006), 'Product market regulation in non-manufacturing sectors in OECD countries: Measurement and highlights', OECD Economics Department Working Paper, No. 530.

De Santis, R.A. (2006), 'The geography of international portfolio flows, international CAPM and the role of monetary policy frameworks', ECB Working Paper Series, No. 678.

De Santis, R.A., R. Anderton and A. Hijzen (2004), 'On the determinants of euro area FDI to the United States: The knowledge-capital-Tobin's q framework', ECB Working Paper Series, No. 329.

De Santis, R.A. and P. Ehling (2007), 'Do international portfolio investors follow firms' foreign investment decisions?', ECB Working Paper Series, No. 815.

De Santis, R.A. and B. Gerard (2006), 'Financial integration, international portfolio choice and the European monetary union', ECB Working Paper Series, No. 626.

De Sousa, J. and J. Lochard (2006a), 'Does the single currency affect foreign direct investment? A gravity-like approach', mimeo, Paris I.

— (2006b), 'The currency union effect on trade and the foreign direct investment channel', mimeo, Paris I.

Devereux, M.P. and R. Griffith (2003), 'Evaluating tax policy for location decisions', *International Tax and Public Finance*, 10, 107–26.

— (1998), 'Taxes and the location of production: Evidence from a panel of US multinationals', *Journal of Public Economics*, 68, 335–67.

Devereux, M.P., R. Griffith and A. Klemm (2002), 'Corporate income tax reforms and international tax competition', *Economic Policy*, 17, 449–95.

Di Giovanni, J. (2005), 'What drives capital flows? The case of cross-border M&A activity and financial deepening', *Journal of International Economics*, 65, 127–49.

ECB (2006), 'Competition, productivity and prices in the euro area services sector', ECB Occasional Paper, No. 44.

European Commission (1996), 'Economic evaluation of the internal market', *European Economy*, No. 4.

Eisfeldt, A.L. and A.A. Rampini (2005), 'Capital reallocation and liquidity', *Journal of Monetary Economics*, 53, 369–99.

Flam, H. and H. Nordstrom (2003), 'Trade volume effects of the euro: Aggregate and sector estimates', mimeo, Institute for International Economic Studies.

Focarelli, D. and A.F. Pozzolo (2008), 'Cross-border M&As in the financial sector: Is banking different from insurance?', *Journal of Banking & Finance*, 32, 15–29.

Glick, R. and A. Rose (2002), 'Does a currency union affect trade? The time-series evidence', *European Economic Review*, 46, 1125–51.

Guimarães, P., O. Fuigueirdo and D. Woodward (2003), 'A tractable approach to the firm location decision problem', *Review of Economics and Statistics*, 85, 201–204.

Head, K. and J. Ries (2005), 'Judging Japan's FDI: The verdict from a dartboard model', *Journal of the Japanese and International Economies*, 19, 215–32.

— (2007), 'FDI as an outcome of the market for corporate control: Theory and evidence', *Journal of International Economics*, 74, 2–20.

Hijzen, A., H. Görg and M. Manchin (2008), 'Cross-border mergers and acquisitions and the role of trade costs', *European Economic Review*, 52, 849–66.

Jovanovic, B. and P.L. Rousseau (2002), 'The q-theory of mergers', *American Economic Review P\&P*, 92, 198–204.

— (2008), 'Mergers as reallocation', *Review of Economics and Statistics*, forthcoming.

Lane, P. (2006), 'Global bond portfolios and EMU', *International Journal of Central Banking*, June 2006, 1–23.

La Porta, R., F. Lopez-de-Silanes and A. Schleifer (2006), 'What works in securities law?', *Journal of Finance*, 61, 1–31.

La Porta, R., F. Lopez-de-Silanes, A. Schleifer and R.W. Vishny (1998), 'Law and finance', *Journal of Political Economy*, 106, 1113–55.

Long, N.V., R. Horst and F. Stähler (2007), 'The effects of trade liberalization on productivity and welfare: The role of firm heterogeneity, R&D and market structure', Kiel Economics Working Paper, No. 2007-20.

Lucas, R.E. Jr (1990), 'Why doesn't capital flow from rich countries to poor countries?', *American Economic Review*, 80(2), 92–6.

MacFadden, D. (1974), 'Conditional logit analysis of qualitative choice behavior', in P. Zarembka (ed.), *Frontiers in Econometrics*, Academic Press: New York, pp. 105–42.

McCallum, J.T. (1995), 'National borders matter: Canada–U.S. regional trade patterns', *American Economic Review*, 85, 615–23.

Micco, A., E. Stein and G. Ordonez (2003), 'The currency union effect on trade: Early evidence from EMU', *Economic Policy*, 37, 315–36.

Neary, P. (2007a), 'Cross-border mergers as instruments of comparative advantage', *Review of Economic Studies*, 74, 1229–57.

— (2007b), 'Trade costs and foreign direct investment', Working Paper, University of Oxford.

Nicita, A. and M. Olarreaga (2007), 'Trade, production and protection 1976–2004', *World Bank Economic Review*, January, 1–7.

Nocke, V. and S.R. Yeaple (2007), 'Cross-border mergers and acquisitions versus greenfield foreign direct investment: The role of firm heterogeneity', *Journal of International Economics*, 72, 336–65.

OECD (2002), *Forty Years' Experience with the OECD Code of Liberalisation of Capital Movements*, OECD, Paris.

Perry, M.K. and R.H. Porter (1985), 'Oligopoly and the incentive for horizontal merger', *American Economic Review*, 75, 219–27.

Petroulas, P. (2007), 'The effect of the euro on foreign direct investment', *European Economic Review*, 51, 1468–91.

Portes, R. and H. Rey (2005), 'The determinants of cross-border equity flows', *Journal of International Economics*, 62, 53–82.

Ramondo, N. (2007), 'Size, geography, and multinational production', mimeo, University of Chicago.

Razin, A. and E. Sadka (2007a), 'Productivity and taxes as drivers of FDI', NBER Working Paper Series, No. 13094.

— (2007b), *Foreign Direct Investment: Analysis of Aggregate Flows*. Princeton University Press, Princeton, NJ.

Razin, A., Y. Rubinstein and E. Sadka (2005), 'Corporate taxation and bilateral FDI with threshold barriers', NBER Working Paper Series, No. 11196.

Rose, A. (2000), 'One money, one market: Estimating the effect of common currencies on trade', *Economic Policy*, 15, 7–45.

Rossi, S. and P.F. Volpin (2004), 'Cross-country determinants of mergers and acquisitions', *Journal of Financial Economics*, 74, 277–304.

Santos Silva, J.M.C. and S. Tenreyro (2006), 'The log of gravity', *Review of Economics and Statistics*, 88, 641–58.

Schiavo, S. (2007), 'Common currency and FDI flows', *Oxford Economic Papers*, 59, 536–60.

Shimizu, K., M.A. Hitt, D. Vaidyanath and V. Pisano (2004), 'Cross-border mergers and acquisitions: Reviews and research issues', *Journal of International Management*, 10, 307–53.

UNCTAD (2006), *World Investment Report 2006 – FDI from Developing and Transition Economies: Implications for Development*, UNCTAD, Geneva.

Household debt

SUMMARY

Despite the lively policy debate on rising household debt, arrears and personal bankruptcy filings, there is relatively little empirical evidence on the determinants of households' debt repayment behaviour, or on the incidence of arrears. Even less is known about how arrears compare between countries, although debt levels are known to vary widely. Using data from the European Community Household Panel, we first show that arrears are frequently associated with subsequent adverse consequences, such as future unemployment or bad health. Second, we find that arrears are often precipitated by an adverse shock to the household's income or health, but that there are large differences between countries in how households react to these events. Finally, we show that these differences can be partly explained by local financial and judicial institutions, as captured by contract enforcement and information sharing indicators. In other words, we show that while adverse shocks are highly important, the extent to which they affect repayment behaviour depends crucially on the penalty for defaulting. This finding suggests that although repayment problems often arise from a genuine inability to repay, some households seem to behave strategically.

— *Burcu Duygan-Bump and Charles Grant*

Economic Policy January 2009 Printed in Great Britain
© CEPR, CES, MSH, 2009.

Household debt repayment behaviour: what role do institutions play?

Burcu Duygan-Bump and Charles Grant

Federal Reserve Bank of Boston; University of Reading

1. INTRODUCTION

Despite the lively policy debate on rising household debt, arrears and personal bankruptcy filings, there is relatively little empirical evidence on the determinants of households' debt repayment behaviour, or on the incidence of arrears. Even less is known about how rates of arrears compare between countries, although debt levels are known to vary widely. The recent turmoil in the household credit market (especially among US sub-prime borrowers) underscores the need to better understand when and why households fail to repay their debts; which households get into repayment difficulties; and how policies and institutions affect debt repayment, arrears and default. Answers to these conundrums have wider importance since they also shed

This paper was presented at the 47th Panel Meeting of *Economic Policy* in Ljubljana, Slovenia. We are very grateful to Clemens Fuest, Jean Imbs, and three anonymous referees for their extremely valuable comments and suggestions, which proved crucial in shaping our ideas and this paper. We would also like to thank Brian Bucks, Guglielmo Weber, and seminar participants at Bilkent University, European University Institute, Federal Reserve Bank of Boston, the Royal Economic Society Meeting, and the Second Italian Congress of Econometrics and Empirical Economics, for helpful comments on a preliminary version of this paper. The views expressed in this paper are those of the authors and do not necessarily reflect the views of the Federal Reserve System or of the Federal Reserve Bank of Boston.

The Managing Editor in charge of this paper was Jan van Ours.

Economic Policy January 2009 pp. 107–140 Printed in Great Britain
© CEPR, CES, MSH, 2009.

light on households' ability to smooth consumption against idiosyncratic shocks. This paper aims to present some evidence from Europe on how arrears affect households in the years that follow and on which types of households enter arrears. Our key contributions are to show both how debt repayment behaviour differs across countries even when households face similar shocks, and how these behavioural variations are related to differences in institutions across Europe.

Many commentators view default as the consequence of a genuine inability to repay. That is, a household's decision to default is determined by adverse events, such as an income or an employment shock, or health problems. However, in the theoretical literature, the decision to default is often modelled to depend on the cost of default (including legal costs and consequences of autarky). For example, in papers by Kocherlakota (1996), Kehoe and Levine (2001), Athreya (2002), and Chatterjee et al. (2007), households compare the punishment for (cost of) default with the benefit from reneging on their debts and do not repay if it is advantageous not to do so.

Relatively few studies, however, analyse the empirical determinants of default, perhaps due to the lack of suitable data. In a seminal paper, Fay et al. (2002) use the Panel Study of Income Dynamics (PSID) to analyse the household's bankruptcy decisions. However, not only is bankruptcy rather rare, it also seems to be significantly under-reported, at least in the PSID. In contrast, Gross and Souleles (2002) use administrative data from US credit card accounts to analyse household delinquency and bankruptcy. While it is more common to observe default in administrative credit card data, these data provide very little information about some potentially important variables (such as changes in employment status) and are not representative of the overall population. Several UK studies have exploited the British Household Panel Survey to investigate financial difficulties, debt burdens, and the evolution of debt problems. Both Boheim and Taylor (2000) and May and Tudela (2005) study housing evictions, while May et al. (2004) look at unsecured credit. Bridges and Disney (2004) exploit data from the Survey of Low Income Families to examine use of credit, default and arrears among low-income families with children; households that often concern policy-makers.

This paper investigates household debt repayment behaviour in different European countries, and shows how judicial and financial institutions affect this behaviour. These institutions, summarized in Box 1, are used as a proxy to capture the differences in the punishment for, and the cost of default. Hence the primary aim of our paper is to understand the role of institutions in household arrears. Several earlier studies have emphasized the role of institutions for credit availability and the general development of financial markets. Examples include La Porta et al. (1998), Jappelli and Pagano (2002), Guiso et al. (2004), and Jappelli et al. (2005). However, institutions will only affect credit availability (lenders will only restrict lending) if they influence the repayment behaviour of borrowers, should their credit application be approved. Of course, if lenders react to the change in institutions by restricting credit, this would weaken the relationship between observed arrears and institutions. Overall, we might expect some combination of reduced credit and increased arrears. Accordingly, by

Box 1. Institutional variables and arrears

Several papers, including Kocherlakota (1996), Kehoe and Levine (2001), Athreya (2002), Chatterjee *et al.* (2007) and Livshits *et al.* (2007), have derived theoretical results about the default behaviour of households who have idiosyncratic income risk, can borrow, and are able to default on their debts. After borrowing, and receiving the income realization, the household must decide whether to repay the loan. In these models, households default when they receive an adverse shock. More precisely, households compare the punishment for default with the benefit from reneging on their debts and do not pay if it is advantageous not to do so. The results from these papers suggest that arrears are more likely after a negative shock, and when the debt is harder (or impossible) to recover. Hence we investigate several candidate institutions which are likely to affect repayment behaviour:

- **Time:** the total number of calendar days it takes, on average, for dispute resolution. We would expect that increasing the amount of time that it takes to complete the judicial process is likely to mean that jurisdictions in which the court process takes longer are less effective at recovering debts, and thus there is less incentive for debtors to repay their debts on schedule.
- **No. of Procedures:** the total number of legal procedures mandated by law that must be followed in order to legally recover a debt. As the number of procedures (or their complexity) increases, we would expect it to become more costly to enforce the debt, reducing the ease with which arrears can be punished, increasing the incentives for arrears.
- **Cost:** the cost (as a percentage of the debt) of judicial proceedings. If the court process is costly, many creditors may prefer not to pursue repayment especially if the debt is small or the prospects of recovering the debt are low, hence increasing incentives for arrears.
- **Public Coverage:** the proportion of the adult population who have information on their repayment history, unpaid debts or outstanding credit recorded in public credit registries.
- **Private Coverage:** the proportion of the adult population who have information on their repayment history, unpaid debts or outstanding credit recorded by private credit bureaus. If other lenders will learn of any failure to repay the debts, then these households have greater incentive to repay their debts since it will be more difficult for them to apply for a loan from alternative lenders.

analysing the response of borrowers to institutions, this paper complements the previous studies that emphasize the response of lenders.

The analysis in this study is based on data from the European Community Household Panel (ECHP), comprising a random sample of EU households observed during the 1994–2001 period for each of the then members of the European Community. Using the ECHP offers several unique advantages. First, rather than analysing bankruptcy – a low probability event that is really a legal status – we use data on arrears to analyse household debt repayment behaviour. After all, relatively few households that default on their debts become bankrupt. Second, the panel nature of the data allows us to investigate how the incidence of arrears evolves as a household experiences income and other types of shocks, while also controlling for unobserved heterogeneity. Moreover, the data allow us to monitor what happens to those households that enter arrears. Third, since we have nationally representative data for each EU country, we can compare the behaviour of households in different countries and assess the role of differences in national institutions. Finally, the data provide separate information on mortgage arrears (which are collateralized) and arrears on unsecured loans. This detail provides a further opportunity to see how different institutional environments might explain why some households choose to repay their loans but other seemingly similar households do not.

After providing a detailed description of our data and institutions in Section 2, we start our discussion in Section 3 by first presenting some preliminary facts about arrears and their correlation with adverse events, such as bad health, unemployment, or a fall in income. In this section, we also present some preliminary evidence on how arrears might be associated with longer-term consequences for households: even four years later, and after controlling for their initial status, our results show that households who fall into arrears are more likely to become unemployed, less likely to be self-employed, more likely to report bad health, and less likely to be home owners. Section 4 investigates the determinants of household debt repayment behaviour in more detail, and especially the role of adverse events. However, our key contribution is to show that there are important differences between countries in how households react to these adverse events. In particular, we show that adverse shocks are important, but the extent to which they matter depends crucially on the punishment associated with default, as measured by our institutional variables. Section 5 concludes with a discussion of these results and some remarks on their policy implications.

2. DATA

2.1 The European Community Household Panel

This paper uses data from the European Community Household Panel (ECHP). The dataset is a nationally representative panel of households, collected between 1994 and 2001, in each of the 14 countries in the EU at that time. The survey asks questions about various demographic characteristics and the income of the household members. Additionally, the survey includes information on households' debts and arrears. In particular, it asks questions on whether the household has any housing debts, and on whether the household is making non-housing loan repayments (such as on a loan or hire purchase agreement). Our key variable of interest is whether the household reports that it has been unable to make a scheduled loan or utility payment during the last 12 months. There are separate questions to capture arrears on mortgage, rent, utility bills, or other scheduled payments on non-housing debt.

There are a number of advantages in using this survey, as discussed in the introduction. First, the data are nationally representative, unlike administrative credit card data. Second, since households are asked the same questions in all EU countries, we can compare the behaviour of similar households in different countries. Third, the survey focuses specifically on arrears over the last 12 months. Few other surveys concentrate on arrears, rather than bankruptcy. For example, Fay et al. (2002) exploited the 1996 wave of the PSID, which asked whether the household had filed for bankruptcy. They found that only 250 households reported having filed, which was only around 1% of their sample (and less than half the national filing rate); suggesting bankruptcy is significantly under-reported. A more serious problem is that only a small proportion of accounts that become delinquent (in which households are more than three months in arrears) result in a filing for bankruptcy. While bankruptcy law sets the punishment for default and thus affects equilibrium behaviour, bankruptcy filings are not an accurate measure of default and/or repayment behaviour. Fourth, the panel component of our data allows us to investigate the evolution of income and arrears for the same household over time. In particular, we can investigate how the incidence of arrears evolves as the household experiences income and other types of shock. Lastly, we can separately study both housing and non-housing debts.

However, some disadvantages remain: arrears are self-reported, and hence likely to be under-reported, as was bankruptcy in the PSID. More importantly, we observe neither the extent of arrears, nor the level of debt. Not knowing the extent of the arrears means that reporting being 'unable to meet a scheduled debt repayment' covers a wide range of different behaviour by borrowers; from bankruptcy at one extreme, to being a few weeks behind on their payments at the other. However, lenders typically view late payment as a signal that the loan could be at risk. Despite these potential shortcomings, we believe that these data are nevertheless informative about arrears and household debt repayment behaviour.

A key relationship we study is the role adverse events play in subsequent arrears. The adverse events we investigate are: the percentage decline in household income over the last 12 months; a dummy variable indicating whether the household's real income has declined by over 7.5% over the last 12 months; and a dummy for whether the household reports its income situation to be worse compared to the previous year. Throughout, household income is measured in real 1996 euros, and each regression includes the three-month money market interest rate for each country.

Table 1. Summary statistics for the ECHP

	All		Borrowers	
	(mean)	(s.e.)	(mean)	(s.e.)
Age	44.47	7.98	43.33	7.60
Tertiary education	0.19	0.39	0.23	0.42
Secondary education	0.32	0.46	0.35	0.47
Less than secondary education	0.48	0.49	0.42	0.49
Homeowner	0.73	0.44	0.83	0.37
No. children	0.94	1.07	1.09	1.12
Couple	0.81	0.39	0.85	0.34
Single woman	0.09	0.29	0.07	0.26
Self-employed	0.17	0.38	0.14	0.35
Change in log-income	0.03	0.52	0.03	0.46
Negative income shock	0.26	0.44	0.26	0.43
Income situation better	0.19	0.39	0.23	0.43
Income situation worse	0.24	0.42	0.23	0.42
Unemployment shock	0.03	0.17	0.03	0.16
Negative health shock	0.02	0.15	0.02	0.14
Real interest rate	5.29	2.52	4.74	2.04
Sample size	101 984		55 389	
Avg. per country	8425		4615	

Notes: Columns under 'All' show the summary statistics for the whole sample, while the last two columns report these only for the sub-sample of households with housing or non-housing debt.

Sources: Authors' calculations based on the 1995–2001 waves of the ECHP.

In constructing our sample, we include all households where the household head (defined as the male in couples) is between the ages of 30 and 60. We exclude households with multiple unrelated adults. Because our focus is on income risk alone, we include only stable households even though divorce may well be an important factor in explaining household default. Due to what looks like measurement problems, we exclude data from Finland and the 1996 wave in the data for Greece. Unfortunately, we must also drop Sweden, Germany and the UK because our key variables of interest were not asked of households in these countries.

After these restrictions, we have over 100 000 observations; on average about 16 500 in each year and about 8500 for each of the included countries. Table 1 summarizes the main variables of interest in our full sample. The table shows that around 80% of households comprised married or co-habiting couples, and the average number of children in each household was slightly less than one. The average age of the household head was 44, while about a fifth of households have completed a university degree, and a further third have finished secondary education. The table shows 73% of the households were homeowners and 17% were self-employed. On average each household's income had increased by 3% over the last year but around a quarter of households had seen their real incomes decline. Table 1 also presents summary statistics for the sub-sample of households with currently outstanding

Table 2. Some basic statistics on debt in the EU

Country	Any debt	Mortgage debt	Other debt	Any arrears	Mortgage arrears	Other arrears
Denmark	88.1	70.8	59.1	3.7	0.7	2.0
Netherlands	78.8	66.1	47.3	2.2	0.4	0.7
Belgium	67.5	55.0	29.3	9.0	4.4	3.3
France	70.2	44.5	45.0	9.5	1.1	2.7
Ireland	69.6	56.0	49.0	8.4	2.4	2.8
Italy	27.7	17.5	14.3	6.2	1.2	1.7
Greece	24.8	13.2	14.8	22.8	2.9	3.5
Spain	46.0	29.4	25.1	5.1	1.6	1.5
Portugal	32.4	21.6	16.1	2.9	0.3	1.7
Austria	46.2	35.0	17.4	2.2	0.5	1.2
Total	54.2	39.5	28.4	6.6	1.4	1.9

Notes: 'Any debt' refers to the proportion of households holding any kind of debt. 'Mortgage debt' refers to the proportion holding a mortgage. 'Any arrears' refers to whether the household has missed a scheduled rent, mortgage, utility or hire-purchase payment in the last 12 months, while 'Mortgage' and 'Other' arrears refer to the proportion that have missed a mortgage or a other loan payment in the last 12 months.

Sources: Authors' calculations based on the 1995–2001 waves of the ECHP.

debts. This sample is smaller, with about 55 000 households. The households in this sub-sample are on average better educated, are more likely to be a couple, are more likely to have children, and to own their homes, and are less likely to be self-employed.

Of key interest for this paper are the wide differences across countries in debt levels and in arrears. Therefore, Table 2 presents the proportion of households with debts and the proportion in arrears by country. These numbers show that the percentage of households with some debt (housing and/or non-housing) is highest in Denmark and the Netherlands, and is lowest in Italy and Greece. This difference between the northern and the Mediterranean countries is fairly well known and is similar to those reported in Crook (2006). The last three columns are the focus of this paper; they report the percentage of households who have missed a scheduled loan or utility payment, a mortgage payment, or a non-housing debt repayment. While the cross-country pattern no longer follows the exact North–South divide, differences remain significant. Moreover, arrears are not always at their highest where the incidence of debt is highest: for example, while the proportion of indebted households is fairly high among Dutch households, they seem to be the least likely to be in arrears. Moreover, reported arrears on 'any loan' are highest in Greece, followed by Ireland and Italy, but Greek households are among the least likely to have debts. The table shows that both the level of debt and the level of arrears differ substantially between EU countries. But more importantly, it also shows that higher arrears are not the necessary corollary of high debt levels, and that some other mechanism must be involved in causing households to fall behind on paying their debts.

2.2. Institutions

To understand the differences in arrears across countries, we follow the law and finance literature and use data on institutions to proxy for differences in the cost of default. Such institutions can affect arrears and default in two ways. First, they can have a direct effect, as making debts more difficult to recover is likely to make default more attractive to borrowers. Second, they may have indirect effects. If borrowers can less effectively be punished for default this might also encourage them to additional borrowing that they might not otherwise have undertaken. Lenders, on the other hand, are likely to reduce their lending and/or react by changing the loan terms that they offer, if they anticipate that recovering the debt might be difficult or expensive. Because our data does not contain information on either the debt level or on the loan terms, this paper will analyse the overall effect of institutions on the rate of arrears. Nonetheless, we note that if lenders restrict credit when institutions are worse, the estimated effect of institutions on arrears will be under-estimated.

We consider three contract enforcement indicators, explained more fully in Box 1, which measure the efficiency of the judicial (or administrative) system in the collection of overdue debt: the total number of procedures mandated by the law; the total number of calendar days it takes, on average, for dispute resolution; and the cost (as a percentage of the debt) of judicial proceedings. We would expect that borrowers are more willing to default as court action becomes more costly. We also look at two additional variables, which measure the coverage of private credit bureaus and of public credit registries, both expressed as a percentage of the adult population. They report the number of individuals and unincorporated firms listed in the respective registry with current information on repayment history, unpaid debts or credit outstanding. While these variables do not directly affect the ability of lenders to enforce repayment through the courts, they capture whether other potential lenders will learn about the debtor's behaviour, and thus affect households' ability to borrow in the future. The data, together with a detailed description of these variables and how they are constructed, can be found on the Doing Business Indicators website (www.doingbusiness.org) and in Djankov et al. (2003 and 2006).[1]

Table 3 summarizes these institutional indicators, and highlights that the differences between the EU countries are large. For example, the average length of trials is only 48 days in the Netherlands but is nearly four years in Italy. The cost is also correspondingly small in the Netherlands but is substantial in Spain and in Belgium. All households are covered by private credit bureaus in Ireland but these institutions do

---

[1] The data set used in our analysis was downloaded from the Doing Business indicators website in May 2006. We have noticed that due to a change in methodology in 2007, our institutional numbers no longer match those that are now listed on this website. Fortunately, however, the ordering across the countries remains constant with these new measures despite the change in levels, which implies that our results should not be affected by this change.

Table 3. Institutions in different EU countries

Country	Time (days)	Cost	No. of procedures	Private coverage	Public coverage
Denmark	83	3.8	15	7.7	0
Netherlands	48	0.5	22	68.9	0
Belgium	112	9.1	27	0	55.3
France	75	3.8	21	0	1.8
Ireland	217	7.2	16	100	0
Italy	1390	3.9	18	59.9	6.1
Greece	151	8.2	14	17.7	0
Spain	169	10.7	23	6.5	42.1
Portugal	320	4.9	24	9.8	64.3
Austria	374	1.0	20	45.4	1.2

Notes: Time is the average number of days to complete the judicial process; Number of procedures refers to the number of legal procedures that must be completed to recover a debt; while 'Cost' is the cost of judicial proceedings in court fees and attorney fees, where the use of attorneys is mandatory or common, expressed as a percentage of the debt value. Public coverage and private coverage refer to the percentage of the population for which public registries and private credit bureaus have information on borrowers.

Sources: These data were downloaded from the Doing Business indicators website (www.doingbusiness.org) in May 2006.

not operate in France or Belgium. However, in France and Belgium, households are recorded on public credit registers (even if relatively few households are included in the public registry in France).

The differences in institutions are likely to influence household behaviour, and the goal of this paper is to understand these effects. Box 1 outlines that we expect all the variables to increase the incidence of arrears through the direct effect on the incentives to default among existing debtors. For the two coverage variables there are additional subtleties. Since these variables affect whether other creditors learn about delinquent behaviour, they can be expected to have a negative affect on arrears. If other lenders will learn of any failure to repay the debts, then these households have greater incentive to repay their debts since it will become more difficult for them to apply for a loan from alternative lenders. A side effect is that creditors will know about the credit history of households to which they have not previously made a loan, which may well increase the overall level of credit in the economy. If households enter arrears due to some unexpected adverse shock then extending credit to more borrowers might instead cause more households to be in arrears. Increasing information about the repayment behaviour of borrowers is likely to improve the operation of credit markets as credit is assigned to households more likely to repay their debts. Overall, a negative coefficient on the coverage variables would suggest that households are more likely to repay their loans if other potential lenders are able to see their debt-repayment history.

3. SOME PRELIMINARY FACTS ABOUT ARREARS

3.1. Descriptive analysis on determinants of arrears

Before the formal regression analysis on determinants of arrears, it is useful to look at some simple sample statistics for arrears. In particular, we informally investigate how arrears are related to income changes and other adverse events, and how the responses to these adverse events differ between countries.

An important reason that households fail to repay their debts on schedule is that they have experienced some shock or adverse event. Households who have been unfortunate may be less able or willing to repay their debts on time. For example, after an unexpected negative shock, they may be unable to repay a loan that would otherwise have been affordable. Even if the debt could still be afforded, immediate repayment may cause substantial hardship, meaning there may be good reasons to delay repayment. However, households may behave differently if the change in income was expected. For instance, a household may default now if it knows that at some future point in time it will be poorer. Moreover, it may delay repayment if it believes that the creditor is unlikely to pursue the debt or if the credit contract is difficult or costly to enforce. Additionally, a household could increase current borrowing, knowing that it will be unlikely to repay the debt at some future date. Unfortunately, the data cannot distinguish whether the shock was fully anticipated, and hence we cannot determine whether an unexpected shock has led to arrears, or whether a (strategic) default precedes the adverse event. Instead we investigate whether a household is in arrears following an adverse event, and keep in mind these two different interpretations.

We consider four adverse events: becoming unemployed, suffering a significant fall in income, falling into bad health, and the worsening of their income situation as reported by the household. The second measure is a dummy variable for whether there has been a significant fall in income, defined as a fall of over 7.5% in real terms. A cut-off of 7.5% is rather arbitrary. An alternative approach would be to estimate earnings process, using a large negative residual from this equation as the 'shock'. Estimating this process, however, requires many more than the relatively few time periods in our data. More seriously, this approach cannot determine whether the change in income was expected by the household rather than the econometrician. To address this, we exploit a fourth variable, where households are asked how their income situation compares with one year previously (constructed as a dummy variable that equals one if the household reports its income situation has clearly deteriorated, and zero otherwise). Unexpected income changes are likely to be captured by this variable. In the regression analysis below, we also include the percentage fall in income (where increases are recorded as zero). After all, we might expect households to be more likely to fall in arrears as they progressively experience larger decreases in income, but households can be expected to repay their debts on schedule if their income has either stayed the same or increased.

Table 4. Percentage of households in arrears by adverse event

	Any arrears	Arrears on mortgages	Arrears on other debt
Overall	6.6	1.4	1.9
Unemployment shock – No	6.4	1.4	1.9
Yes	12.8	2.6	3.4
Negative income shock – No	6.1	1.3	1.8
Yes	7.9	1.7	2.3
Negative health shock – No	6.5	1.4	1.9
Yes	12.8	2.3	3.1
Income situation worse – No	5.0	1.1	1.5
Yes	11.6	2.2	3.1

Notes: 'Any' arrears refers to the proportion of households who missed a mortgage payment, a loan payment, rent or a utility payment in the last 12 months, while 'Arrears on mortgage' and 'Arrears on other debt' refer to the proportion who have only missed a mortgage or other loan payment, respectively.

Sources: Authors' calculations based on the 1995–2001 waves of the ECHP.

Table 4 reports the simple relation between these various shocks and the incidence of different types of arrears. Mortgage arrears are arrears on mortgage debt. 'Other arrears' are arrears to financial institutions and include arrears on credit card payments, hire-purchase agreements, and other financial loans made by banks. 'Any arrears', in addition to mortgage and 'other arrears', includes arrears on utility bills and rent. The table shows that, on average, 6.6% of households are in arrears in our sample. It also shows that households who have lost their job are almost twice as likely to be in arrears, compared to households who have not. For any debt, nearly 13% of recently unemployed households are in arrears compared with only 6.4% of households that did not lose their jobs. While the differences between the incidences for mortgage arrears are similar, they are nevertheless higher for those households who have suffered a job loss. These numbers are much larger for other debts: 3.4% of households that suffered unemployment shocks are in arrears compared to 1.9% for households who did not face any unemployment shock. The table also shows that households are more likely to be in arrears on their other (non-housing) debts compared to their mortgage debts, which are collateralized.

We obtain similar results when analysing households whose real income fell, however the differences are much smaller compared to the effects of the unemployment shock. For health shocks the results are much stronger: for each of the different types of debts, households with a negative shock are over 50% more likely to default than households who did not suffer the shock. As before, arrears are more likely for 'other' debts than for mortgage debts. Similarly, households that report a worsening in their income situation are three times more likely to have missed any scheduled payment than those households who believe their income situation is either about the same as the previous year, or it has improved.

Table 5. Percentage of households in arrears by adverse event and by country

Country	Unemployment shock	Negative income shock	Negative health shock	Income situation worse
Denmark	6.6	5.5	9.4	6.1
Netherlands	3.5	3.3	9.2	4.9
Belgium	15.4	9.3	20.6	16.6
France	20.7	12.4	21.1	15.2
Ireland	16.0	7.9	17.0	14.5
Italy	11.5	7.3	11.4	10.3
Greece	34.6	24.4	34.3	34.0
Spain	12.0	6.0	13.7	8.7
Portugal	5.1	3.3	3.7	4.5
Austria	5.0	2.4	3.6	3.3

Notes: This table shows the arrears on any debt in each country when they experience an adverse event.
Sources: Authors' calculations based on the 1995–2001 waves of the ECHP.

To capture how these responses may vary across countries, Table 5 presents summary statistics for the proportion of households in each country who are in arrears after each of the four possible adverse events. The table shows that households in each country are highly affected by adverse events, but there are large differences between countries: over 34% of Greek households fall into arrears after an unemployment shock compared to only 3.5% of Dutch households facing the same shock. A primary goal of this paper is to explain this variation. We want to understand why households with similar shocks should be so much less likely to pay their debts on schedule in Greece than in the Netherlands.

3.2. Correlations between arrears and future outcomes

Before studying the effect of institutions, we first investigate the relationship between arrears and several different outcomes – employment, home ownership, self-employment and health – up to four years after the initial incidence of arrears. These outcomes may indicate some of the consequences that befall debtor households and further motivates our focus on understanding the micro-dynamics of arrears.

In assessing the implications of arrears for future outcomes, it is crucial to consider the timing of arrears and of home ownership, employment, self-employment or health. For example, households may enter arrears and enter unemployment at the same time. To address this issue, we use a fully dynamic random effects specification in which we investigate the relationship between arrears for household i between time $t - 1$ and time t denoted A_{it}, and a dummy for employment a time $t + 1$, denoted by z_{it+1}, controlling for the current value of the outcome value and also for a full set of household characteristics. We follow the same procedure for home ownership, self-employment, and health, and also investigate the effect on household i at $t + 2$, $t + 3$ and $t + 4$. Accordingly, we estimate the relationship:

$$\Pr(Z_{it+1} = 1) = \Phi(\alpha X_{it} + \delta A_{it} + \varphi Z_{it} + f_i + u_{it}) \tag{1}$$

where X_{it} is a set of household characteristics and other controls (age, age-squared, the number of children in the household, dummy variables indicating the marital status of the household head, whether the household owns their home, whether the household head is self-employed, the interest rate, log-household income in the previous period, as well as a full set of time dummies). The f_i and u_{it} capture the time invariant and time-varying idiosyncratic errors, while α, δ and φ are parameters to be estimated. Because Z_{it+1} is a dummy variable, and the panel is relatively short, the model is estimated using the random effects probit model, hence $\Phi(\cdot)$ denotes the cumulative normal distribution.

The dynamic probit random effects regression suffers from the initial conditions problem highlighted in Hyslop (1999). We address this by adopting the procedure of Wooldridge (2005) where the initial state of the left-hand side variable is modelled as a function of the time-invariant variables as well as the time-varying variables in the initial time period. Separate regressions are run for the three types of arrears we discussed above – 'any arrears', mortgage arrears, and 'other arrears'.

Table 6 reports the results from this exercise. The four sets of rows correspond to the future outcomes we are exploring, and the three sets of columns correspond to the three types of arrears. The results suggest that arrears indeed may have long-term effects on households, even after controlling for the initial status of the household. The first row of Table 6 shows that households in 'any arrears' are significantly less likely to be employed one and two years ahead, though the effect is significant at four years later only at 10%. 'Any arrears' seem to reduce employment one year later by 1.5%.[2] 'Other arrears' reduce employment one year ahead by 1.9%, and the effect remains significant two years ahead. However, there is no statistically significant correlation between mortgage arrears and future outcomes.

The second panel in Table 6 shows that arrears are negatively correlated with home ownership in the future, with similar effects across all arrears types. The coefficients reported in this panel imply that, one year ahead, 'any arrears' reduce home ownership by 2%, mortgage arrears reduce home ownership by 1.7%, and 'other arrears' reduce home ownership by 2%. These effects persist even after four years. The third panel of Table 6 shows that all types of arrears are negatively correlated with self-employment one year ahead, but the size of the effect is rather small and does not persist: self-employment is reduced by 0.5% with 'any arrears'; and 1% with either mortgage or 'other' arrears. Finally, the results in the last panel imply that arrears are also positively correlated with bad health in the future: both 'any' and 'other' arrears

---

[2] To calculate the size of the marginal effects, we predicted the level of unemployment holding all variables at their current level except assuming first that the household was in arrears and then that the household was not in arrears (the household specific effect, by necessity, is held at zero). The difference between these two numbers was calculated to be the effect of arrears on unemployment. A similar procedure is adopted throughout the paper such that they reflect the mean marginal effect computed at actual levels, rather than the marginal effect computed at the mean.

Table 6. Correlation between arrears and future outcomes, full dynamic probit model results

	'Any arrears'				Mortgage arrears				Arrears on 'other' loans			
	(1) 1-year	(2) 2-year	(3) 3-year	(4) 4-year	(5) 1-year	(6) 2-year	(7) 3-year	(8) 4-year	(9) 1-year	(10) 2-year	(11) 3-year	(12) 4-year
Future employment												
Arrears	-0.212***	-0.276***	-0.126*	-0.153*	-0.089	0.020	0.004	-0.114	-0.271***	-0.406***	-0.123	-0.200
	(0.043)	(0.054)	(0.067)	(0.078)	(0.092)	(0.116)	(0.141)	(0.160)	(0.071)	(0.090)	(0.113)	(0.132)
No. observations	81 242	59 883	42 308	28 009	81 440	60 042	42 444	28 109	81 378	59 987	42 393	28 074
No. households	21 953	18 261	14 840	12 164	21 963	18 268	14 855	12 178	21 959	18 267	14 850	12 176
Home ownership												
Arrears	-0.277***	-0.349***	-0.455***	-0.396***	-0.238***	-0.224*	-0.348**	-0.404**	-0.281***	-0.425***	-0.537***	-0.522***
	(0.036)	(0.059)	(0.075)	(0.101)	(0.076)	(0.126)	(0.168)	(0.220)	(0.062)	(0.101)	(0.128)	(0.196)
No. observations	99 037	72 852	51 350	33 764	99 260	73 033	51 499	33 873	99 188	72 969	51 443	33 834
No. households	25 945	21 660	17 730	14 563	25 953	21 668	17 743	14 577	25 951	21 666	17 740	14 574
Self-employment												
Arrears	-0.093**	-0.030	0.029	-0.043	-0.171**	-0.065	-0.033	-0.123	-0.194**	-0.273***	0.065	-0.040
	(0.041)	(0.066)	(0.083)	(0.106)	(0.080)	(0.121)	(0.153)	(0.191)	(0.075)	(0.116)	(0.145)	(0.192)
No. observations	99 051	72 860	51 353	33 767	99 274	73 041	51 502	33 876	99 202	72 977	51 446	33 837
No. households	25 946	21 662	17 730	14 564	25 954	21 670	17 743	14 578	25 952	21 668	17 740	14 575
Bad health												
Arrears	0.227***	0.232***	0.234***	0.320***	0.072	0.103	0.137	0.434**	0.217***	0.122	0.345***	0.156
	(0.047)	(0.057)	(0.069)	(0.087)	(0.097)	(0.117)	(0.144)	(0.172)	(0.077)	(0.097)	(0.116)	(0.157)
No. observations	98 411	72 390	51 033	33 575	98 630	72 570	51 182	33 684	98 560	72 506	51 126	33 645
No. households	25 830	21 554	17 645	14 501	25 838	21 562	17 658	14 515	25 836	21 560	17 635	14 512

Notes: The first four columns show the effect of having 'any arrears' (on loans, rent or utility) on various future outcomes (as defined in the respective rows) one, two, three, and four periods into the future, respectively. Columns 5–8 repeat this for the effect of mortgage arrears alone, and columns 9–12 for arrears on other loans. All regressions include a full set of year dummies, and a set of controls for household characteristics and other variables (age, age-squared, no. of children, couple, self-employed and homeowner where applicable, household income in previous period, and interest rate together with a constant). The sample includes all households, and the results reported are from the full dynamic probit model, estimated including lagged employment, home ownership, self-employment, and bad health, and a full set of additional regressors to account for the initial conditions problem. We adopt the convention that * means significant at 10%, ** significant at 5%, and *** significant at 1%.

Sources: Authors' calculations based on the 1995–2001 waves of the ECHP.

seem to increase the incidence of bad health by 1.1% one year ahead. However, mortgage arrears are not associated with changes in future health.

These correlations, as reported in Table 6, are often persistent for several periods. One interpretation of this finding is that household shocks are persistent: when households are hit by an idiosyncratic shock, the household continues to suffer for many periods after the first incident of arrears. The employment and health consequences of arrears, in particular, raise serious concern. The results for the self-employed are also interesting – the findings here suggest some support to the common argument that reducing the punishment for debtors will encourage entrepreneurial activity since arrears decrease self-employment one year ahead, but they do not have longer-term consequences. We believe that the interpretation of the results is least ambiguous when considering health: the results are significant and may well concern policy-makers if they believe that poor health is a direct consequence of the problems associated with the original arrears. An alternative view, however, is that households who anticipate shocks, such as unemployment, for example, may rationally react by not repaying their current debts, as predicted by Kocherlakota (1996) and by Kehoe and Levine (2001). However, this presumes that households are strategic about repayment, rather than merely reacting to an adverse event. Thus the interpretation of these results on the persistent effects of arrears is not straightforward. Fundamental to disentangling these different views is an understanding of why and under what circumstances households default. This provides an important motivation to our analysis of household default in the next section.

4. DETERMINANTS OF ARREARS: ADVERSE EVENTS AND INSTITUTIONS

4.1. Regression analysis of arrears and adverse events

The descriptive statistics reported above hint at some of the determinants behind household debt repayment behaviour. The regression analysis of this section controls for the effect of other variables, and enables us to analyse the micro dynamics behind household arrears. We start by exploring the effect of household characteristics at time t, on arrears between time t and $t + 1$. Our regressions include age, age-squared, the number of children in the household, the interest rate, log-income in the previous period, and dummy variables indicating the marital status of the household head, whether the household owns their home, whether the household head is self-employed, as well as a full set of time dummies. Using age and time dummies precludes estimating cohort effects. Boheim and Taylor (2000) and May and Tudela (2005) report similar regressions for arrears in the UK.

This section investigates the role of adverse events and arrears. For this analysis, the timing of adverse events and of arrears is crucial. The household is asked about their arrears during the past 12 months (e.g. the 12 months prior to when the arrears were reported). Hence in our regressions, we measure household i's income at time

$t - 1$, the adverse event S_{it} between time $t - 1$ and t, and the subsequent arrears A_{it+1} between time t and $t + 1$. The regressions thus take the form:

$$Pr(A_{it+1} = 1) = \Phi(\beta X_{it} + \theta S_{it} + f_i + \varepsilon_{it}) \qquad (2)$$

where X_{it} is a set of household characteristics and other controls (including household income at $t - 1$) discussed earlier, the f_i and ε_{it} capture the time invariant and time-varying idiosyncratic errors, while β and θ are the parameters to be estimated. As before, $\Phi(\cdot)$ denotes the cumulative normal distribution, and the regression is estimated using random effects probit, which allows for the fact that different households can have different propensities to fall behind on their repayments.[3]

Throughout, the regressions include the full sample of households, rather than only the sample of borrowers. Modelling the selection decision of lenders would require finding suitable exclusion restrictions; that is, finding variables that affect the lending decision but not arrears (see Grant and Padula, 2006). Any candidate exclusion restriction seems inherently implausible if we suppose that lenders restrict credit based on their assessment of likely repayment behaviour, in which case they would grant loans to relatively lower risk households. Hence we keep all the households in our sample. If lenders react to changes in institutions by reducing credit then our regressions results will underestimate the true effect of these institutions and our results will be a lower bound on the true effect of institutions on borrower behaviour.

Results for the basic regression are reported in the first column of Table 7. It shows that the incidence of arrears increases with age but falls with age-squared (where age is measured in decades). The coefficients (although not significant) imply that arrears are highest for households aged around 50. Renters are four times more likely to be behind on their payments than homeowners. Although large, this effect is unsurprising since homeowners have an asset that could, in principle, be liquidated and used to repay the households debts. Couples are also less likely to be in arrears compared to singles, though the effect is smaller than the effect of home ownership. The coefficients imply that couples are around half as likely to be in arrears as other types of house-holds. Having children also reduces the incidence of arrears. However, there is no significant difference in the repayment behaviour of the self-employed and of other types of households. As might be expected, the interest rate (measured using each country's specific three-month money market interest rates) increases the incidence of arrears: increasing the interest rate by 1% raises the incidence of arrears in the population by 0.3%.

---

[3] Fixed effects estimators of panel models are severely biased because of the well-known incidental parameters problem when panel data has only limited observations across time, as discussed in detail in Hahn and Newey (2004). The inconsistency occurs because there are only a finite number of observations that are available to estimate each individual fixed effect. In fact, Fernandez-Val (2007) estimates that the bias is at least 20% for 4-period panels, and 10% for 8-period panels. Because we have a 6-period panel, we chose to estimate our models using a random effects specification. However, we also repeat our analysis using a conditional-logit fixed effect specification. While the magnitudes of the estimated effects become smaller in the latter case, the main conclusions remain the same. These conditional-logit results are available from the authors upon request.

Table 7. The incidence of household arrears (standard errors in parentheses)

	Any arrears		Mortgage arrears		'Other' arrears	
	(1)	(2)	(3)	(4)	(5)	(6)
	Baseline	Including adverse events	Baseline	Including adverse events	Baseline	Including adverse events
Age	0.247		1.076***		0.325	
	(0.196)		(0.347)		(0.254)	
Age-squared	−0.026		−0.127***		−0.04	
	(0.022)		(0.039)		(0.029)	
Homeowner	−0.587***				−0.520***	
	(0.029)				(0.037)	
No. children	0.190***		0.110***		0.163***	
	(0.014)		(0.023)		(0.017)	
Couple	−0.291***		−0.008		−0.183***	
	(0.037)		(0.065)		(0.047)	
Self-employed	0.025		0.189***		0.049	
	(0.034)		(0.055)		(0.044)	
Interest rate	0.124***		0.043***		0.037***	
	(0.005)		(0.009)		(0.007)	
ln-income	−3.142***		−1.828***		−1.736***	
	(0.188)		(0.309)		(0.255)	
Unemployment shock		0.343***		0.358***		0.261***
		(0.045)		(0.086)		(0.066)
Percentage fall in income		0.253***		0.198***		0.155***
		(0.024)		(0.037)		(0.034)
Large fall in income		0.253***		0.232***		0.163***
		(0.022)		(0.040)		(0.031)
Negative health shock		0.281***		0.215**		0.097
		(0.053)		(0.101)		(0.080)
Income situation worse		0.365***		0.281***		0.267***
		(0.022)		(0.039)		(0.030)

Notes: Estimated using random effects probit regression using the 1995–2000 waves of the ECHP. All regressions include a full set of year dummies. Columns 2, 4 and 6 report only the coefficients of the adverse events, and not the coefficients on the controls outlined in the baseline model to preserve space and because the results are pretty similar to those of the baseline model. More precisely, columns 2, 4 and 6 essentially correspond to five separate regressions, where the type of the shock included is either of the events described, and where only the dependent variable changes from 'any arrears' to 'mortgage arrears' to 'arrears on other loans'. In other words, the shocks are not all included at the same time. We adopt the convention that * means significant at 10%, ** significant at 5%, and *** significant at 1%.

Sources: Authors' calculations based on the 1995–2001 waves of the ECHP.

Table 7 also shows that log-income, measured at $t-1$, is highly significant. Households that are initially poorer are significantly more likely to miss scheduled debt payments between time t and $t+1$. This might not seem surprising, but it does require comment. One reason for arrears is that households find it difficult to repay their debts when some unforeseen adverse event occurs. Therefore, we would expect households whose income is currently low to be more likely to miss their scheduled debt repayments. Moreover, households will only be in arrears if they have borrowed in the previous period. One reason to borrow is to smooth consumption when income is temporarily low, hence we would expect households with low income in period t to be in arrears more often simply because these households are more likely to borrow. In taking income one year prior to this, we hope to (at least partially) eliminate this effect that temporarily poor households are more likely to borrow. Hence finding that poorer households at $t - 1$ are more likely to be in arrears between t and $t + 1$ is genuinely striking and need not be predicted from a strict interpretation of the life-cycle consumption model.

The second column of Table 7 reports the effect of including an adverse event in the baseline model, where each row corresponds to a separate regression (we also adopt this convention in columns 4 and 6). Because the estimated effects of the household characteristics are substantially unchanged, we report only the coefficients of, in turn, each adverse event (the full results are available from the authors). The results show that households that report an unemployment shock are significantly more likely to be in arrears over the next year. In fact, if we held all the other characteristics constant, and compared households if they had received the shock and if they had not, then the unemployment shock would lead to an increase by around 2.8% in the level of 'any arrears'. Similarly, we consider the percentage fall in income that the household has experienced (recall increases are recorded as zero), and again find that it increases the incidence of arrears. For the large fall in income, we find the effect of the adverse event to be large and significant: the coefficient implies that having a significant fall in income increases arrears by 1.9%. The results are also similar for the health shock and if the income situation is worse: in both cases such households are significantly more likely to be in arrears. The estimated coefficients imply that a health shock increases the incidence of arrears by 2.8%, while an 'income situation worse' shock increases arrears by 3.3%. These effects are substantial.

The third and fourth columns of Table 7 look at mortgage arrears alone. As before, arrears increase with age and decrease with age-squared. But this time the coefficients are highly significant, and imply that arrears peak when the household head is around 44. Having children and being self-employed also increase the incidence of mortgage arrears. Similarly, single households and couples are no more likely to be in arrears. The table also shows that households that were initially poor are less likely to be in arrears, and that arrears are more likely as the interest rate rises. Arrears are again more likely when the household experiences an adverse event. The results suggest that the unemployment shock increases the proportion of households in mortgage arrears by 0.8%; the income shock by 0.5%; the health shock by 0.5%; and a worsened income situation by 0.6%. Although the size of these effects is smaller than for 'any arrears', fewer households enter mortgage arrears.

Arrears on 'other' loans are reported in the last two columns. These numbers indicate that age has no effect (neither age nor age-squared are significant) but couples and homeowners are much more likely to be in arrears. Having children, on the other hand, significantly increases the incidence of arrears. In the table, self-employed households are not significantly different from other households, but initially poor households are much more likely to miss a scheduled debt repayment. Again, higher interest rates are associated with higher rates of arrears. Of the five different shocks we investigate, all except the health shock significantly increase arrears, although the implied marginal effect is smaller than in the case of mortgage arrears. As for 'other' loans, households that experience an adverse event frequently respond by falling behind on their repayment: for unemployment shocks by 0.9%; for the negative income shock by 0.5%; for the health shock by 0.3%; and by 0.9% when the income situation was reported to be worse. These numbers are large considering that only 2% of households have arrears on 'other' debts.

Because we are interested in seeing whether there are differences across countries in household response to shocks, as discussed in the descriptive section, we repeat these analyses by adding interaction terms between country dummies and the adverse events. In other words, we estimate a separate effect for the shock in each country. We do not report the results from this exercise due to space considerations, but the findings indicate that for each of the shocks and for each type of arrears, there are indeed significant differences in how households in each country react to the same shock, even after controlling for other household characteristics. This includes the health shock, which, for 'other arrears' wasn't significant by itself. These results suggest that adverse events are strongly associated with arrears, but the extent of the reaction is different in different countries.

Another interesting observation is that the results reported in Table 7 suggest that the size of the effects is similar for mortgage arrears and for 'other' arrears. This is surprising since if households are strategic, we might expect them to default on their unsecured debts more readily than on the mortgage debts. However, there could be an unobserved supply effect as a rational lender would react by reducing unsecured credit. We do not disentangle these supply and demand effects, but note that overall, the default rates are in both cases considerably larger for households experiencing the adverse event.

4.2. Arrears and the role of institutions

Table 7 shows that while there are differences in the incidence of arrears for households with different characteristics, in all cases adverse events make households significantly more likely to miss a scheduled debt payment. Households fall into arrears if their income has fallen or if their income situation has become worse. However, the degree to which households react to these adverse events differs substantially between countries. As we said before, a primary goal of this paper is to understand why households with similar shocks should be so much less likely to pay their debts on schedule in Greece than in the Netherlands. Could it be related to the way that credit markets are regulated in these different countries, and the fact that households are more likely to default if they can be less effectively punished? To assess this, we investigate how some of the regulatory differences across countries are related to the incidence of arrears. We do this by exploiting the Doing Business measures of institutions in different countries (as reported in Box 1) discussed in the data section.

Ideally, we would also consider the evolution of these institutional variables over time. Unfortunately, there is no time-series variation in these variables for the relatively few years that are in the data. As a result, in the regressions, these variables are indistinguishable from a country specific effect. Accordingly, our formulation includes these institutions interacted with the adverse events, where the interaction term shows how institutions mediate the effect of a shock on arrears. More specifically, if A_{it+1} is a dummy variable indicating whether household i missed a payment between period t and period $t + 1$, the regression takes the form:

$$\Pr(A_{it+1} = 1) = \Phi(\beta X_{it} + \theta S_{it} + \gamma I_i S_{it} + f_i + \varepsilon_{it}). \tag{3}$$

This is the same regression as in Equation (2) except for the additional term where the shock S_{it} is interacted with I_i, a matrix representing all of the institutional variables where household i lives. As before, f_i and ε_{it} capture the time invariant and time varying idiosyncratic errors, while β, γ, and θ are the parameters to be estimated using the random effects probit model.

Relevant institutions are those pertaining to the legal enforcement of contracts. Hence, we investigate the effect on arrears of three contract enforcement indicators that measure the efficiency of the judicial system in the collection of overdue debt: the total number of calendar days for dispute resolution ('time'), and the cost of judicial proceedings ('cost') and the number of procedures necessary to enforce the repayment of any debt. On information sharing, we investigate the role of coverage through either private credit bureaus or public credit registries.

Table 8 reports the results from this exercise. In order to save space, and since the effects of household characteristics are largely unchanged, they are not reported further; we report only the coefficients of our key variables of interest, the interaction term between adverse events and the institutions. Thus the five sets of three columns correspond to the effect of each of our five shocks on the three types of arrears we consider. The first shock, in the first three columns, is the effect of losing a job. Only 'cost' and public coverage seem to have statistically significant effects for 'any debt'. No institution, interacted with the unemployment shock, is significant when considering either 'mortgage arrears' or 'other arrears'. To measure the size of the marginal effect, we measure the difference in the predicted level of arrears with the institution held at its lowest level, and at its highest level. All other variables are held at their actual observed level. The results for 'any arrears' suggest that 'cost' increases the incidence of 'any arrears' in the whole population by 0.2% in general, or by 6.7% among those who receive the shock. Similarly, public coverage reduces arrears by 0.2% in general and by 7% among those who have become unemployed.

Columns 4–6 of Table 8 investigate the effect of institutions interacted with falling income. For any arrears, only 'cost' (at 10%) and 'public coverage' are significant,

Table 8. Institutions and arrears (standard errors in parentheses)

	Unemployment shock			Percentage fall in income			Large drop in income			Negative health shock			Income situation worse		
	(1) Any arrears	(2) Mortg. arrears	(3) 'Other' arrears	(4) Any arrears	(5) Mortg. arrears	(6) 'Other' arrears	(7) Any arrears	(8) Mortg. arrears	(9) 'Other' arrears	(10) Any arrears	(11) Mortg. arrears	(12) 'Other' arrears	(13) Any arrears	(14) Mortg. arrears	(15) 'Other' arrears
Shock × Time	0.009 (0.012)	−0.005 (0.022)	0.006 (0.016)	−0.001 (0.007)	0.013 (0.011)	0.023** (0.010)	0.008* (0.005)	0.015* (0.009)	0.015** (0.007)	0.008 (0.013)	0.028 (0.030)	−0.032 (0.020)	0.003 (0.005)	0.016* (0.009)	−0.001 (0.007)
Shock × Cost	0.068*** (0.023)	0.044 (0.038)	0.050 (0.031)	0.020* (0.011)	0.062*** (0.023)	0.022 (0.017)	0.065*** (0.01)	0.098*** (0.018)	0.038*** (0.013)	0.079*** (0.025)	0.211*** (0.064)	0.037 (0.034)	0.085*** (0.010)	0.122*** (0.018)	0.061*** (0.012)
Shock × No. Procedures	0.017 (0.024)	−0.07 (0.047)	0.059 (0.036)	0.007 (0.014)	0.039 (0.030)	0.054** (0.022)	0.036*** (0.010)	0.050** (0.020)	0.032** (0.014)	0.078*** (0.028)	0.207*** (0.079)	−0.002 (0.039)	0.039*** (0.010)	0.087*** (0.021)	0.035** (0.014)
Shock × Private Coverage	−0.265 (0.187)	0.359 (0.359)	0.153 (0.259)	−0.215 (0.137)	0.438* (0.244)	−0.338* (0.198)	−0.325*** (0.079)	0.006 (0.136)	−0.331*** (0.111)	−0.218 (0.221)	0.168 (0.474)	0.820*** (0.306)	−0.483** (0.082)	−0.122 (0.154)	−0.020 (0.107)
Shock × Public Coverage	−1.299*** (0.471)	1.107 (0.852)	−0.975 (0.643)	−0.717*** (0.239)	−0.603 (0.565)	−1.118*** (0.362)	−1.447*** (0.201)	−1.238*** (0.403)	−0.956*** (0.268)	−1.898*** (0.471)	−3.155** (1.436)	0.153 (0.624)	−1.760*** (0.187)	−1.708*** (0.389)	−0.895*** (0.243)

Notes: Estimated using Random Effects Probit regression using the 1995–2001 waves of the ECHP. All regressions include a full set of year dummies, and a set of controls for household characteristics and other variables (age, age-squared, no. of children, couple, self-employed, homeowner, household income in previous period, and interest rate, as in the baseline model). Time is the number of days on average to complete the legal process; Cost is the proportion of the principle it costs to recover the debt; No. Procedures are the number of procedures to complete the legal process; while Coverage is the coverage of private credit bureaus or public registries, respectively. Each row reports only the coefficients of the interaction term between adverse events (as defined in each of the five sets of columns) with the corresponding institution, and not the coefficients on the controls outlined in the baseline model to preserve space and because the results are pretty similar to those of the baseline model. More precisely, each column corresponds to a separate regression which includes simultaneously all institutions interacted with each shock, where the type of the shock is reported at the head of the column, and where the dependent variable is either 'any arrears', 'mortgage arrears', or 'arrears on other loans'. We adopt the convention that * means significant at 10%, ** significant at 5%, and *** significant at 1%.

Sources: Authors' calculations based on the 1995–2001 waves of the ECHP.

while for mortgage arrears, 'cost' and private coverage (at 10%) are significant. In column 6, which investigates the effect on 'other arrears', all institutions except cost are significant. Columns 7–9 instead look at whether the household suffered a large fall in income, interacted with each institution. This time all the institutions are significant for all three types of debt, except private coverage for mortgage arrears. The coefficients imply that 'time' increases any arrears by 0.2%, cost by 1.4% and number of procedures by 1.0% across the population, (0.9, 5.4, and 3.8% among those who receive the shock). Similarly, private and public coverage reduces the level of arrears in the whole population by 0.6 and by 2.4 respectively (by 1.6% and by 6.3% among those households who have received the negative income shock). Similarly, for mortgage arrears, time increases arrears by 0.1% (0.5% if receive the shock), cost increases arrears by 0.6% (2.4% if experience the shock), procedures increases arrears by 0.4% (1.5%) and public coverage reduces arrears by 0.4% (1.6% if receive the shock). For 'other' arrears, the effects on time, cost and procedures are 0.2%, 0.4% and 0.4% across the whole population, and 0.7%, 1.3% and 1.4% among the affected households. Increasing private and public coverage leads to a reduction in 'other' arrears by 0.3% and 0.5% in general, and 1.0% and 1.8% among those who receive the shock, respectively. In other words, cost and public coverage seem to have the largest effect.

For the negative health shock, cost, procedures and public coverage are both significant for both 'any arrears' and for mortgage arrears. The size of the coefficients suggests that cost increases both any arrears and mortgage arrears by 0.2% (8.1% and 6.1% if receive the shock); procedures increases any arrears and mortgage arrears by 0.2% (9.7% and 7.7%); while public coverage reduces any arrears by 0.2%, and mortgage arrears by 0.1% (10.2% and 4.7% if receive the shock). However, for other arrears, only private coverage is significant, and the sign suggests that increasing coverage actually increases the incidence of arrears.

Lastly, we investigate institutions interacted with whether the household reports a worsening income situation. For all three types of arrears, cost, procedures, and public coverage are significant. Moreover cost increases any arrears, mortgage arrears and other arrears by 2.1%, 0.8% and 0.6% respectively in general, and 8.1%, 3.4%, and 2.7% among those who reported a worsening income situation. Procedures increases these arrears by in turn, 1.2%, 0.8%, 0.5% (4.8%, 3.1%, 1.9%); while public coverage reduces each arrears in turn by 2.2%, 0.6% and 0.5% (9.0%, 2.3%, and 2.0% if receive the shock). The results are never significant for time (at the 5% level), and public coverage is only significant in column 14, increasing any arrears by 1.0% (or 4.3% if receive the shock).

These results are broadly consistent with the theoretical predictions summarized in Box 1.[4] An increase in the amount of time taken to recover debts reduces the incentives

---

[4] We check the sensitivity of these results to inclusion of country fixed effects. The results from this exercise show that the effects of institutions on arrears remain broadly the same, though they do become somewhat weaker as can be expected. These results are available from the authors upon request.

to pursue unpaid debts, thereby encouraging arrears, and this is often found in the data. Similarly, increasing either cost or the number of procedures is also predicted to increase arrears, and this again is mostly found in the data. Likewise, public coverage mostly has a negative and significant sign, which is consistent with the view that if arrears become widely publicized then households become less willing to miss their payments. In other words, households care about their reputation and the potential punishment of, for example, being excluded from other credit agreements, and are less likely to default if other lenders can learn of their failure to repay their debts. An alternative explanation is that households that have defaulted in the past can be effectively excluded from credit markets and thus will not be in arrears. That is, the coverage of private credit bureaus may reduce default because they increase the penalty (or reputational cost) of defaulting, or they may reduce default because they facilitate better borrower loan matches. Our regressions cannot distinguish between these two explanations. We would expect private coverage to have similar effects as public coverage. While we often find this to be true, the positive effect reported in columns 5 and 12 are surprising exceptions. Here the results conflict with the theoretical predictions of Box 1: we would expect that increasing coverage (information sharing) would have increased the incentives to pay debts on time, thereby discouraging arrears. However, lenders are likely to react by reducing the availability of credit in these cases. Accordingly, the coefficient provides a lower bound on the true effect. In other words, finding a positive effect suggests that the effect on credit supply dominates that on arrears.

Overall, while the size of the responses to mortgage arrears and 'other' arrears are often strikingly similar, some subtle differences nevertheless remain. For example, the judicial enforcement related variables consistently explain mortgage arrears for most of our cases, while private coverage is always more important for 'other' arrears. This might not be surprising since mortgage loans are larger in volume and are backed by collateral. However, given the small size of other consumer loans, and the fact that they are unsecured, it seems more likely that banks rely more heavily on credit information sharing systems to 'blacklist' individuals and to exclude them from future borrowing in formal credit markets, rather than going through the judicial system. Similarly, from a borrower's perspective, an individual will be less likely to default on their mortgages because they have an invested equity in the property. However, these differences are quite small.

5. CONCLUSIONS AND POLICY IMPLICATIONS

This paper has shown that arrears are associated with subsequent adverse consequences for the household in terms of employment, home owning and health. However, the interpretation of these results as causal relationships is problematic since we cannot rule out the possibility that households react strategically to anticipated future adverse events by defaulting. We have also shown that although certain types of household (such as renters) are more likely to be in arrears, falling behind on repayments is often precipitated by an adverse shock to the household's income or health. This supports the argument made by many policy professionals that repayment problems arise from a genuine inability to repay, and hence that the long-run consequences suffered by defaulting households ought to be of genuine concern. However, we believe that the behaviour of households is more subtle than this simple story since households in different countries respond differently to these adverse shocks, as shown in this paper. This suggests that at least some households behave strategically: if households merely reacted to the adverse events that they suffer, then there should be no differences in behaviour between countries among households facing similar shocks.

To further confirm our hypothesis, we provide a mechanism to explain these differences. Many papers, such as the papers by La Porta *et al.* (1998), Guiso *et al.* (2004), and Jappelli *et al.* (2005), have found that institutional factors that capture differences in how effectively default can be punished are important in explaining credit availability. This paper has shown that similar factors are also important in explaining arrears. With some institutions households default when they suffer an adverse event, while with other institutions, seemingly similar households repay their debts on schedule. Of course, this does not necessarily mean all households behave strategically, but it does support the idea that at least some households are strategic since they are less likely to repay on time when institutions are less effective at punishing default.

Our findings highlight the crucial role of institutions for consumer credit, both in terms of household borrowing and for debt repayment behaviour. Guiso *et al.* (2004) argue that reforming institutions can help credit markets work more effectively, and raise output if they improve the allocation of credit to businesses. Similarly, strong institutions can enable creditors to recover their loans and hence improve the operation of consumer credit markets. A well-functioning credit market enables households to borrow when needed and to smooth their consumption over time, improving welfare. Poorly designed institutions, conversely, both encourage households to default on their debts, and discourage lending.

When thinking about institutions and policy design, however, one should also recall that there is a trade-off. While good institutions are important for credit supply, good institutions can also mitigate the effects of adverse shocks. Our paper has shown that arrears often occur when a household that has borrowed is surprised by an adverse event, such as a wage earner's unemployment or ill health. Under such circumstances, it may well be optimal to allow such households to default on their debts. With incomplete markets, bankruptcy provisions can help households to insure against some of their income fluctuations. Of course, there are many other institutional arrangements that affect household consumption, borrowing, and default, besides the institutions investigated in this paper. These include social insurance schemes, such as unemployment insurance, and employment legislation. The latter, for example, affects the incidence of default through increased protection from job loss (hence reduces labour income risk) and lowers the need for insurance through default.

The theoretical study by Athreya and Simpson (2006) is one of the first papers to demonstrate that public insurance and personal bankruptcy should be studied jointly. They show that generous public insurance improves welfare when default is prohibited, and that generous bankruptcy law can be an important barrier to the efficacy of social insurance policies. Similarly, Grant and Koeniger (2007) study the interaction between bankruptcy and labour market risks, and provide empirical evidence that these different institutional arrangements are substitutes. Using data from the US, they show that not only do different US states have dramatically different rules about the assets that households can keep in bankruptcy, but that these states differ with respect to their social insurance schemes as well.

Given these trade-offs, and that at least some households are strategic about when they default, policy-makers face a mechanism design problem: credit market institutions can be designed so that households default when it is socially desirable for them to do so, and welfare is optimized. The European Commission is one such policy-making institution, and it has committed itself to creating a single market for consumer credit throughout Europe. Undoubtedly there is some potential for cross-national legislation on credit market issues. For example, information sharing across the EU is likely to become increasingly important as workers become more mobile across national borders, and we have shown that information sharing is an important factor that affects arrears. However, since countries in the EU differ in their social insurance schemes and their labour market structures, and given the trade-offs that policy-makers face, we suggest that credit market institutions and bankruptcy provisions should be allowed to differ across the EU since the types of risks that consumers face also differs. In other words, the exact nature of institutional arrangements will need to accommodate the specific needs of each country.

We, of course, acknowledge that these policy conclusions should be read cautiously, especially since the analysis is limited by the lack of time-series variation in the institutions in our study. Similarly, the analysis may have some limitations caused by the use of approximate indicators, which possibly pick up spurious effects. However, given the heightened debate in the press and among policy makers about rising levels of household debt and bankruptcies and the recent credit crunch, we remain convinced that this paper makes an important contribution to understanding the microdynamics of repayment difficulties and the role of policies and institutions.

Discussion

Clemens Fuest
Universität zu Köln

The issues of excessive private household debt and personal bankruptcies are a matter of increasing concern, and the current financial sector crisis has brought this topic to the very top of the economic policy agenda. The present paper is therefore a timely and highly interesting contribution. The most important results are the following. Firstly, households are more likely to fall into arrears if they are affected by adverse income or health shocks. At the same time, households are more likely to experience adverse shocks like unemployment or illness after falling into arrears. Secondly, the extent to which negative shocks correlate with the failure to meet financial obligations differs considerably across countries. Thirdly, credit market institutions, which differ across countries, seem to be an important factor determining the repayment behaviour of households.

What are the implications of these results for economic policy? It is certainly not the purpose of this paper to produce direct and clear-cut policy conclusions. The analysis in this paper rather highlights some key issues the policy debate should address. These include the mere fact that arrears are a much more widespread phenomenon than explicit bankruptcies, the correlation between arrears, poor health and unemployment and, most interestingly, the huge differences in the debt repayment behaviour of households in different European countries and under different institutional regimes.

If it is true that the institutional environment determines the extent to which households fall into arrears if they are affected by economic shocks, the proper design of this institutional framework becomes a matter of high importance. Of course, many credit market institutions are generated by private markets, not the government. But public policies do affect the development of these institutions through regulations and other interventions, and some institutions like, for example, bankruptcy laws, are directly designed by governments.

Which are the trade-offs involved in the design of 'good' credit market institutions related to private household debt? One issue raised by this paper is why the judicial systems of European countries differ so much in the number of procedures, the time required to enforce contracts and so on. Does this just reflect X-inefficiencies, or is there a trade-off between reducing the cost of contract enforcement and avoiding enforcement errors? Of course, this issue relates to the overall efficiency of the judicial system and goes well beyond the problem of household arrears.

Whatever the efficiency of the judicial system as such, governments have to decide to what extent the law should protect households which fail to repay their debt. Here, the key policy trade-off seems to be between, on the one hand, the protection of the property rights of creditors and, on the other hand, the deliberate restriction of these property rights to protect debtors. One policy instrument which addresses this trade-off is the level of bankruptcy exemptions. The advantage of 'strong' institutions, i.e. institutions which facilitate debt enforcement, is that they protect the property rights of creditors, improve access to credit and avoid credit constraints. They also set incentives for debtors to do everything they can to avoid falling into arrears or going bankrupt.

But there are also important economic reasons to protect debtors and to release them from their debt under certain circumstances. The first reason, emphasized by

Burcu Duygan-Bump and Charles Grant, is that debtor protection may act as an insurance against adverse economic events. Of course, this raises the question of why private markets do not provide this insurance and why these risks are not covered by public health or unemployment insurance.

A second reason for releasing households from the obligation to pay back their debt is usually referred to as the 'fresh start' idea. If a highly indebted individual is forced to use all income above a given threshold to repay debt, this obligation may destroy incentives to work and supply effort. If the overall debt is sufficiently high, the obligation to repay the debt has the same incentive effect as a confiscatory income tax. Giving debtors a fresh start by discharging them from their debt may therefore enhance economic efficiency. Of course, doing so comes at the cost of reducing incentives to avoid bankruptcy in the first place.

It is interesting to consider the empirical results of Burcu Duygan-Bump and Charles Grant in the light of the 'fresh start' concept. One important finding is that households falling into arrears are more likely to be unemployed than other households for several years. One interpretation of this finding would be that these households are exposed to pressures to repay their debt which reduce their incentives to work or search for a job.

Finding the policy which optimally deals with the trade-off described above is a complex task and seems to require a process of trial and error. US bankruptcy legislation offers an illustrative example for this trial and error process. In the 1970s, the US policy debate very much emphasized the necessity of protecting indebted households (see, e.g., Gropp et al., 1997, p. 218). As a result, the Bankruptcy Reform Act of 1978 made the law much more protective for debtors. During the following decades, however, the number of personal bankruptcy filings increased significantly. As Gropp et al. (1997) report, there were 313,000 personal bankruptcy filings in 1983. During the period 1983–92, approximately 5.3 million households, nearly 6% of all US private households, experienced a personal bankruptcy. In the following years, the number of bankruptcies continued to grow and reached a peak of more than 1.4 million bankruptcies in the year 2006.[5]

In 2005, the US Federal Government reacted to this development. The Bankruptcy Abuse Prevention and Consumer Protection Act of 2005 makes it much more difficult for debtors to be discharged from their debts after a bankruptcy. Interestingly, in 2008, the number of bankruptcies declined to 560,000.[6] Whether this is considered as an improvement depends on the assessment of the trade-offs described above. In a recent paper, Chatterjee et al. (2007) developed a credit market model and mapped

---

[5] The reporting period is 1 April 2005 to 31 March 2006. These are only chapter 7 bankruptcies; see Administrative Office of the US Courts, News Release of 3 June 2008, Bankruptcy Filings up in March, available at http://www.uscourts.gov/Press_Releases/2008/BankruptcyFilingsMar2008.cfm.

[6] Ibid.

the model to US data in order to study the welfare effects of the 2005 reform. Their model suggests that the reform significantly increased the welfare of the average US household, by 1.6% of consumption. Gropp *et al.* (1997) exploit the differences in bankruptcy laws across US states[7] to study the impact of debtor protection on different household types. They find that generous bankruptcy exemptions primarily exclude low income and low asset households from the credit market. This implies that, even from a distributional perspective, a high level of debtor protection may be undesirable.

These results suggest that bankruptcy legislation in the US may have put too much emphasis on debtor protection and the 'fresh start' idea. The huge differences in credit market institutions across European countries documented in the present paper suggest that there may also be room for welfare improving reforms in European countries. Where these reforms should go, however, towards more or less debtor protection, is an open question. To investigate this is a challenging and interesting agenda for future research.

Jean Imbs
HEC Lausanne

This paper proposes a description of the events that precede and follow entry into arrears. To do so, it brings to bear a remarkable dataset, the European Community Household Panel, which keeps track of a representative cross-section of individual households over time. The data make it possible to date precisely entry into arrears, rather than into bankruptcy. That is important, what with the differences in the legal definitions of bankruptcy across countries, and some clear evidence that bankruptcy is vastly under-reported. Second, the same questions are surveyed across several European countries. This helps to identify roughly identical shocks for households living in different countries. The information is crucial in assessing whether the response to a given shock differs according to the institutional environment. In particular, results in the paper suggest that institutions that make default more costly affect the reported incidence of arrears negatively. Third, the data informs arrears on both secured and unsecured loans, which is not made much of in the paper.

It is interesting from a descriptive standpoint that entry into arrears be associated with subsequent adverse shocks, like exit of employment, health issues or lower home ownership. But care should be taken when drawing a conclusion, especially of a policy nature. After all, the decision to default on interest payments may well be endogenous, in particular to expected future events that are known to the borrower, but not directly observable. The adverse shock may well be expected, yet recorded in the dataset much later – perhaps even several years after the default decision is

---

[7] The Bankruptcy Reform Act of 1978 did permit the states to opt out of the Federal exemption.

reached. Thus the sequencing documented in this paper is essentially silent about causality. Subsequently observed adverse shock may in fact be the cause for default.

Duygan-Bump and Grant are upfront about this difficulty of interpretation. It is when they turn to an analysis of the factors that predate default that they propose more of a causal analysis. When institutions make default costly (debt contracts are well enforced), entry into arrears is less likely in response to the same adverse event. In other words, irrespective of whether it is strategic or not, fewer borrowers choose to default. This is once again interesting from a descriptive standpoint, but interpretation remains problematic. The identification scheme does not inform the reasons for default. It is inconclusive as to whether default is optimal, as it would be under a conventional overhang argument, or if it is forced by a sudden adverse event. As a result, we do not know much about the welfare consequences of the institutional environment in this context. Since it is not clear either whether the observed consequences of arrears are causal, policy implications are hard to draw.

Duygan-Bump and Grant focus on the international response of the level of arrears to a given observed shock, and relate this cross-section with measures of contract enforcement. Of course, the quality of institutions is likely to affect the overall depth of financial markets, and in particular the level of debt as a whole. For instance, Greece has among the highest rates of arrears in the sample, but also among the lowest prevalence of indebtedness. The two must be correlated, with causality going both ways. High arrears rates must deter lenders, and/or the resulting rationing of credit may create borrowing terms that foster default. In other words, contract enforcement can affect jointly the levels of arrears and of total indebtedness. Duygan-Bump and Grant ignore this supply response, arguing that it acts to attenuate the estimated effect of institutions on arrears. But that is not necessarily the case: if the overall debt level rises with good institutions, then it is possible that the level of arrears should increase correspondingly. But not necessarily because the incentives to default have altered.

In short, two identification difficulties are central to the exercise: the possibility of strategic default, and the response of debt to the institutional environment. Duygan-Bump and Grant fully recognize the existence of both, and are careful to discuss the scope of their results accordingly. But the ECHP data may have warranted more ambition. Suppose the supply effect of good institutions on the provision of credit affects equally all kinds of debt, secured or not. Consider then the differential response of default on mortgage loans versus others. Under the assumption, the differential purges the common effect of institutions on the overall provision of credit. It controls for the response of supply to institutions, and makes it possible to focus on demand effects across countries and institutions.

In addition, strategic borrowers will presumably default asymmetrically on secured or unsecured loans. For instance, it is interesting that default on mortgage loans is not followed by negative health shocks, whereas default on any other kind of debt is. The asymmetry is entirely consistent with strategic default on unsecured loans only, in anticipation of an expected negative health shock. A significant differential effect within country could therefore be indicative of strategic borrowers, while a significant international differential response would indicate an effect of institutions on *borrowing* behaviour. Duygan-Bump and Grant begin to illustrate the existence of such asymmetries in the data, but more can be done with this remarkable dataset. And more should be.

Panel discussion

Ray Rees opened the panel discussion by noticing that there is likely to be at least a partial insurance against the shocks mentioned in the paper, to an extent that differs across countries. He suggested including household data to account for the possibility that the incidence of job loss differs in two-income families. Agreeing on the importance of structural features, Christian Gollier added that credit arrangements could help insure and improve welfare in an incomplete-markets world. Given that in the US people defaulted on mortgages because of housing prices shocks, he wondered whether these shocks could be relevant in Europe, too. Then, he argued that since many people have variable-rate debts in most countries, it would be interesting to account for changes in interest rates: the latter may affect the decision to repay the loan and lead the timing of repayments to differ across countries and over time. Among directions for further improvements, Ekaterina Zhuravskaya suggested that individual characteristics are a potentially relevant factor if one is interested in assessing the *ex-ante* aspects of credit markets. Barbara Petrongolo noticed that the large size of the estimated coefficients concerning future employment in Table 6 may indicate an effect of unemployment, and that a simple way to check for the persistence of the difference between employment and unemployment would be to include such a term in the regression. Georges de Ménil suggested looking at the correlation between default and future employment. Morten Ravn argued that becoming unemployed has very different implications in Denmark, where the unemployment spell is short, with respect to countries with less generous unemployment benefits such as Italy. He suggested including the level of debt, which is affected by supply-side effects, in the regression, as well as an interaction term with the shock. On religious beliefs, Christian Schultz noticed that survey information about law-abiding values is available and could be usefully included into the equation. Jacques Melitz asked how much of the cross-country heterogeneity can be explained by the paper with the variables it considers. He also suggested trying to put all the elements summarized in Table 2 together, in a composite index, to have a more informative picture. Following on the interpretation of results, Klaus Adam wondered whether, besides providing statistically significant evidence, the authors could be more explicit about which coefficients are economically meaningful. Pierre-Yves Geoffard noticed that although there are a few empirical studies on defaults, there must be a lot of relevant information about default in banks' databases and credit scoring algorithms. However, as Richard Portes remarked, the behaviour of credit market institutions, which have not been able to predict the subprime crisis, does not indicate that they are really experts in the field. Portes concluded the panel discussion noticing that the kind of evidence presented in the paper would have been useful before the subprime crisis.

REFERENCES

Athreya, K.B. (2002), 'Welfare implications of the Bankruptcy Reform Act of 1999', *Journal of Monetary Economics*, 49(8), 1567–95.

Athreya, K.B. and N.B. Simpson (2006), 'Unsecured debt with public insurance: From bad to worse', *Journal of Monetary Economics*, 53(4), 797–825.

Bridges, S. and R. Disney (2004), 'Use of credit and arrears on debt among low income families in the United Kingdom', *Fiscal Studies*, March, 25, 1–25.

Boheim, R. and M.P. Taylor (2000), 'My home was my castle: Evictions and repossessions in Britain', *Journal of Housing Economics*, 9, 287–319.

Chatterjee, S., D. Corbae, M. Nakajima and J.V. Rios-Rull (2007), 'A quantitative theory of unsecured consumer credit with risk of default', *Econometrica*, 75, 1525–89.

Crook, J. (2006), 'The supply and demand for household debt: A cross country comparison', in G. Bertola, R. Disney and C. Grant, (eds.) *The Economics of Consumer Credit*, Cambridge, MA: MIT Press.

Djankov, S., C. McLiesh and A. Shleifer (2006), 'Private credit in 129 countries', *Journal of Financial Economics*, 84(2), 299–329.

Djankov, S., R. La Porta, F. Lopez-de-Silanes and A. Shleifer (2003), 'Courts', *Quarterly Journal of Economics*, 118(2), 453–517.

Fay, S., E. Hurst and M. White (2002), 'The household bankruptcy decision', *American Economic Review*, 92(3), 706–18.

Fernandez-Val, I. (2007), 'Fixed effects estimation of structural parameters and marginal effects in panel probit models', Boston University mimeo.

Grant, C. and W. Koeniger (2007), 'Redistributive taxation and personal bankruptcy in US states', mimeo.

Grant, C. and M. Padula (2006), 'Bounds on repayment behaviour: Evidence for the consumer credit market', mimeo.

Gropp, R., J.K. Scholz and M.J. White (1997), 'Personal bankruptcy and credit supply and demand', *Quarterly Journal of Economics*, 112, 217–51.

Gross, D. and N. Souleles (2002), 'An empirical analysis of personal bankruptcy and delinquency', *Review of Financial Studies*, 15(1), 319–47.

Guiso, L., T. Jappelli, M. Padula and M. Pagano (2004), 'Financial market integration and economic growth in the EU', *Economic Policy*, October, 523–77.

Hahn, J. and W. Newey (2004), 'Jackknife and analytical bias reduction for nonlinear panel models', *Econometrica*, 72, 1295–319.

Hyslop, D.R. (1999), 'State dependence, serial correlation and heterogeneity in intertemporal labor force participation of married women', *Econometrica*, 67, 1255–94.

Jappelli, T. and M. Pagano (2002), 'Information sharing, lending and defaults: Cross-country evidence', *Journal of Banking and Finance*, 26, 2023–54.

Jappelli, T., M. Pagano and M. Bianco (2005), 'Courts and banks: effect of judicial enforcement in credit markets', *Journal of Money, Credit, and Banking*, 37(2), 223–44.

Kehoe, T.J. and D. Levine (2001), 'Liquidity constrained vs. debt constrained markets', *Econometrica*, 69, 575–98.

Kocherlakota, N. (1996), 'Implications of efficient risk sharing without commitment', *Review of Economic Studies*, 63, 595–609.

La Porta, R., F. Lopez-de-Silanes and A. Shleifer (1998), 'Law and Finance', *Journal of Political Economy*, 106, 1113–55.

Livshits, I., J. MacGee and M. Tertilt (2007), 'Accounting for the rise in consumer bankruptcies', NBER Working Paper No. 13363.

May, O. and M. Tudela (2005), 'When is mortgage indebtedness a financial burden to British households? A dynamic probit approach', Bank of England Working Paper No. 277.

May, O., M. Tudela and G. Young (2004), 'British household indebtedness and financial distress: A household-level picture', Bank of England Quarterly Bulletin, Winter, 414–28.

Wooldridge J.M. (2005), 'Simple solutions to the initial conditions problem in dynamic, non-linear panel data models with unobserved heterogeneity', Journal of Applied Econometrics, 20, 39–54.

Regional inflation

SUMMARY

Inflation differentials across regions of an integrated economy can reflect a proper response to demand and supply conditions, but can also indicate distortions with negative welfare implications. Using a novel dataset of regional inflation rates from six euro area countries, we examine the size and persistence of their differentials and find that they appear to be related to factor market distortions and other structural characteristics, rather than to cyclical and growth dynamics. Our empirical analysis shows that only about half of inflation rates variation is accounted for by area-wide factors such as monetary policy or oil price developments. National factors (such as labour market institutions) still play a very important role, and a regional component accounts for about 18% of inflation variability.

— Guenter W. Beck, Kirstin Hubrich and Massimiliano Marcellino

Regional inflation dynamics within and across euro area countries and a comparison with the United States

Guenter W. Beck, Kirstin Hubrich and Massimiliano Marcellino

Goethe University Frankfurt and CFS; Research Department, European Central Bank; European University Institute, Bocconi University and CEPR

1. INTRODUCTION

In recent years, heterogeneous inflation developments across the euro area have received considerable attention in the economic literature and in economic policy debates. The size, persistence and origins of inflation differentials across euro area countries and their potential policy implications have been analysed extensively both from a theoretical and an empirical perspective.[1] In the absence of the country-specific nominal exchange rate channel and in the presence of low labour mobility, differences in inflation rates play an important role as a macroeconomic adjustment

---

For helpful comments on previous drafts we thank three referees, Klaus Adam, Guenter Coenen, Gabriel Fagan, Tohmas Karlsson, Lutz Kilian, Diego Puga, Lucrezia Reichlin, participants at the 47th *Economic Policy* Panel and at seminars at the European Central Bank and the Dutch Central Bank, as well as participants of the CEF 2006, the EEA-ESEM 2006 and the ECB-European Commission 2007 conferences. The usual disclaimer applies. The views expressed in this paper are those of the authors and do not necessarily reflect those of the European Central Bank.

The Managing Editor in charge of this paper was Giuseppe Bertola.

[1] In Section 3 we review the literature on the sources of inflation differentials.

Economic Policy January 2009 pp. 141–184 Printed in Great Britain
© CEPR, CES, MSH, 2009.

mechanism in response to asymmetric shocks. Thus, inflation differentials within a monetary union such as the European Monetary Union (EMU) can be seen as 'the product of an equilibrating adjustment process . . . and, as such, are not only unavoidable, but also desirable'.[2] Inflation differentials might also be an implication of the process of convergence in per-capita incomes between relatively poor and rich regions. Inflation differentials stemming from this so-called Balassa–Samuelson effect can be considered to be benign as well, even if they are potentially quite long-lasting.

Inflation differentials can, however, also be the result of economic distortions which cause welfare losses. For example, diverging regional developments in the prices of production input factors such as labour or rents, which are not the implication of pure market forces but are caused by structural inefficiencies in factor markets, could lead to production costs and therefore goods prices in the affected regions to diverge. This can have negative implications for the competitiveness of the high-inflation regions, particularly if the inflation differentials are long-lasting.

Harmful inflation differentials can also arise from rigidities in nominal wages and prices. If adjustments to shocks are staggered and non-synchronized, a symmetric impulse will lead to differences in inflation rates. These differences can cause relative price distortions and thus inefficient allocations of households' spending. Moreover, not only differences in levels of inflation but also variations in inflation rates over time can lead to considerable welfare losses in the presence of nominal price rigidities for the same reason. As a consequence, their reduction is considered as an important objective for policy-makers by the recent New Keynesian literature on stabilization policy.[3]

Differences in inflation rates within a monetary union can also have another, potentially destabilizing, effect. Since short-term nominal interest rates are identical in a monetary union, differences in inflation rates directly transmit into differences in real interest rates. As a consequence, regions with relatively high inflation rates experience relatively low real interest rates. These relatively low real interest rates can boost investment and thus aggregate demand which in turn might lead to even higher inflation rates. Of course, these effects are more pronounced the more long-lasting inflation differentials are and would then need to be addressed by policy-makers.

The goal of this paper is to contribute to the existing literature on inflation differentials within EMU in several ways. We complement the existing literature on national inflation rates by providing a systematic analysis of inflation rates at the regional level. Use of regional CPI data allows us to see whether European regions cluster across national borders along this as well as other dimensions.[4] It also makes it possible to identify the empirical importance of the national factor for within-country inflation developments.

[2] See ECB (2005, p. 61).

[3] A standard assumption in this literature is that the policy-maker's objective is to minimize a loss function where losses depend on quadratic deviations of inflation rates from target and on quadratic deviations of output from its natural level. A utility based derivation of such a function is given in Woodford (2003, ch. 6). A more detailed discussion of this point is given in Section 5.

[4] See, e.g., the work by Overman and Puga (2002) on unemployment rates or by Quah (1996) on income growth rates.

Using a novel monthly dataset of regional inflation rates from six euro area countries, namely Austria, Germany, Finland, Italy, Portugal and Spain, we document the extent of long-run inflation rate heterogeneity. Our results indicate that inflation differentials across European regions are not only large but also long-lasting. Moreover, it turns out that regional heterogeneity is substantially larger than national heterogeneity, so that the potential problems mentioned above could be further amplified, and affect in a different way the regions of a given nation.

To determine the potential sources of the observed long-run differences in regional inflation rates and understand whether or not they are worrisome, we regress them on a set of region-specific variables which we use as proxies for sources of inflation differentials within a monetary union. Our findings suggest that labour market variables and the Balassa–Samuelson effect do not play an important role in explaining long-lasting inflation differentials.[5] Instead, we find evidence in favour of the importance of the costs of input factors other than wages, and of both the competitive and economic structure of a region. These results suggest that the observed long-run differences in regional inflation rates do not reflect the response of integrated markets to economic shocks and are not the result of a convergence process in regional incomes but that they are caused by inefficiencies in factor markets and region-specific structural characteristics. Our analysis thus implies that to reduce long-lasting, potentially damaging inflation differentials structural reforms in factor markets are needed to avoid inappropriate factor price movements.[6]

A second major contribution of our paper is that we quantify the extent to which observed inflation variations are caused by area-wide, national and regional factors. In the presence of nominal rigidities, variations in inflation cause relative price distortions and can thus create considerable welfare losses, so that they should be addressed by policy-makers.[7] Before being able to take appropriate measures to stabilize inflation rates, one first has to identify its sources. Thus, following the study by Forni and Reichlin (2001) on output fluctuations, we adopt a factor model to decompose regional inflation rates into a common area-wide, a country-specific and an idiosyncratic regional component. We find that the bulk of the variation in regional inflation rates (at least 50%) is explained by one area-wide factor. However, also the national and regional components considerably contribute to variations in regional inflation rates: The national factor explains on average 32% of observed inflation variations while the remaining 18% is due to regional elements. Furthermore,

---

[5] Honohan and Lane (2003) do not find an important role of the Balassa–Samuelson effect for national inflation differentials, either.

[6] Our finding that factor market distortions and differences in the competitive and economic structure are an important source of inflation differences gains renewed interest in the light of recent shocks in energy and food inflation. Our results suggest that we should observe an increase in inflation divergence across regions. A similar conclusion follows for the recently observed upward trend of the euro relative to the US dollar, a finding which is in line with previous results by Honohan and Lane (2003) obtained for national data. A more detailed investigation of these issues during the more recent period would be of great interest for further research based on a longer sample to be collected.

[7] See reference to Woodford (2003, ch. 6) in n. 3.

we find that the area-wide and the national factors affect regional inflation dynamics heterogeneously. There are two major conclusions that can be drawn from these results. First, our results suggest that the area-wide monetary policy can considerably contribute to regional inflation stabilization even though it cannot take regional developments into account when making its decisions. Secondly, our results show that in order to address welfare-affecting inflation variations national policies such as fiscal and labour market policies still play a crucial role in addition to the area-wide policy.

The result that about one-third of inflation variation is still determined at the national level is striking. However, one might wonder whether, as a consequence of EU harmonization policy and globalization, other regional characteristics such as the average level of unemployment, unit labour costs, initial income or income growth play an even more important role. From a policy perspective, if regions grouped according to these characteristics are more homogenous than regions within a nation, then, as pointed out by Overman and Puga (2002) EU regional policy should include a transnational dimension and national policies should take regional economic disparities into account. Our empirical analysis shows that nationality based groups remain more homogenous, confirming that national policies keep a major role for inflation developments.

We also evaluate the consequences of the EMU on regional inflation heterogeneity. The national component of regional inflation could reflect heterogeneous monetary policies, so it should be less important after introduction of the euro. In our data, which span the period 1995–2004, EMU inception has virtually no effect on the extent of regional heterogeneity. The most likely explanation for this finding is that (at least at the national level), inflation convergence mostly occurred before 1995. Unfortunately, comparable regional data are not available before 1995.

The last question that we examine is how our results for the euro area compare to similar findings for a monetary union which is of similar size but was established a long time ago, that is, we repeat the analysis for the United States and compare the results with those for the euro area. We find a somewhat smaller degree of dispersion in regional inflation rates across US regions than across euro area regions. Moreover, regional US inflation rates exhibit slightly less persistence than euro area inflation rates. However, the extent of heterogeneity and co-movements in the United States are similar to those for the euro area.

The remainder of the paper is organized as follows. In Section 2 we give a description of our regional dataset and document the extent of long-run differences in inflation rates across European regions. In Section 3 we provide a theoretical discussion of potential sources and implications of differences in inflation rates and inflation dynamics within a monetary union. In Section 4 we analyse to what extent the observed regional inflation differentials can be related to the theoretical causes identified in Section 3. Then, in Section 5, we decompose the dynamics of regional inflation rates into a common area-wide, a country-specific and an idiosyncratic regional component. Furthermore, we examine whether the degree of commonality in inflation rate dynamics has experienced major changes after the introduction of the euro. In Section 6, we investigate whether national borders are still important for inflation developments in the monetary union by comparing the degree of commonality in groups of regions composed by economic characteristics with groups of regions of the same country. In Section 7, we compare our findings for the European regions with analogous results for US metropolitan areas. Section 8 summarizes our results and draws some policy conclusions.

2. HOW LARGE ARE REGIONAL INFLATION DIFFERENTIALS WITHIN THE EURO AREA?

To investigate and document systematically differences in regional inflation rates in the euro area, we collected a large set of regional and national price data. The data set contains consumer price index (CPI) data from six EMU member countries (Austria, Finland, Germany, Italy, Norway and Spain), and comprises a total of 70 locations. These data cover about two-thirds of the euro area in terms of economic activity and span the period 1995(1) to 2004(10) on a monthly frequency. For the remaining euro area countries comparable regional data are not available or at least not for a similar time span.[8]

All data are monthly, non-seasonally adjusted and are available in index form. Inflation rates π_t are computed as year-on-year percentage changes in the price index in the following way:

$$\pi_t = 100 * (\ln P_t - \ln P_{t-12}),$$

where P_t represents the respective price index in month t. Year-on-year inflation rates are plotted in Figure 1 on a monthly basis.

Figure 1 illustrates the importance and extent of regional inflation rate dispersion for our sample. It shows that short-run regional dispersion is considerable. Over the whole sample, regional year-on-year inflation varies between −1% and 7%. Additionally, there does not seem to be a tendency for overall inflation dispersion to decrease over time (no σ-convergence). There is a tendency for inflation dispersion to increase over the later part of the sample.

So far we have shown that there exists significant dispersion in inflation rates across European regions and that there is no tendency for this dispersion to decline over time. We now assess the persistence of the existing inflation differentials. As we will discuss in more detail in the next section, inflation differentials within a monetary

---

[8] More specifically, we are using price data for 12 German states (*Länder*), 9 Austrian regions, 5 Finnish regions, 19 Italian cities, 18 Spanish regions (*communidades*), and 7 Portuguese regions. In all cases the regions correspond to NUTS-II regions (in Eurostat's terminology), except for Germany where only data for NUTS-I regions are available. As data for Austria were only available at a city level we compiled NUTS-II level data for Austrian regions by computing a weighted regional CPI index. Weights were given by the number of inhabitants of the respective cities. Data for Italy were available for a sufficiently long time period only for the main cities in each of the NUTS-II regions. All data were provided either by a country's national statistical office (Austria, Finland, Italy, Spain and Portugal) or by the respective region's statistical office (Germany).

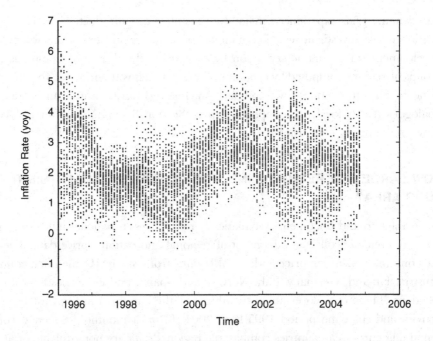

Figure 1. Regional European inflation rates: 1996(1)–2004(10)

Note: Figure 1 plots cross-sectional inflation rates for Germany, Austria, Italy, Spain, and Portugal. Inflation rates are computed as year-on-year percentage changes in the underlying consumer price index.

union are particularly troublesome if they are long-lasting, since they then can cause inappropriate changes in the real exchange rate and thus the competitiveness of the respective economies.

We have computed for each region the average year-on-year inflation over the whole sample period. The results, plotted in Figure 2, illustrate that regional differences in inflation rates are still considerable even when a relatively long time horizon is considered. The figure also shows that long-lasting inflation differentials exist not only across countries but also within countries. This is particularly true for Italy and Austria, but also applies to a smaller extent to Germany, Portugal and Spain.[9]

To quantify the extent of existing long-lasting inflation differentials across EMU regions Table 1 provides some descriptive statistics. The figures in this table confirm the graphical impression from Figure 2 that there is considerable inflation rate dispersion not only across countries but even within countries, and even at the relatively long time horizon of almost nine years. Looking at the reported cross-sectional dispersion,[10] we can see that dispersion at a national level is admittedly lower than at the EMU level; nevertheless, it is still important also at the national level. This

---

[9] For expositional reasons the data for Finland were omitted in Figure 2.

[10] Dispersion is measured as the standard deviation of regional mean inflation rates.

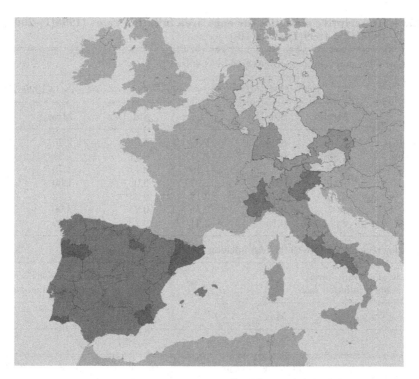

Figure 2. Mean regional European inflation rates: 1996(1)–2004(10)

Note: Figure 2 plots regional mean inflation rates for Germany, Austria, Italy, Spain, and Portugal. Inflation rates are computed as average year-on-year percentage changes in the underlying consumer price index over the period 1996(1)–2004(10). The dark colour indicates regions with average inflation rates above 2.5%, the lightest colour represents regional inflation rates below 1.5% and for the other regions average inflation is between 2.0 and 2.5%.

indicates that regional data might contain information that is not available in national data alone.

Moreover, the reported figures about long-lasting mean inflation rates in Table 1 imply that large changes in the competitive structure of EMU regions might have occurred over the sample period. Looking at the mean inflation rates reported in the upper panel of Table 1, we can see that there have been large differences in the average national inflation rates across EMU countries over the sample period: The lowest average inflation rate prevailed in Germany (1.35), followed by Finland (1.41), Austria (1.62), Italy (2.26), Portugal (2.85), and Spain (2.87, in that order). If one follows the most widely used approach in the vast purchasing power parity (PPP) literature and uses CPI data to construct the real exchange rate between two economies then the observed differences in inflation rates across countries/regions within the EMU correspond to changes in the real exchange rate between these countries/regions. Since the real exchange rate is an important indicator to assess the foreign-trade competitiveness of an economy the observed long-lasting inflation differentials might have strong implications for the relative competitiveness of the countries/regions of

Table 1. Descriptive statistics for euro area inflation rates (1996(1)–2004(10), 1996(1)–1998(12), 1999(1)–2004(10))

Results for all regions and regions grouped by countries

	1996–2004		1996–1998		1999–2004	
	Mean	Std. Dev.	Mean	Std. Dev.	Mean	Std. Dev.
All regions	2.18	0.63	1.89	0.61	2.26	0.70
Germany	1.35	0.15	1.21	0.21	1.31	0.20
Austria	1.62	0.1	1.19	0.17	1.73	0.11
Finland	1.41	0.09	1.07	0.05	1.60	0.13
Italy	2.26	0.22	2.13	0.33	2.22	0.22
Spain	2.87	0.22	2.45	0.25	3.06	0.24
Portugal	2.85	0.15	2.41	0.28	3.09	0.12

Results for regions with lowest/highest inflation rates

Regions with lowest/ highest inflation rate		Group of five regions with lowest/ highest inflation rates	
Min	Max	Min	Max
1.11	3.83	1.37	3.68

Note: The mean year-on-year CPI inflation rate (mean) is computed as the cross-sectional mean of all regional mean inflation rates (geometric mean) included in the respective sample. The computation of the standard deviation (std. dev.) is likewise based on the cross-section of the geometric means of all regional mean inflation rates included in the respective sample.

our sample. The reported difference in the inflation rate between an average German and an average Spanish region correspond to a cumulative depreciation in the real exchange rate between an average German and an average Spanish region of around 15% over the sample period.[11]

The numbers become even more striking when one not only looks at differences in inflation rates between the 'average' region of a country but also compares differences in inflation rates of individual regions. To this end, the lower panel of Table 1 reports differences in inflation rates between the region with the lowest and the region with the highest average inflation rate. Additionally, it documents differences in inflation rates between the group of regions with the lowest and the group of regions with the highest inflation rates.[12] According to the reported numbers the region with the lowest inflation rate experienced a real depreciation of about 25% over the sample period.

[11] To compute the reported cumulative change in the real exchange rate between an average German and an average Spanish region we define the real exchange rate, Q_t, between a German region and a Spanish region as $Q_t = P_t^G/P_t^S$, where P_t^G corresponds to the CPI of a German region in period t and P_t^S corresponds to the CPI of a Spanish region in period t. The cumulative percentage change in the real exchange rate between the two regions between period t and period $t + k$ is then computed as $(Q_{t+k} - Q_t)/Q_t$.

[12] Each group consists of five regions. Admittedly, the chosen number of five members in each group is very arbitrary. However, it solely serves to illustrate that it is instructive to take a look at the regional rather than only the national level when analysing inflation differentials within EMU. Therefore, we think that our approach is justified.

The gain in the competitiveness of the average region belonging to the group of the five regions with the lowest inflation rates is somewhat smaller but still amounts to 22%.

To gain some insights whether there have been major changes in cross-regional inflation dynamics after the introduction of the euro we split the sample into a 'pre-EMU' (1996(1) – 1998(12)) and an 'EMU' (1999(1) – 2004(10)) subsample. The results of this exercise are reported in the upper panel of Table 1. From the reported figures two observations can be made. First, mean inflation rates are always lower in the 'pre-EMU' subperiod (see Table 1). Second, inflation dispersion remains more or less stable across the two subperiods, in line with the visual impression from Figure 1. The first observation probably reflects the large efforts of EMU countries to meet the Maastricht criteria before 1999. The second observation shows that, despite substantial harmonization efforts, considerable heterogeneities across EMU regions continue to exist.[13] Our discussion and empirical investigation of the sources of those regional inflation differentials in Sections 3 and 4 gains renewed interest in the light of recent shocks in energy and food inflation as well as the recently observed upward trend of the euro relative to the US dollar.[14]

Overall, the results we have obtained so far based on regional inflation rates within and across euro area countries show that there are large and very long-lasting differences in inflation rates across EMU countries implying potentially considerable changes in the competitive structure between the considered economies. Moreover, our results demonstrate that the differences are substantially more pronounced across regions than across country averages.

Before we proceed to the next section in which we discuss potential reasons underlying these observed differences in inflation rates, we discuss whether our choice of the overall CPI data can influence the analysis. In particular, as we will discuss more in detail in the next section, one of the most-cited potential causes of inflation differences, the Balassa–Samuelson effect, has different predictions on the behaviour of the prices of goods in the tradable and non-tradable sectors. More specifically, if there is convergence in per-capita income levels between relatively poorer and richer regions, then the Balassa–Samuelson effect would imply that only the relative price of non-traded goods would increase by more in the poorer than in the richer regions. However, even if this is the case, there should still be a negative relationship between a region's initial income level and subsequent changes in the overall price level, a relationship that we will test in our econometric analysis.

---

[13] Since inflation rates are generally very persistent, close to unit-root processes we performed Augmented Dickey Fuller (ADF) unit root tests on the regional inflation rate series. As is well-known, the power of single-equation unit root tests is low in small samples like ours. Panel unit root tests on the other hand might not be well suited in our context due to the substantial comovement across regional inflation rates, evident in Figure 1 which would bias the tests substantially (see Banerjee et al., 2005). Given the low power of the single-equation unit root tests and given the results from the panel-unit root tests we decided to base most of our analysis on inflation level data rather than first differences. However, as a sensitivity check we also repeated the analysis for first differences. The results were qualitatively similar to those reported below and can be obtained from the authors upon request.

[14] Previous results by Honohan and Lane (2003), for example, indicate that national inflation differentials can to a large extent be attributed to exchange rate effects, in particular the dollar depreciation.

Moreover, to assess whether the descriptive statistics on inflation differentials that we have reported can be distorted by the use of the overall CPI data, we have also collected comparable regional data for the sectors Food (as an example of mostly tradable goods) and Hotel and Recreation (as an example of mostly non-tradable goods).

It turns out that the dispersion in regional inflation for the food sector is about 30% higher than for the overall CPI; for the hotel sector, it is about 80% higher than for overall CPI. These results are in line with the common wisdom that trade has an equalizer effect on inflation, but also suggest that the use of the overall CPI, if anything, underestimates the extent of regional inflation heterogeneity, likely due to averaging effects in the construction of the overall price index.

Two other empirical approaches to assess the empirical importance of the Balassa–Samuelson effect are based on either absolute price data, or on PPI data. The former would allow examining to what extent observed inflation differences are the result of a convergence in price levels. The latter are assumed to contain a larger share of tradable goods, such that one should observe smaller differences in PPI inflation rates than in CPI inflation if the Balassa–Samuelson effect is underlying the large observed inflation differentials.[15] Unfortunately, absolute price data are not available at a regional basis, but the best available absolute price data normally cover only selected goods and thus are not as representative as CPI data.[16] Similarly, PPI data are not available on a regional basis, but the previously reported sectoral analysis did not highlight any substantial qualitative changes in the extent of inflation differentials with respect to the use of CPI data.

In summary, we think that our CPI data are informative and representative of inflation differentials. Even if the latter were due to the Balassa–Samuelson effect, we should observe a negative relationship between the initial income of a region and its CPI inflation rate, a hypothesis that will not find empirical support.

3. INFLATION HETEROGENEITY IN A MONETARY UNION

In this section we discuss from a theoretical point of view the potential sources of the large and long-lasting differences in inflation rates across EMU regions that we have detected, and the reasons for the differences to be considerably more pronounced across regions than across countries. In particular, we will see that inflation differentials could be either benign, for example reflecting convergence processes or adjustment to asymmetric shocks, or malign, related to market rigidities and other imperfections.

---

[15] The PPP literature has used both CPI and PPI data but normally does not find significant differences in the results.

[16] One of the best data sources for absolute price data are the EIU (Economist Intelligence Unit) data which were, e.g., used by Engel and Rogers (2004). This database provides complete pricing information on 160 products and services across 123 cities in 79 countries. Its major goal is to deliver information for the personnel departments of firms to enable them to calculate what staff working abroad should be earning and what prices firms' core customers. The selection of the goods included in the database is therefore biased towards these needs of the personnel departments.

The two possibilities have very different policy implications, but they can be only discriminated empirically, which will be the topic of the next section.

Given the importance of heterogeneity of inflation developments within the EMU, its possible sources have received considerable attention in the academic literature in recent years.[17]

The focus of almost all the existing papers is, however, on country data rather than on regional data, at least partly due to the lack of regional data, a gap that we close with this paper.[18] We argue that, while national borders within the euro area are relevant for inflation developments in different regions, it is instructive to look also at regional developments for three main reasons. First, the understanding of the behaviour of regionally disaggregated inflation rate series helps to understand aggregate inflation, since the construction of the latter is based on the regional series. Second, as we will see in Section 5, the use of regional data enables us to disentangle the importance of national from purely regional factors for inflation rate variability, and therefore provides policy-makers aiming at stabilizing inflation rates with useful information. Third, the larger regional than national heterogeneity in economic conditions and production structures can help the identification of the sources of inflation heterogeneity.

The literature has identified several potential sources of inflation differentials:

(a) Differences between the actual positions of the economies within their business cycles, asymmetric shocks, and asymmetric effects of area-wide impulses such as monetary policy impulses, exchange rate movements or oil price changes.

(b) The Balassa–Samuelson effect.

(c) Inappropriate domestic policies or other unwarranted domestic developments such as misaligned fiscal policies, immoderate wage evolution, or other production input factor price developments.

(d) Nominal wage and price rigidities.

Whereas the first two mentioned sources of inflation differentials are normally not worrisome from a policy point of view, since they are either only transitory (point (a)) or reflect the result of convergence dynamics (point (b)) the other two factors can lead to undesirable economic outcomes and should therefore be properly addressed by policy-makers.[19]

---

[17] See, e.g., the papers by Altissimo *et al.* (2005), Benigno (2004), Duarte and Wolman (2008), ECB (2003, 2005), Honohan and Lane (2003).

[18] Two notable exceptions are provided by Alberola and Marques (2000) and Beck and Weber (2005). The focus of these two papers is different from ours, though. Whereas the analysis of Alberola and Marques (2000) is purely on Spanish regions, Beck and Weber (2005) examine the dynamics of regional inflation rates within the euro area but do not relate their results on the persistence of regional inflation rate deviations from the euro area mean to potential explanatory variables.

[19] For example, the European Commission (2004) identifies problems arising, e.g., from the structural inefficiencies. European regional policies aim to address structural weaknesses of regions that limit their competitiveness. One inflation related aspect of achieving a more balanced spread of economic activity across the Union is that it will reduce bottlenecks in a growing economy and lessen the likelihood of inflationary pressure.

From an empirical point of view, due to the nature of the potential explanatory variables for inflation differentials, it is sometimes not possible to find an exact match between the theoretical variable and the variable for which data are available. For this reason, we sometimes need to proxy the variable of interest. Moreover, since our focus is on the regional rather than on the national level, we face additional data limitations both with respect to the amount of available time series and the frequency at which they are collected. Nevertheless we have been able to collect a set of regional variables which allows us to proxy the major variables that are responsible for inflation rate differentials.

In the following we present a more extended exposition of each of the theoretical factors possibly underlying inflation differentials, and of the variables we will use to proxy them in the empirical analysis of the next section. In most cases, the data for the regional real variables were obtained from Eurostat's Regio database. The original data series are mostly annual, a detailed description of the empirical variables used is given in the Data Appendix.

3.1. Asynchronous business cycles and asymmetric shocks

An important determinant of the inflation rate of a region is its position within the business cycle. A region that experiences a high aggregate excess demand is also likely to experience (due to capacity constraints and the price-setting power of the firms) an increase in goods prices whereas a region that experiences a low aggregate excess demand might experience falling prices. As a consequence, the lack of synchronization of business cycles across regions, or more generally the presence of asymmetric shocks, might represent an important reason for differences in inflation rates.

The increased cost of production which results from existing capacity constraints will not only lead to higher prices in the domestic market but will also very likely be passed on to prices of goods which are exported. As a consequence, the external demand for the goods of the region will decrease, and the increase in prices will be mitigated. The opposite is true for a region which experiences a slow-down in economic activity. Hence, inflation rate differentials are part of an equilibrium adjustment process and should vanish over time, even though in practice the process can be long. They therefore represent one of the channels through which adjustment to asymmetric shocks must occur in a monetary union where national governments no longer have the possibility to offset the effects of asymmetric economic disturbances by adjusting nominal exchange rates.[20]

---

[20] Alternative mechanisms are high labour mobility, wage flexibility or a monetary union-wide fiscal transfer system. However, none of these mechanisms is very likely to play a role in EMU. There is little evidence of significant labour mobility across and often even within countries and wages normally exhibit downward rigidities. Likewise, a significant centralization of national budgets at the European level has not taken place after the introduction of the euro. A fourth alternative mechanism to insure against asymmetric shocks is a high degree of financial market integration across member countries. If residents of the member countries of a monetary union hold monetary union-wide diversified portfolios the costs of asymmetric shocks will be born by all residents. Since adjustment via relative goods prices often takes very long, the achievement of a high degree of financial market integration has been the focus of European policy-makers in recent years. Empirical evidence shows that much progress has been made in this respect in recent years.

A major explanation for asynchronous business cycle developments is that the economic structures of the regions differ. Differences in the economic structure might, for example, be the result of sectoral specialization as a consequence of the higher integration of European markets.[21] These differences in the production structure can be the origin of asymmetric shocks, and of differences in the transmission of the same shocks. For example, the more open a region is and the more it trades with countries outside the euro area, the stronger will be the effect of a change in the nominal euro exchange rate on its inflation rate. Similarly, the production structure of a region also determines how strong the effect of energy shocks, such as oil price shocks are. The more energy-intensive the production is, the larger will be the influence of changes in energy prices.

Since inflation differentials caused by asymmetric shocks are part of an equilibrium adjustment process, no policy measures are required to offset them. Moreover, inflation differentials of this type should be only temporary.

This discussion suggests regional business cycle measures and indicators of production structures as potential empirical explanatory variables for regional inflation differentials. To proxy for business cycle movements we use regional GDP growth, and to proxy for differences in the production structure we use data on the relative sizes of the agriculture, industry and services sector for the regions of our sample.

3.2. Balassa–Samuelson effect

Another reason for differences in regional inflation rates is related to the process of convergence in incomes. As pointed out, for example, in ECB (2003, 2005), the process of economic convergence in per-capita income levels within a monetary union can lead to differences in inflation rates. As initially shown by Balassa (1964) and Samuelson (1964), economies that experience relatively higher productivity growth in the traded goods sector than in the non-traded goods sector will experience a higher increase in the relative price of their non-traded goods. As a consequence, the overall price levels of the relatively fast-growing economies will rise by more than those of the relatively slow-growing economies, and we will therefore observe inflation differentials between these economies.

Since there are strong differences in per-capita incomes across European countries and even within countries, and since there have been large efforts at the European-wide level to narrow these differences, it can be expected that regions with relatively low initial incomes will experience relatively higher inflation rates. Inflation differences due to this convergence process will, however, not be a major concern from a policy point of view, since they can be seen as the by-product of a desirable adjustment

---

[21] See, for example, Krugman (1993) or Krugman and Venables (1996). On the other hand, authors such as Frankel and Rose (2002) and Rose and Engel (2002) find that more international trade is likely to result in more highly correlated business cycles. If the latter authors are correct, then we should see a decline in European inflation differentials over time.

process. It should also be noted that inflation differentials arising from the Balassa–Samuelson effect can be expected to be relatively long-lasting. Moreover, since large income differences exist even within our sample countries (such as between Northern and Southern Italian regions or West and East German states) we should expect that inflation differentials arise not only at a national but also to a large extent at a regional level.

Since the Balassa–Samuelson effect implies a negative relationship between initial income levels (or income growth rates) and subsequent inflation rates, we have collected per-capita income series for each region to examine the empirical importance of the Balassa–Samuelson effect. We use these series to construct two different measures, which we employ as potential explanatory variables in our regression analysis: the average level of (log) per-capita income in 1995 and the average per-capita growth rate between 1995 and 2003.

3.3. Diverging prices of input factors

Diverging developments in input factor prices can lead to diverging inflation rates through their impact on marginal production costs. In the following we will discuss the two groups of input factors that can potentially lead to diverging inflation rates: regionally divergent developments in wages, and the cost of other non-traded input factors, such as renting, heating or electricity. The net price of electricity might differ across countries and even across regions (e.g. Germany), and taxes, regulations and market structure in the energy sector are also likely to differ across countries and regions.

3.3.1. Diverging regional wage developments.   Different regional developments in the prices of input factors matter for inflation developments. In this context wage developments, but also other labour market variables such as unemployment rates or labour productivity, are of particular importance. Calmfors and Driffill (1988), for example, argue that differences in labour market institutions can give rise to different inflation rate outcomes. More specifically, they argue that economies with either strong centralization or strong decentralization of wage bargaining are better equipped to face supply shocks than economies with an intermediate degree of centralization. To support their hypothesis they compute what they call 'misery indices' which show that economies with intermediate degree of centralization indeed exhibit a worse performance in terms of inflation and unemployment figures than economies with extreme centralization or decentralization. As differences in wage changes are reflected in differences in labour costs, the prices of goods produced in economies with relatively higher wages will increase relatively strongly, and thus external demand for their goods will decrease.

Labour market institutions within EMU are still largely determined nationally. However, there is also some evidence for pronounced regional differences in labour market developments. Various aspects of the geographical segmentation of labour markets across European and US regions have been analysed and discussed. For instance, Overman and Puga (2002) document the regional and transnational dimension of European unemployment, i.e. geographical unemployment clusters that do not respect national boundaries. They argue that this reflects agglomeration effects of economic integration. Bertola (2006) argues that in Europe unemployment tends to be both higher and regionally dispersed in large and heterogeneous countries than in smaller, homogeneous ones. Layard *et al.* (2005, ch. 6) document persistent regional unemployment differences in the UK. For the United States, Clark (1998) finds that a large part of the cyclical employment variation is region-specific even after controlling for industry differences, while Blanchard and Katz (1992) find regional persistence differences in employment growth, but more transitory differences in unemployment rates. Decressin and Fatás (1995) find greater persistence in the regional relative participation following a shock to regional demand in Italy than in Germany and the UK. Jimeno and Bentolila (1998) find that regional Spanish wages and relative unemployment and participation rates are very persistent.

To capture the potential effects of labour market heterogeneity on inflation differentials, in the next section we will also consider the role of average levels of unemployment, average wage growth, and average changes in unit labour costs over 1995–2004.

Low labour mobility is presumably also important for explaining regional differences. For instance, it has been pointed out in Jimeno and Bentolila (1998) that the responses of migration and participation rates to labour demand shocks are slower in Spain than in the United States. Unfortunately, migration data on a regional level are only available for some of the regions we analyse, and for those only for parts of our sample period. For example, for Germany data are only available until 1994 (for an analysis of migration between euro area countries, see e.g. Heinz and Ward-Warmedinger, 2006, and references therein).

To avoid welfare losses caused by asymmetric wage developments, structural reforms in labour markets aimed at increasing competition and equalizing labour market institutions are necessary. Since labour market institutions within EMU are still mostly determined nationally, these decisions have to be taken at a national or coordinated area-wide level.[22]

3.3.2. Other costs of non-traded input factors. A second important factor for regional price developments are the costs of non-traded input factors other than wages, e.g., the cost of renting, in particular for stores, and the costs of maintaining distribution and production facilities. Input cost changes may differ across regions, both as a result of supply and demand in segmented but freely adjusting markets, or

---

[22] It must be noted that asymmetric wage developments will occur in the context of the adjustment process following asymmetric shock (see Subsection 3.1). These asymmetries can, however, be considered to be temporary.

because of different and changing structural inefficiencies in regulated markets (such as in the energy sector). Those lead to regional differences in input factor cost changes.

No data are available on a regional level from our data sources on the rents and energy costs for firms and producers. Therefore, we cannot draw any firm conclusion regarding the relevance of inflation in the costs of those input factors for regional inflation differentials. However, as an empirical proxy for these effects, we will approximate inflation in factor rental costs by the average year-on-year change in the COICOP (Classification of Individual Consumption by Purpose) index 'Housing, water, electricity, gas and other fuels'.

3.4. Nominal wage and price rigidities

The existence of nominal wage and price rigidities can result in high persistence in inflation rates. When wages and prices are sticky and react only in a slow manner to exogenous shocks, the adjustment to such shocks takes a long time, and persistent inflation differentials across regions can arise. As a consequence, the functioning of the equilibrating real exchange rate channel can become less efficient. Empirical evidence on the degree of price rigidities shows the existence of sizeable, even though not dramatic, nominal rigidities in the euro area.[23] As a consequence, we observe that inflation rates exhibit a relatively high degree of persistence, which can give rise to persistent inflation differentials.[24] An additional negative implication of the existence of nominal wage and price rigidities is that they decrease economic efficiency because they lead to relative price distortions in response to economic shocks. As Woodford (2003, ch. 6) analytically shows, a policy concerned about maximizing social welfare therefore aims at stabilizing inflation rates. To reduce nominal wage and price rigidities there should be structural reforms that enhance the degree of competition. In other words, the competitive structure of a region might be a crucial factor determining the degree of prevailing nominal inertia.

Typically, nominal rigidities are associated with imperfect competition in the goods and labour markets, which in turn can be approximated by the number of suppliers, i.e., the market density, in a market. Therefore, as an available regional empirical proxy for nominal rigidities, we propose a measure of market density in the manufacturing and in the wholesale sectors.

4. EMPIRICAL EVIDENCE ON THE SOURCES OF REGIONAL INFLATION DIFFERENTIALS

In the previous two sections we have seen that there exist long-lasting and sizeable inflation rate differentials across European regions, we have discussed their potential

---

[23] See, e.g., Altissimo *et al.* (2006).

[24] Evidence for the persistence of inflation rates is, e.g., provided later in Table 2.

sources from a theoretical point of view, and we have shown that, depending on their sources, the inflation rate differentials can be good or bad. In this section we wish to assess empirically which are the main sources of inflation differentials, whether the differentials are good or bad, whether policy intervention is needed, and if needed whether it should be at the area wide, national or regional level.

We start this section with a discussion of some descriptive statistics for the empirical counterparts of the theoretical sources of inflation differentials that we have introduced in Section 3. In the second subsection we present a more formal regression based analysis.

4.1. Descriptive statistics

We start our empirical analysis of the possible sources of regional inflation differentials with the proxies for labour market heterogeneity introduced in Section 3, namely, average levels of unemployment, average wage growth, and average changes in unit labour costs. Table 2, columns 1 to 3, documents regional heterogeneity of labour market variables for the countries and regions that are included in our new regional inflation dataset presented in Section 2. In the first two columns of Table 2 we report mean regional unemployment rates and mean growth rates of wages for all regions as well as grouped by country, together with the respective cross-regional standard deviation. Moreover, we report the mean correlation of unemployment and wage growth with the respective regional inflation rates. The figures indicate that there is considerable dispersion of regional wage growth and unemployment rates across regions of different countries, but also across regions within a given country. For wage growth, the within country dispersion is particularly pronounced for Portugal. For unemployment rates we find very large regional dispersion in Germany, Italy and Spain. Since relatively higher unemployment rates might dampen wage increases, and since wage changes directly influence firms' marginal costs, the documented large differences in labour market variables at the regional level likely contribute to the substantial differences in regional inflation rates documented in Section 2. Actually, there is substantial negative correlation between regional unemployment and inflation, in particular in Germany and Spain. The figures on the correlation between wage growth and inflation are more varied, with positive values for Spain, close to zero for Portugal, and negative for Austria and Germany.

To capture the cost pressures from the labour market, the change in unit labour costs is a useful additional indicator since it relates nominal wages to labour productivity. For Eurostat's regional measure of changes in unit labour costs a similar pattern as for unemployment rates and wage growth is found. We detect large regional dispersion in unit labour costs developments both across and within countries, and we find a slightly positive correlation with regional inflation rates at the area-wide level. For individual countries, on the other hand, we find both positive (Spain, Portugal) and negative (Austria, Germany, Spain, Finland and Italy) correlations. Of course, a more formal econometric analysis is required (see Box 1 and the following section), but these findings are already interesting.

Overall, dispersion in regional unemployment rates, wage growth, change in unit labour costs seem likely to have contributed to regional inflation differentials. Those at least in part are likely reflecting differences in the adjustment process to common economic shocks or adjustment to asymmetric shocks.

Let us now consider the average year-on-year change in the COICOP index 'Housing, water, electricity, gas and other fuels', which, as mentioned, we use as a representative for other costs of non-traded input factors. Descriptive statistics on this variable are reported in column 4 of Table 2 (under the heading DP_HOUS). The reported numbers suggest that changes in the housing index are in all cases positively correlated to the overall inflation rate. The observed cross-regional and cross-country patterns reflect those of the overall index. We therefore can conclude that differences in housing costs developments are likely one major driving force not only for the levels but also for the differences in regional inflation rates. Given our discussion above, this result points to the fact that some regions have experienced major increases in their marginal costs which might have led to losses in their competitiveness.

Next we move to the relative sizes of the agriculture, industry and services sector for the regions of our sample, which we have proposed as proxies for the economic structure that in turn can determine asymmetric effects from similar shocks or business cycle asymmetries. The results are reported in columns 5 to 7 of Table 2. It turns out that there are significant differences in the economic structure across regions, both across and within countries. These differences are particularly pronounced in the agriculture and in the industry sectors. Another interesting finding is that the share of industry seems to be positively correlated with inflation, while that of services negatively correlated, though with marked differences in size across countries. This result indicates that asymmetric shocks caused by sectoral specialization might be one of the sources of regional differences in inflation rates. As we outlined above, inflation differences of this type could be considered to be part of the adjustment process in response to the asymmetric shock.

As noted in the previous section, the competitive structure of a region is approximated with a measure of market density. In columns 8 and 9 of Table 2 we report descriptive statistics on the 'market density' in the manufacturing and in the wholesale sectors.[25] Again, the figures confirm that there is considerable heterogeneity across regions. Given our reasoning in the previous section, this observation suggests that goods market imperfections might play a role for inflation heterogeneities.

Finally, we consider the average level of (log) per-capita income in 1995, and the average per-capita growth rate between 1995 and 2003, which could capture Balassa–Samuelson effects. From columns 11 and 12 of Table 2, there is considerable dispersion in both income levels and growth rates within and across countries.

---

[25] Please see the Data Appendix for a description of how these two variables are constructed.

Table 2. Descriptive statistics for regional real data

		U [1]	DW [2]	DULC [3]	DP_HOUS [4]	AGR [5]	IND [6]	SERV [7]	DENS_D [8]	DENS_G [9]	Y_95 [11]	DY [12]
All	Mean	9.76	2.94	-0.63	2.51	4.12	28.30	67.58	1.75	6.66	9.62	39.02
	Std.dev	5.93	0.89	0.70	0.69	3.36	7.22	7.68	3.60	11.95	0.28	12.97
	Corr	-0.01	0.57	0.08	0.81	0.36	-0.12	-0.04	0.26	0.27	-0.29	0.49
AU	Mean	3.46	2.40	-1.08	2.07	2.72	32.24	65.04	0.55	1.66	9.83	35.09
	Std.dev	1.23	0.34	0.57	0.42	1.97	7.02	7.84	0.36	1.08	0.23	5.58
	Corr	-0.42	-0.30	-0.41	0.65	0.32	0.34	-0.39	-0.22	-0.17	-0.32	0.30
DE	Mean	11.54	2.41	-0.73	1.69	1.64	29.21	69.15	0.07	–	9.68	28.44
	Std.dev	5.74	0.29	0.95	0.24	1.16	4.66	4.56	0.06	–	0.26	9.55
	Corr	-0.55	-0.18	-0.12	0.43	-0.01	0.83	-0.85	0.39	–	0.11	0.35
ES	Mean	11.89	2.88	-0.77	3.10	5.38	28.80	65.83	2.90	11.48	9.49	54.96
	Std.dev	4.38	0.34	0.53	0.55	3.83	7.79	9.28	4.70	17.90	0.21	4.85
	Corr	-0.52	0.54	0.08	0.32	-0.14	0.43	-0.31	0.09	0.03	0.52	-0.08
FI	Mean	11.08	–	-0.27	1.71	5.59	33.01	61.41	0.74	1.80	9.61	49.15
	Std.dev	2.87	–	0.39	0.10	3.22	4.57	4.87	0.50	0.65	0.16	3.69
	Corr	-0.27	–	-0.62	0.36	0.23	-0.46	0.28	-0.43	-0.51	-0.11	-0.72
IT	Mean	10.55	–	-0.43	2.71	3.66	26.51	69.84	2.44	5.22	9.73	29.84
	Std.dev	7.40	–	0.47	0.40	1.48	6.53	6.07	4.59	7.68	0.27	4.77
	Corr	-0.30	–	-0.17	0.55	-0.59	0.30	-0.18	-0.13	0.00	0.46	-0.28
PO	Mean	5.12	4.73	-0.28	2.83	7.36	22.57	70.07	1.97	7.38	9.32	42.60
	Std.dev	1.58	0.66	1.11	0.60	5.72	9.26	10.47	2.55	10.82	0.20	14.60
	Corr	0.11	0.01	0.60	0.67	0.12	0.21	-0.26	-0.29	-0.25	0.17	-0.55

Note: Table 2 reports means and standard deviations of the respective regional variables. Moreover mean correlations with the respective regional inflation rates are reported for all real variables for all regions as well as for the respective countries. *U*: Unemployment rate; *DW*: Year-on-year changes in quarterly monthly wages; *DULC*: Change in unit labour costs; *DP_HOUS*: Year-on-year change in COICOP index 'Housing, water, electricity, gas and other fuels'; *AGR*: Percentage of Agriculture in Gross value added at basic prices; *IND*: Percentage of Industry in Gross value added at basic prices; *SERV*: Percentage of Services in Gross value added at basic prices; *DENS_D*: Number of local units (Manufacturing)/Total population; *DENS_G*: Number of local units (Wholesale and retail trade; repair of motor vehicles, motorcycles and personal and household goods)/Total population; *AR1*: Persistence of inflation measured as estimated coefficient in AR(1) model; *Y_95*: (Log of) PPP 1995 GDP per inhabitant; *DY*: Growth of PPP GDP per inhabitant. See the Data Appendix for more details.

Moreover, initial income levels are on average associated with higher consecutive growth rates. This holds both across and within countries. However, whereas there is a clear negative (positive) correlation between initial income at a regional level (consecutive growth rates) with inflation area-wide (as suggested by theory), the correlation patterns within countries are less clear-cut. However, inflation differences due to the convergence process are benign and are not a major concern from a policy point of view, since they will become less pronounced over time and ultimately disappear.

4.2. A more formal evaluation

After the descriptive analysis, we now present the results of a more formal cross-sectional regression based approach to explain average (over time) regional inflation, see Table 3 (see also Box 1 for the overall econometric framework considered in this paper). We focus on a specification that does not include all the variables listed in Table 2. The selection of the variables was based on the following criteria: First, we omitted average wage changes (DW) since we do not have data for Finnish and Italian regions on this variable. Second, we dropped variables that created collinearity problems due to the presence of national dummy variables.

The results indicate that, contrary to our intuition and the descriptive analysis, labour market variables do not play an important role in explaining long-lasting regional inflation differentials. Both unemployment and unit labour costs are insignificant, unit labour costs even have the wrong sign. The results do not change if we repeat the analysis for the smaller set of regions where DW is also available. Moreover, for these regions DW is also not statistically significant. This result suggests that differences in labour market institutions do not seem to have caused long-lasting differences in inflation rates due to their impact on marginal costs.

Table 3. Regression of mean inflation rates on mean economic structural variables

	Area wide analysis	
Variable	Estimate	Std. Error
U	−0.00679	0.005798
DULC	−0.02321	0.036111
DP_HOUS	0.227631	0.064476
DENS_D	−0.01197	0.005862
SERV	−0.00723	0.0034
DY	0.002051	0.004318
R-squared:	0.952	Obs. 66
Rbar-squared:	0.943	

Note: National fixed effects included. White HAC standard errors. *U*: Unemployment rate; *DULC*: Change in unit labour costs; *DP_HOUS*: Year-on-year change in COICOP index 'Housing, water, electricity, gas and other fuels'; *SERV*: Percentage of Services in Gross value added at basic prices; *DENS_D*: Number of local units (Manufacturing)/Total population; *DY*: Growth of PPP GDP per inhabitant.

Likewise, we do not find evidence in favour of the Balassa–Samuelson effect. Even though our proxy for this effect, the average per-capita income growth rate, has the correct sign it does not turn out to be significant. We have also used initial per-capita income, the results were, however, also not supportive for the Balassa–Samuelson effect. Our results on the empirical relevance of the Balassa–Samuelson hypothesis is similar to findings of Rogers (2007), who concludes that the process of price level convergence does not explain much of observed inflation rates differentials across European cities.

However, we find strong evidence for the importance of the costs of non-wage input factors. Our proxy for the cost of this variable (DP_HOUS) has the expected positive sign and is highly significant. This result suggests that prices of some input factors such as rents, gas or electricity have risen systematically more in some regions than in other regions. Since we do not find evidence in favour of the Balassa–Samuelson effect which would justify increases in non-traded input factor prices, we can conclude that the observed differences in non-wage input factor prices have led to changes in the competitive structure of our sample regions: High inflation regions have experienced considerable competitiveness losses whereas low-inflation regions have experienced considerably competitiveness gains. Unfortunately, the available data do not allow the identification of the factors that have played a particularly important role.

The extent of competitiveness of the economy also seems to play an important role for inflation differentials. The sign for our proxy of the extent of competitiveness (DENS_D) is negative and significant at a 5% level. Given our discussion of this variable in the previous section, this result suggests that markets in which there are more suppliers experience relatively lower inflation rates. Our discussion on the implications of nominal rigidities suggests that regions which are more competitive thus experience relatively smaller welfare losses through inflation.

The results in Table 3 also show that the economic structure of a region plays a significant role for inflation differentials. Our proxy for sectoral specialization, the size of the service sector (SERV), is statistically significant. This finding shows that asymmetric shocks caused by sectoral specialization also seem to be one source of inflation differences across regions. However, as we argued in the previous section, this type of inflation differentials is not worrisome from a welfare-theoretic point of view.

It should also be remarked that our results are based on a specific and fairly short sample period, with limited business cycle fluctuations, so that it could be that labour market variables become relevant over a longer horizon, or when using producer rather than consumer prices.

However, overall, our regression results indicate that the observed long-lasting inflation differentials are the outcome of different developments in the costs of non-wage input factors and are due to differences in the competitive and economic structure of the regions. Therefore, as previously discussed, we think that a reduction in the potentially damaging long-lasting regional inflation differences can be achieved by policy reforms which aim at increasing competition in non-wage factor input and goods markets. Our analysis suggests that these measures would help to reduce long-lasting welfare-impeding inflation differentials in the future.

5. CO-MOVEMENT AND HETEROGENEITY IN EURO AREA REGIONAL INFLATION DYNAMICS

In the econometric analysis of the previous section we have focused on long lasting (average) inflation and argued that the detected long-lasting differences in inflation rates across the member countries/regions of a monetary union are mostly harmful because they lead to competitiveness losses of high-inflation regions and relative price distortions. In this section we turn our attention to another aspect of the behaviour of inflation rates that is of interest from a welfare-theoretic aspect, namely, the variation of inflation rates over time. In the presence of nominal rigidities, policy should aim at stabilizing not only economic activity, i.e. the output gap, but also inflation rates (see Woodford, 2003, ch. 6). Across regions, as we argued above, nominal rigidities and inflation differentials similarly imply relative price distortions which are welfare-reducing. Recent evidence on the degree of nominal rigidities for the euro area suggests that prices are changed on average every 13 months.[26] This considerable nominal rigidity implies that stabilization of inflation rates is an important policy objective.

Our discussion of the various determinants of regional inflation variation in Section 3 suggests that the variables which are responsible for movements in inflation rates differ with respect to their geographical impact. It is therefore useful to group the different variables into three groups, namely into area wide, national and region specific variables. The objective of this section is to provide some insights into the relative importance of these three groups of factors for the dynamics of regional inflation rates. The results of the analysis will provide important guidelines for a policy aiming at stabilizing inflation rates.

As Forni and Reichlin (2001) have done for the analysis of regional European output volatility, we use a factor model and represent the standardized regional inflation rates as a linear combination of one (or several) area-wide factor(s), one (or several) national factor(s) and a region-specific component. The common, national and regional factors are assumed to be uncorrelated, while their effects on the inflation rates are unconstrained. While there can be economically interesting correlations between the different types of factors, our assumption is needed to identify the factor model and make its parameters and the factors estimable. Other identification restrictions are feasible, as in any simultaneous equation model, but orthogonality of the factors is the standard choice in the factor literature. The econometric factor model that we use as well as a more detailed motivation underlying this approach are presented in Box 1.[27]

---

[26] See, e.g., Dhyne *et al.* (2006).

[27] For a more technical discussion of the approach the reader is referred to Beck *et al.* (2006).

In the first two subsections the decomposition of regional inflation dynamics into area wide, national and regional components is presented. Since we find that there are significant differences in the extent to which regional inflation dynamics are explained by area-wide and national factors, in the third subsection we assess alternative potential reasons for the observed differences. In the final subsection, we evaluate whether and why the monetary union has had a substantial impact on the extent of commonality. We post-pone to Section 6 a discussion of whether the determinants of long lasting inflation differentials that we have discussed theoretically in Section 3 and empirically in Section 4 could also play a role in shaping the temporal evolution of inflation variations.

Box 1. Econometric framework

We model the inflation rate in region i of country j at period t, denoted by x_{ijt}, as follows:

$$x_{ijt} = \mu_{ij} + q_{ijt},$$

$$q_{ijt} = \lambda_{ij} f_t + \eta_{ij} g_{jt} + e_{ijt}, \tag{1}$$

$$i = 1, \ldots, N_j, j = 1, \ldots, 6, t = 1, \ldots, T.$$

Therefore, each regional inflation rate is decomposed into a region specific mean (a fixed effect), μ_{ij}, and a term that represents the deviation of inflation from its mean, namely, $q_{ijt} = x_{ijt} - \mu_{ij}$.

The deviation of inflation from the mean, q_{ijt}, can be further decomposed into a common component, $\lambda_{ij} f_t$, a nation specific component, $\eta_{ij} g_{jt}$, and a region specific (idiosyncratic) component, e_{ijt}. The common component is driven by few factors common to all regions, f_t, which represent economic forces such as the common monetary policy within the euro area (and similar monetary policies across countries in the convergence to the euro), and common external developments such as oil prices and the exchange rate. Notice that the common factors can have a differentiated impact on different regions, measured by the loadings λ_{ij}. The national component is driven by few factors common to all regions in a nation, g_{jt}, which can be related for example to fiscal policy and remaining labour and goods markets heterogeneity within the euro area members. The residual purely region specific component, e_{ijt}, is related to regional variables such as local labour market conditions, which could matter even more than their national counterparts due to the low labour mobility across European regions.

In order to identify the model for q_{ijt}, we assume that the common and national factors are orthonormal (namely, orthogonal, with zero mean and unit variance), and orthogonal to the idiosyncratic component e_{ijt}. Under these assumptions, it is possible to estimate each region specific mean μ_{ij} as the sample average (over time) of x_{ijt}; the common factors f_t as the principal components of the standardized x_{ijt}; the national factors g_{jt} as the principal components of the residuals of a regression of the standardized x_{ijt} on the estimated common factors; the loadings λ_{ij} and η_{ij} as the coefficients in a regression of each standardized x_{ijt} on the estimated common and national factors; the residuals of these regressions represent the estimated regional components e_{ijt}. See Stock and Watson (2002b) and Beck *et al.* (2006) for details. In particular, Stock and Watson (2002b) show that the principal component based estimators of the factors have good properties even in the presence of a rather short temporal dimension of the sample, given a rather large cross-sectional dimension, as in our case. While more sophisticated factor estimation techniques are available, see e.g. Forni *et al.* (2000, 2005b), the differences are usually minor both in simulation experiments and in empirical applications, see e.g. Kapetanios and Marcellino (2004), Favero *et al.* (2005).

The choice of the number of common and national factors, say p and v, can be made either based on specific information criteria, such as those introduced by Bai and Ng (2002), or using less formal methods, such as the fraction of variance of all series explained by the first p principal components. In our case, the information criteria suggest one common and one national factor, while the less formal methods would favour three factors of each type. We present results based on the former choice in the main text, but qualitatively the findings do not change with more factors, see Beck *et al.* (2006) for details.

It is worth mentioning that a more common modelling approach is the regression of the regional series on macroeconomic variables, possibly at different levels of disaggregation, rather than on the unobservable factors. However, this approach is empirically dominated in our application by the factor specification, in terms of both explanatory power and properties of the resulting residual component e_{ijt}, see Beck *et al.* (2006) for details.

Finally, besides evaluating the decomposition of q_{ijt} into euro area level, national and regional components, it is also interesting from an economic point of view to try and explain the heterogeneity both in the mean regional inflation rates, μ_{ij}, and in the loadings of the common factors, λ_{ij}. This can be achieved by means of cross-sectional regressions, where (the estimated values of) these variables are regressed on nation specific effects, d_j, and on temporal averages of regional macroeconomic characteristics, z_{ij}. Hence the regression models are

$$\mu_{ij} = d_j + az_{ij} + u_{ij}, \tag{2}$$

and

$$\lambda_{ij} = d_j + bz_{ij} + \varepsilon_{ij}, \tag{3}$$

with $i = 1, \ldots, N_j, j = 1, \ldots, 6$. The parameters a and b can be estimated by OLS, and we compute HAC standard errors around the point estimates in order to account for possible heterogeneity and correlation in the errors u and ε.

5.1. How much co-movement is area wide?

The starting point of our empirical analysis is the estimation of the area wide and national common factors, which are denoted by f_t and g_{jt} in Equation (1) of Box 1. Stock and Watson (2002a) proved that, under mild regularity conditions that also allow for temporal correlation in the idiosyncratic regional errors, the factors can be consistently estimated by principal components of the variables. Therefore, to estimate the area wide factors, we extract the principal components from the pooled regional dataset, which contains a total of 70 time series.

To decide on the number of area wide factors to be used in our analysis we use the statistical information criteria for the selection of the number of factors proposed by Bai and Ng (2002). These criteria suggest that one factor is sufficient. This is a common finding in this type of analyses, see e.g. Forni and Reichlin (2001), Kose et al. (2003), and Ciccarelli and Mojon (2005). We therefore assume there is one area wide factor, and estimate it by the first principal component of the regional inflation rates.[28]

The first panel of Table 4 reports the proportion of the variance in all inflation rates that is explained by the first area wide factor. It turns out that almost 50% of the overall variance in regional inflation rates is due to movements in this factor. We consider this number to be a lower limit, since other selection criteria than the one by Bai and Ng (2002) might suggest using more than only one area wide factor.

When the area wide factor is regressed on area wide variables such as the short-term interest rate, M3 growth, the exchange rate and the growth in oil prices, these variables have, as expected, a good explanatory power. However, it is not possible to associate this factor with a single, specific, area wide macroeconomic variable. Additional insight into the economic interpretation of the factors could be provided by a structural factor approach along the lines of Forni et al. (2005a). However, our data set is not rich enough for such an approach to be implemented, since most real variables are not available on a monthly basis on the regional level.

To obtain a better understanding of the underlying structure of our common factor and the area wide inflation rate that would be computed based on our sample data we have compared the weights of each regional inflation rate in the first principal component with the economic weight of the respective region based on its GDP.[29] The results show that there are large differences between these two types of weights.

---

[28] More precisely, the criteria suggested by Bai and Ng (2002) can produce unreliable results in medium size samples with enough heterogeneity. Under these conditions, the information criteria tend to indicate either just one or the maximum pre-specified number of factors. Therefore, we also performed our econometric analysis based on alternative, less formal, methods for the selection of the number of factors. These methods suggest that three area wide factors should be used rather than only one. The results are qualitatively comparable to those based on one factor. Basically, as expected, there is an increase in the importance of the area wide factor, and a corresponding decreasing role for the national and regional factors, which remain important though. The interested reader is referred to Beck et al. (2006), where the results from both analyses are reported and compared.

[29] The results are available from the authors upon request.

Table 4. Variance explained by euro-area, national and idiosyncratic factors

	All regions					
Proportion of variance explained	48.46					

	Austria		Germany		Spain	
	National	Regional	National	Regional	National	Regional
Proportion of variance explained	30.36	21.18	37.11	14.43	26.88	24.66

	Finland		Italy		Portugal	
	National	Regional	National	Regional	National	Regional
Proportion of variance explained	48.80	2.74	28.73	22.81	34.78	16.76

Note: The area wide factor ('All Regions') is estimated as the first principal component extracted from a dataset with the inflation rates of all the regions of all countries, over the monthly sample 1996–2004. Each national factor is estimated as the first principal component extracted for each country from the residuals of a regression of regional inflation rates on the area wide factor, over the same sample period. We report the proportion of variance explained by the area wide factor (that is the same for all countries) and, for each country, the proportion of variance explained by the national factor and the residual idiosyncratic regional contribution.

This is to be expected since the principal component analysis maximizes the explained variance rather than representing the relative economic importance of a region. Thus, Spanish regional inflation series, for example, obtain a relatively large weight in the first principal component, whereas German regional inflation series obtain a relatively low weight. Nevertheless, there is a very high correlation between the area wide factor and the euro area HICP inflation rate (about 0.90). We will also discuss in the next subsections how the relative importance of the area wide, national and regional components differs geographically.

5.2. National factors and regional heterogeneity

After having obtained the area wide factor, we now discuss estimation of the national factor.

For each country, we clean the regional series from the common area wide effects by regressing them on the estimated area wide factor. The principal components of the resulting residuals can be used to estimate the national factors. This procedure is justified by the assumed orthogonality of the area wide, national and regional components.

Again we use the information criteria by Bai and Ng (2002) and find that for all countries one national factor seems to be sufficient. In the lower panels of Table 4 we report the proportion of the (overall) variance in regional inflation rates of a specific country that is explained by the national factor. We additionally report the proportion of the variance in regional inflation rates that is not explained by either the area wide or the national factor and is thus region-specific.

The results show that the national factors play an important role in explaining regional inflation rates. The proportion of variance in regional inflation rates that is explained by the national factor ranges from about 25% for Spain to almost 50% for Finland. These differences are partly due to economic reasons, such as the economic size of the regions and the different degree of policy decentralization/independence, and partly purely to the lower number of regions in smaller countries. The low value for Spain, for example, can probably be explained by the high degree of independence that Spanish communities enjoy. On the other hand, the large value for Finland can be explained by the fact that the individual provinces have little significance.

On average, 32% of regional inflation variation is explained by the national factors. This result shows that national policies are still very important for regional inflation rate dynamics despite the fact that monetary policy is no longer conducted at the national level and despite the fact that fiscal policy is considerably constrained by the Growth and Stability Pact. The strong influence of the national factor very likely results both from nationally conducted fiscal policy and nationally determined labour market institutions. As for the area-wide factor, our data is unfortunately not rich enough to associate the national factor with a single, specific, national macroeconomic variable. However, labour market variables such as unit labour costs or unemployment have a good explanatory power for the national factors in simple regression analysis.

The results of Table 4 also show that there remains a relevant regional component in all countries, except Finland. In particular, the proportion of region specific inflation variance ranges from about 14% for Germany to about 25% for Spain.

5.3. Do common area-wide and national factors affect inflation symmetrically across regions?

In the previous subsections we found that at least 50% of the variance in regional inflation rates can be attributed to area wide factors and that at least another 25% can be attributed to national factors. An interesting question that arises in the context of this analysis is whether the estimated area wide and national factors have the same effects across all regions. From an econometric point of view, this requires examining whether the loadings of the factors, denoted by λ_{ij} in Box 1, are equal across regions. If this is not the case, deviations of regional inflation from a common average value can partly be attributed to developments that affect the euro area as a whole, such as monetary policy or oil price shocks.[30]

A graphical illustration of the different loadings of the area wide and the national factors is given in Figure 3, which reports the regional loadings of the area wide

---

[30] Potential reasons for asymmetric effects of area wide developments are discussed in Section 3.

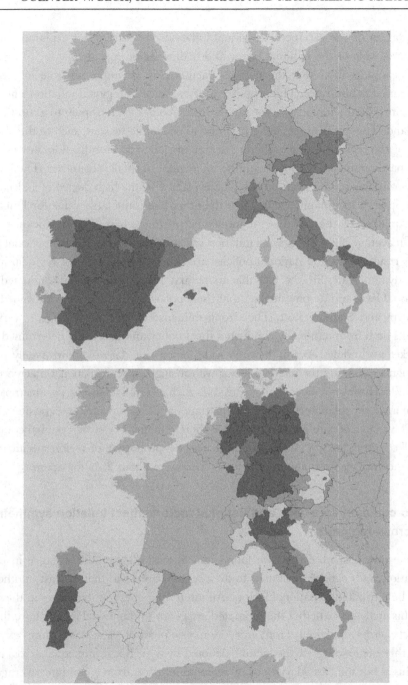

Figure 3. Percentage of inflation variance explained by the area wide component (upper panel) and national factors (lower panel)

Note: Figure 3 plots the percentage of inflation variance that is explained by the euro area wide component (upper panel) and national component (lower panel). The darker a region the higher is the percentage of explained inflation variance. Limits for colour changes are 30%, 50% and 70% (upper panel) and 20%, 30% and 40% (lower panel).

factor in the upper panel, and those for the national factors in the bottom panel. The upper panel shows that there is a lot of heterogeneity in the effect of the euro area component within nations, except in Spain and Portugal (see Forni and Reichlin, 2001, for similar findings for output growth). In particular, in Spain the euro area wide component is quite large in all regions. The lower panel shows that there is also a lot of heterogeneity in the effect of the national component within nations. One can see that the lighter areas in the bottom panel correspond roughly to the dark areas of the upper panel, that is, a region with larger area wide component of inflation will have a smaller national component. Overall, Figure 3 shows that there are large differences across regions in the proportion of overall variance explained either by the area wide or national factors.

The observed differences in the extent to which regional inflation rate dynamics are determined by area wide, national and regional factors are very likely due to asymmetries in the regional input factor prices, the economic structure and the business cycle position and the convergence of the respective regions. To obtain some intuition for the potential causes of the observed differences in the relative importance of the area wide and national factors we follow Kose *et al.* (2003), and relate the observed differences across regions to structural characteristics of the respective economies in a more formal econometric analysis.

More specifically, to characterize the relationship between the structural characteristics of economies and the relative importance of the area wide factors, we regress the loading of each region associated either with the area wide or the national factor on a set of explanatory variables that are related to regional characteristics.

In Table 5, the panel labelled 'Area wide analysis' reports results when the loadings of the area wide factors are used as the dependent variable, while the panel labelled 'Country analysis' reports analogous results when the loadings for the respective country specific factors are used as dependent variables. For each region, we consider five explanatory variables: the unemployment rate (U), the change in the COICOP housing cost index (DP_HOUS), the market density ($DENS\_D$), the share of service production in overall production ($SERV$), and the GDP growth (DY).[31] The choice of these variables is based on data availability and on their economic relevance according to the discussion in Section 3. There we grouped the variables that can cause differences in inflation rates across regions into different classes. For our econometric analysis we decided to choose at least one variable from each group in Section 3.

Our discussion in Section 3 suggests that market density ($DENS\_D$) should have a positive sign, whereas all the other variables should have a negative impact on the loadings of a region. This intuition is fully confirmed in the upper panel of Table 5, and mostly confirmed in the lower panel of Table 5. However, based on the *t*-statistics of the

---

[31] See the Data Appendix for a more detailed description of how the individual variables are constructed.

Table 5. Regression of regional loadings on economic structural variables

Variable	Estimate	Std. Error	
Area wide analysis			
U	−0.02009	0.302386	
DP_HOUS	−5.79983	4.468402	
DENS_D	0.160733	0.291991	
SERV	−0.17253	0.204821	
DY	−0.23461	0.185649	
R-squared:	0.709	Obs.	66
Rbar-squared:	0.656		
Country analysis			
U	0.046803	0.389653	
DP_HOUS	−3.91473	3.616188	
DENS_D	0.345413	0.495333	
SERV	−0.43577	0.425553	
DY	−0.13273	0.224306	
R-squared:	0.068	Obs.	66
Rbar-squared:	−0.009		
Regional analysis			
U	−0.08519	0.486083	
DP_HOUS	−5.94433	3.737456	
DENS_D	−0.45333	0.665835	
SERV	0.734198	0.519539	
DY	−0.24208	0.251536	
R-squared:	0.157	Obs.	66
Rbar-squared:	0.087		

Note: The upper panel of Table 5 results (estimated coefficient, White HAC Standard Error, t-test for non-significance and associated p-value) from regressing the proportion of variance explained by the area-wide factor on the unemployment rate (U), the growth rate of the COICOP index (DP_HOUS), the market density in the manufacturing sector (DENS_D), the share of the service sector in total production (SERV), and output growth between 1996 and 2003 (DY). The middle panel results from regressing the proportion of variance explained by the national factor and regional factor on the same variables as in the upper panel. The lower panel results from regressing the residual regional proportion of variance on the same variables as in the upper panel. The regression equation of the area wide analysis includes national dummy variables in addition to the variables listed above. The regression equation for the country analysis additionally includes a constant. An overview on the sources of the data and how they are constructed is given in the Data Appendix.

estimated coefficients, no variables are statistically significant at the conventional level.[32] Overall, the coefficients in the lower panel of Table 5 are somewhat more significant than those in the upper panel, and in this respect our results are similar to those in Kose *et al.* (2003). A major reason for the poor estimation results might be the poor quality of the available regional data.

In summary, the results of this subsection show that there is considerable heterogeneity in the economic structures of euro area regions such that even symmetric impulses such as a monetary policy shock can have heterogeneous effects.

---

[32] Similarly, Kose *et al.* (2003) only get indicative results when regressing the fraction of variance of output, consumption and investment attributable to a world, regional or country-specific factor on a variety of country characteristics.

5.4. The effects of the EMU

The introduction of the euro in 1999 and the associated delegation of monetary policy to the ECB represent major institutional changes that can have a large impact on inflation dynamics. In particular, we would expect a larger area wide component for inflation and a decline in dispersion in the long run. However, since the formation of a European Monetary Union was to some extent expected since the early 1990s, the convergence process has been a continuous, slowly evolving process such that there could be no major changes in regional inflation dynamics after the formal introduction of the euro.

A nice feature of the econometric model and estimation procedure we adopt is that it requires a large longitudinal dimension rather than a large temporal dimension. Therefore, we can split our already short sample into two subsamples, and evaluate whether the figures before and after 1999 differ. In particular, we consider the samples 1996–1998 and 1999–2004.

The main result is that the fraction of variance of regional inflation rates explained by the first area wide factor remains constant over 1999–2004 in comparison with 1996–1998, at about 54%. In each country, the role of the national factor is also fairly stable over the two subsamples. On this basis, we believe that our full sample results are reliable and not affected by major structural breaks.

6. HAVE NATIONAL BORDERS BECOME LESS IMPORTANT FOR INFLATION DYNAMICS?

The analysis we have conducted so far assumed that the dynamics of regional inflation rates is caused by an area wide, a national and a region-specific factor. However, in Sections 3 and 4 we have seen that the economic characteristics of a region play a relevant role for long-lasting inflation differentials. Hence, it could be that they are also relevant to shape inflation dynamics. To assess whether this is the case, now we investigate whether grouping the regions on the basis of other criteria than nationality could increase the homogeneity of the resulting aggregates, enhancing the relevance of the common component of inflation in a given group and, more generally, highlighting different schemes of inflation dynamics. For example, regions that experience high wage or unit labour cost growth or tight labour market conditions (low unemployment) might experience high inflation rates. The same can be expected when the prices of other input factors such as renting costs experience relatively high growth. From an economic point of view, it is also interesting to consider whether higher inflation persistence is associated with a larger role of the common component of inflation or with a more important regional component. Moreover, regions that grow faster or have lower per capita income can be expected to experience higher increases in prices and higher inflation.

Therefore, we will now repeat our analysis of the determinants of regional inflation variation by grouping the regions on the basis of either their average unemployment

Table 6. Proportion of total variance explained by first principal component when inflation rates are grouped by economic variables

		U		DW		DULC	
	National	Low	High	Low	High	Low	High
Variance explained	34.17	20.37	16.56	18.64	24.16	17.76	16.51

	DP_HOUS		AR1		Y_95		DY	
	Low	High	Low	High	Low	High	Low	High
Variance explained	22.55	16.62	16.55	16.47	16.59	23.17	21.01	20.92

Note: Low (High) indicates the group of one-third of regions characterized by the lowest (highest) values of the economic variable used for the grouping. The economic variables used for the groupings are: average unemployment rate (U), wage growth rate (DW), unit labour cost growth rate ($DULC$), growth rate of the COICOP index (DP_HOUS), degree of inflation persistence ($AR1$), per capita income in 1995 (Y_95) and growth rate over the period 1995–2001 (DY).

rates, wage growth rates, unit labour cost growth rates, housing cost growth rates, their degree of inflation persistence, their growth rate over the period 1995–2001 and their per capita income in 1995. For each category, we will consider six groups, containing each one-sixth of the regions.

In Table 6 we present the results of the principal component analysis for groupings based on the variables discussed above. For each variable, we report the proportion of variance that is explained by the first common component, focusing on the groups with the lowest and highest values for the economic variable used for the grouping. As a comparison, the average proportion of the variance that is explained by the national factors is about 34%, with the lowest value of 26.88% for Spain and the highest value of 48.8% for Finland.

The main feature that emerges from Table 6 is that the fraction of variance of the inflation rates in each group explained by the first factor is lower than the corresponding figure based on the national grouping. This implies that national features of a region, related, for example, to the institutional and social environment, generate more commonality than the economic features we consider.

It is also worth mentioning that the economic groups with the highest commonality are those characterized by low wage changes, unemployment, and low growth in unit labour costs.

In summary, the results we have obtained with the national grouping of the regions appear to be robust also to changes in the grouping criterion. In particular, aggregating the regions on the basis of various economic characteristics does not increase the commonality of the variation in their inflation rates or the explanatory power of the group specific factors. Therefore, these regional characteristics appear to be more related to the level of inflation than to its variation. These findings imply that, despite strong political efforts to create a Europe of regions and despite delegation of powers to the European Commission and Parliament, national policies still play an important role for the dynamics of prices in their country.

7. WHAT ARE THE DIFFERENCES BETWEEN THE EURO AREA AND THE UNITED STATES?

To benchmark and compare our results with a long established common currency area, we have examined disaggregate inflation series for the United States. Unfortunately, consumer price data at the state level are not available over a comparable period, and those for the main metropolitan areas also present several problems of availability. We will base our analysis on a bi-monthly dataset for the same sample as for the euro area regions, 1995–2004, for eleven metropolitan areas, see the Data Appendix for details.

Average inflation over the period 1995–2004 is somewhat higher for US areas than for euro area regions, 2.50% compared to 2.18%. However, the major difference between the euro area and the United States is in the measured degree of inflation dispersion, which is about twice as large in the euro area than in the United States. This suggests that the degree of segmentation across European regional markets is considerably larger than that across US regional markets. National policies are the candidate variable to explain the larger degree of heterogeneity across euro area inflation rates, since we have seen that a national component is still very relevant to explain regional inflation in the euro area. However, the euro area data set contains a much larger number of regions, which can also contribute to the higher dispersion.

For the United States, the first principal component explains a large fraction of the variance of the metropolitan areas inflation rates, 57% versus 48% for the euro area. Therefore, we will assume that one common factor is driving all the metropolitan areas' inflation rates, and estimate it by the first principal component of the data.

When the estimated factor is used to explain the inflation dynamics in the different US areas, it is strongly significant, the average adjusted R^2 is about 0.72, and there are basically no signs of misspecification of the models, which provides support for the factor model representation of disaggregate inflation dynamics also for the United States.

In summary, with respect to the euro area, in the United States there is less dispersion in inflation rates, but this is likely due to the smaller sample available, and only a rather small increase of about 10% in the relevance of the common area wide component. Therefore, overall, the results for the euro area and for the United States are fairly similar.

8. CONCLUSIONS

In this paper we analyse regional inflation dynamics in the euro area using a novel disaggregate dataset. It contains CPI data at a regional level within euro area countries, on a monthly frequency, covering two-thirds of the euro area in terms of economic activity. The additional regional dimension of our data allows us to gain useful insights which cannot be obtained in this form from national data only. Only by using regional data we are, for example, able to identify the empirical importance of the national factor for within country inflation rates. Moreover, the regional perspective enables us to evaluate the relative importance of national borders versus region-specific economic characteristics for within euro area inflation dynamics.

We use this regional dataset to provide insights into a variety of issues and assess whether the existing inflation differentials within the euro area have potentially welfare-damaging implications. Therefore, we provide results of interest both from an economic and a policy point of view.

In the first part of the paper, we show that there exist large and long-lasting differences in inflation rates across European regions, implying changes in the real exchange rate across individual regions of up to 25% over our sample period from 1996 to 2004. Since inflation differences even of this size and persistence can be part of a benign adjustment process, particularly if they reflect convergence in per-capita income across regions, we then examine the empirical significance of a variety of factors that can be made responsible for the observed inflation differences. Our results indicate that these differences are not related to business cycle or income growth dynamics. Somewhat surprisingly, neither our labour market related variables nor our proxy variables for the Balassa–Samuelson effect turn out to be significant in our regression analysis. Rather, our results suggest that the observed differences in regional inflation rates are primarily caused by increases in non-wage input factor prices, which do not reflect market-driven forces, and by limited competition in goods markets. From a normative point of view these results imply that the observed inflation differentials are associated with welfare losses. Whereas the first mechanism negatively impacts the com-petitiveness of high-inflation regions, the second one can give rise to relative price distortions due to nominal price rigidities. A welfare improving policy should aim at increasing competition in both non-wage factor and goods markets. We also find that sectoral specialization plays a significant role for the existence of regional inflation differentials.

Therefore, the key conclusion of the first part of the paper is that the main sources of long-lasting inflation differentials within the euro area are factor market distortions and other structural characteristics, which implies that inflation differentials within the euro area are welfare affecting and should be addressed by policy-makers. Moreover, in the absence of policy interventions, there should be an increase in inflation dispersion across regions in response to external shocks, such as the pronounced changes in the value of the euro or in the price of energy as recently observed in the euro area.

In the second part of our paper we analyse the role that area-wide, national and purely regional factors play for inflation variations. This is important because those factors may originate in policy-making at the three levels, and because variations in inflation rates are harmful for economic welfare in the presence of the empirically well documented rigidities in nominal goods prices. We find that about 50% of regional inflation variation is explained by the common area-wide factor, which can be related to the common monetary policy in the euro area and to external developments, such as changes in oil prices, and the euro exchange rate. Our results further suggest that national policies still have a very significant impact on within-country inflation variations despite the constraints imposed on fiscal policy by the Growth and Stability Pact and the delegation of the conduct of monetary policy to the European Central Bank. The national factor explains on average 32% of regional inflation rate variance. This large contribution is very likely due to nationally determined fiscal policies and labour market institutions. These results on the sources of inflation variations over time imply that both a stability-oriented area-wide monetary policy and national fiscal policy can considerably contribute to a reduction in welfare-affecting inflation volatility.

The importance of the national factor is confirmed when we compare its role with that of other economic characteristics. In particular, we find that being within the national borders of a particular country is still more important for regional inflation developments than economic characteristics such as the unemployment rate, wage changes, unit labour cost changes, or output growth. We also show that the relative importance of area wide and national factors for explaining regional inflation developments is heterogeneous across euro area regions. This result implies that regional inflation rates respond differently even to a common area wide or common national impulse.

Our findings do not differ substantially before and after the formal introduction of the euro in 1999, even though the average level of regional inflation has changed. This indicates a limited effect of EMU on inflation dynamics from the mid 1990s onwards. However, both the average level of inflation and the regional dispersion were substantially higher in the early 1990s, suggesting that convergence has largely taken place before the mid 1990s.

Finally, to benchmark and compare the results for the euro area with a long established common currency area, we examined disaggregate inflation series for the United States. Apart from smaller dispersion in the United States, which could be a smaller sample problem, the results regarding heterogeneity and co-movements are similar to those for the euro area.

Discussion

Klaus Adam
Mannheim University and CEPR

The paper by Beck, Hubrich and Marcellino is a welcome study of a new data set on regional inflation rates. The data covers approximately two-thirds of the euro area (in terms of GDP), starts 4 years prior to the creation of the euro and extends 6 years beyond its creation. One of the most compelling findings of this paper is that the introduction of the euro area seems to have had no discernible impact on regional inflation dynamics, both in terms of the cross-regional dispersion of inflation over time and in terms of the cyclical behaviour of regional inflation rates along the time series dimension. This suggests that the concerns that have been expressed prior to the creation of the euro area regarding the loss of the nominal exchange rate as a potentially important adjustment mechanism fail to receive support in the data to date.

The analysis of the data set proceeds in two meaningful steps. The first part of the analysis documents differences in regional-specific inflation means and makes an effort to link these differences to a number of regional economic indicators that proxy for a variety of economic factors giving rise to inflation differentials. Some of these factors are associated with benign and desirable relative price adjustments across regions, while others point more towards potential inefficiencies in product or factor markets. The main conclusion drawn from this part of the analysis is that it is unlikely that the observed mean inflation differences are the outcome of benign relative price adjustments. Instead, they rather reflect inefficiencies in non-labour factor input markets, while labour market factors (unemployment, wage growth) show surprisingly little explanatory power for the regional variation of mean inflation. While I generally agree with the conclusions that are reached, the interpretation of inflation differentials as non-benign and indicative of inefficiencies in non-labour factor input markets appears a bit stretched. I will suggest below that a possibly more plausible interpretation of the evidence is that the long-lasting inflation differentials are mainly the result of benign relative price adjustments in non-traded goods.

In a second step, the authors provide a comprehensive analysis of the time series behaviour of regional inflation rates (in deviation from their region-specific means) and decompose it into an aggregate, a national and a region specific 'factor'. The paper documents that prior to and after the introduction of the euro, there is strong area wide comovement in regional inflation dynamics explaining roughly 50% of the time series variability at the regional level. Another 30% of regional inflation variability is attributable to a common national factor and only about 20% of regional inflation variability is region specific. This is an intriguing set of facts and highlights that a substantial part of regional inflation might be attributed to some national component.

Which relative prices to look at?

A main task of the paper is to assess whether the observed inflation differentials can be attributed to benign relative price adjustments or whether they are due to inefficiencies or frictions in factor or product markets that should be addressed by policy. To assess this issue the paper studies differentials in CPI inflation across regions. In a currency union, inflation differentials give rise to movements in the real exchange rate, so that the paper effectively studies regional real exchange rate movements in the euro area. One issue with the real exchange rate is that it is simply not an economically relevant relative price because the CPI contains a large share of non-traded components, including housing and local service inputs. Ideally, one should thus focus on relative price adjustment in traded goods to be able to assess whether or not relative price adjustments across regions are efficient. Relative price adjustments for traded goods could potentially point towards inefficient relative price movements. Yet, even when narrowing down the analysis to traded goods, this conclusion is not foolproof: since the initial relative price of traded goods may be distorted as well, inflation differentials in traded goods can be benign to the extent that they reduce these initial price distortions. It is important to keep these issues in mind, even if data availability appears to require using CPI data to determine the causes and desirability of regional inflation dispersion.

A crude first look at the inflation data

To illustrate the concerns mentioned above let us compare the country in the sample with the highest average inflation rate (Spain) to the one with the lowest mean inflation (Germany). Looking at the Harmonized Index of Consumer Prices (HICP) for all items, see Table 7, reveals a real exchange rate appreciation for Spain of 16% over the considered sample period. Decomposing this real exchange rate movement into the goods and services category reveals, however, that the real exchange rate appreciation in services, which tend to be less tradable than goods, was 24% and thus twice as high as that for the goods category. This suggests that a large part of the real exchange rate appreciation occurred in a sector with relatively more non-tradable components. Indeed, for housing services – a particularly non-tradable service – the Spanish appreciation was 31% and thus even larger than for the services category at large. Such an appreciation of the relative price of Spanish homes may have many economically plausible reasons, including increased demand from the Spanish population for a second home due to rising incomes, or the increased popularity of Spain as a holiday resort among foreigners. The relative price adjustments induced by such demand shifts are hardly the result of inefficiencies in the national (housing) markets.

This is not to say that there was no Spanish appreciation in traded goods prices at all. Table 7 reveals that within the goods category the price of industrial goods – a relatively more tradable goods subcomponent – still appreciated by 9% versus Germany. This is considerably less than the 16% appreciation recorded for all items and may not even be a sign of inefficiency because industrial goods likely contain a sizeable non-tradable service component as well (e.g. retail services). Moreover, one cannot rule out the possibility that Spanish industrial goods were underpriced by roughly 10% in 1996.

Table 7. Cumulative HICP inflation (1996(1)–2004(10))

	Germany	Spain	Differential
All items	+12%	+28%	+16%
Goods	+11%	+23%	+12%
– Food	+11%	+29%	+18%
– Industrial goods	+11%	+20%	+9%
Services	+14%	+38%	+24%
– Housing	+14%	+45%	+31%

Non-traded goods are significant drivers of inflation differentials

When it comes to relating the cross-regional variation in mean inflation rates to a number of economic variables, the paper documents that the change in the COICOP 04 price index (capturing the price of housing, water, electricity, gas and other fuels) is by far the most significant explanatory variable for regional variation in mean inflation (see Table 3). For Germany, the expenditure weight for housing and housing repairs in the COICOP 04 index is close to 70% (as of 2005). Other non-tradable services account roughly for an additional 10% in the index, so its tradable component (mainly fuels and electricity) is just below 20%. This index is thus largely an index of housing costs. Given the importance of housing in the overall price index, it is hardly surprising that it captures well regional variation in inflation. Moreover, this finding is just another indication that regional inflation differentials are well associated with relative price changes in non-tradable goods. In the light of this evidence, the call for national policies that aim at reducing regional inflation differential is slightly surprising. It cannot be welfare improving if national policies interfere with the relative price adjustment between non-tradable and tradable goods and services for the sake of stabilizing the real exchange rate between regions.

Overall, the picture emerging from the paper is rather reassuring: variation in regional inflation rates appears to be associated with fluctuations in non-tradable goods and there is nothing wrong with that. Of course, whether and to what extent goods and services are tradable is partly endogenous to the policy framework and it is possible that policies that aim at increasing the tradability of goods and services may improve welfare, as well as reduce real exchange rate fluctuations.

Panel discussion

Kevin O' Rourke argued that the finding that the Balassa–Samuelson effect does not play a role in terms of income levels does not necessarily dismiss the effect itself: it might have been simply absorbed by the services component, housing prices, and other control variables. Julia Darby suggested looking at inflation differentials across sectors for countries. She also noticed that disaggregating by type of goods and considering the role not only of housing but also of energy and food prices may be more relevant than disaggregating by region. Philippe Martin asked whether price index baskets are the same in different regions.

DATA APPENDIX

Regional euro area data

- *U*: Unemployment rates by sex and age, at NUTS level 3 (%, 15 years and over, total). Reported number is average unemployment of the years 1999 to 2003. Source: Eurostat.
- *DW*: Year-on-year changes in quarterly monthly wages from national statistical offices (Missing data: Spain (data start in 1996, no data for ES Ceuta), Portugal (data start in 1998), Finland (no data), Austria (data start in 1996), Italy (no data)). Reported number is average year-on-year wage change monthly of the years 1995 to 2004. Sources: National statistical offices.
- *DP_HOUS*: Year-on-year change in COICOP index 'Housing, water, electricity, gas and other fuels'. Reported value is the average between January 1996 and October 2004 (Austrian data start in 2001, Italian data start in 1997). Sources: National statistical offices.
- *DULC*: Change in unit labour costs. Unit labour costs are computed as the growth rate of the ratio: compensation per employee in current prices divided by GDP in current prices per total employment. Source: Eurostat.
- *DENS_D*: Number of local units, NACE D, (Manufacturing)/Total population. Reference year: 2003. Source: Eurostat.
- *DENS_G*: Number of local units, NACE G, (Wholesale and retail trade; repair of motor vehicles, motorcycles and personal and household goods)/Total population. Reference year: 2003. Source: Eurostat.
- *AGR*: Gross value added at basic prices at NUTS level 2 – Agriculture, hunting, forestry and fishing (NACE A-B, millions of euro (from 1.1.1999)/millions of ECU (up to 31.12.1998)/Gross value added at basic prices at NUTS level 2 – All NACE branches – Total (excluding extra-territorial organizations and bodies, millions of euro (from 1.1.1999)/millions of ECU (up to 31.12.1998). Reported number is average between 1995 and 2003. Source: Eurostat.
- *IND*: Gross value added at basic prices at NUTS level 2 – Industry (NACE C–F, millions of euro (from 1.1.1999)/millions of ECU (up to 31.12.1998))/Gross value added at basic prices at NUTS level 2 – All NACE branches – Total (excluding extra-territorial organizations and bodies, millions of euro (from 1.1.1999))/millions of ECU (up to 31.12.1998). Reported number is average between 1995 and 2003. Source: Eurostat.

- *SERV*: Gross value added at basic prices at NUTS level 2 – Services (NACE G-P, millions of euro (from 1.1.1999)/millions of ECU (up to 31.12.1998))/Gross value added at basic prices at NUTS level 2 – All NACE branches – Total (excluding extra-territorial organizations and bodies, millions of euro (from 1.1.1999)/millions of ECU (up to 31.12.1998)). Reported number is average between 1995 and 2003. Source: Eurostat.
- *AR1*: Estimate of AR(1) coefficient of regional inflation rate time series (Estimated model: $\pi_{ijt} = a + \pi_{ijt-1} + \varepsilon_{ijt}$). Source: Own computation.
- *Y_95*: (Log of) Gross domestic product (GDP) at current market prices at NUTS level 2, purchasing power parities per inhabitant. Reference year: 1995. Source: Eurostat.
- ΔY: Log change of gross domestic product (GDP) at current market prices at NUTS level 2, purchasing power parities per inhabitant between 2003 and 1995. Source: Eurostat.
- *AW1*: Squared loadings of first area-wide PC ($\lambda^2_{ij,1}$). Source: Own computation.

Regional US data

US consumer price index data: Monthly CPI data are available for Chicago–Gary–Kenosha, New York–Northern New Jersey–Long Island, and Los Angeles–Riverside–Orange County. For Detroit–Ann Arbor–Flint, Houston–Galveston–Brazoria, Miami–Fort Lauderdale, Philadelphia–Wilmington–Atlantic City, and San Francisco–Oakland–San Jose CPI data are released in even-numbered months. For Boston–Brockton–Nashua, Cleveland–Akron, and Dallas–Fort Worth data are available in odd-numbered months. For US areas for which data are available monthly only even month data are used. Also, at the beginning of the sample, data for Philadelphia–Wilmington–Atlantic City and San Francisco–Oakland–San Jose were monthly, but switched to even month. For Dallas–Fort Worth data were released in even-numbered months at the beginning of the sample, while the reverse is true for Miami–Fort Lauderdale.

REFERENCES

Alberola, E. and J.M. Marques (2000). 'On the relevance and nature of regional inflation differentials: The case of Spain', Banco de Espana, Servicio de Estudios n. 9913.
Altissimo, F., P. Benigno and D.R. Palenzuela (2005). 'Long-run determinants of inflation differentials in a monetary union', Working Paper 11473, National Bureau of Economic Research.
Altissimo, F., M. Ehrmann and F. Smets (2006). 'Inflation persistence and pricesetting behaviour in the euro area: A summary of the IPN evidence', Occasional Paper Series 46, European Central Bank.
Bai, J. (2003). 'Inference on factor models of large dimensions', *Econometrica*, 71(1), 135–72.
Bai, J. and S. Ng (2002). 'Determining the number of factors in approximate factor models', *Econometrica* 70(1), 191–221.
— (2004). 'The PANIC attack on unit roots and cointegration', *Econometrica*, 72(4), 1124–77.

Banerjee, A., M. Marcellino and C. Osbat (2005). 'Testing for PPP: Should we use panel methods?', *Empirical Economics*, 30, 77–91.

Beck, G. and A.A. Weber (2005). 'Price stability, inflation convergence and diversity in EMU: Does one size fit all?', Goethe University Frankfurt, mimeo.

Beck, G., K. Hubrich and M. Marcellino (2006). 'Regional inflation dynamics within and across euro area countries and a comparison with the US', ECB Working Paper No. 681.

Balassa, B. (1964). 'The purchasing power parity doctrine: A reappraisal', *Journal of Political Economy*, 72, 584–96.

Benigno, P. (2004). 'Optimal monetary policy in a currency area', *Journal of International Economics*, 63, 293–320.

Bertola, G. (2006). 'Europe's unemployment problems', in M. Artis and F. Nixson (eds.), *Economics of the European Union*, 3rd edn, Oxford University Press, Oxford.

Blanchard, O.J. and L.F. Katz (1992). 'Regional evolutions', *Brookings Papers on Economic Activity*, I, 1–61.

Calmfors, L. and J. Driffill (1988). 'Bargaining structure, corporatism, and macroeconomic performance', *Economic Policy*, 6, 13–61.

Ciccarelli, M. and B. Mojon (2005). 'Global inflation', Working Paper 537, European Central Bank.

Clark, T.E. (1998). 'Employment fluctuations in the US regions and industries: The roles of national, region-specific and industry-specific shocks', *Journal of Labor Economics*, 16(1), 202–29.

Decressin, J. and A. Fatás (1995). 'Regional labor market dynamics in Europe', *European Economic Review*, 39, 1627–55.

Dhyne, E., L.J. Alvarez, H. Le Bihan, G. Veronese, D. Dias, J. Hoffmann, N. Jonker, P. Lünnemann, F. Rumler and J. Vilmunen (2006). 'Price changes in the euro area and the United States: Some facts from individual consumer price data', *Journal of Economic Perspectives*, 20(2), 171–92.

Duarte, M. and A.L. Wolman (2008). 'Fiscal policy and regional inflation in a currency union', *Journal of International Economics*, 74(2), 384–401.

Engel, C. and J.H. Rogers (2004). 'Euro's price dispersion', *Economic Policy*, July, 347–84.

European Central Bank (2003). 'Inflation differentials in the euro area: Potential causes and policy implications'.

— (2005). 'Monetary policy and inflation differentials in a heterogenous currency area', ECB Monthly Bulletin, May, 61–78.

European Commission (2004). 'A new partnership for cohesion convergence competitiveness cooperation', Third Report on Economic and Social Cohesion, February.

Favero, C., M. Marcellino and F. Neglia (2005). 'Principal components at work: The empirical analysis of monetary policy with large data sets', *Journal of Applied Econometrics*, 20, 603–20.

Forni, M., D. Giannone, M. Lippi and L. Reichlin (2005a). 'Opening the black box: Structural factor models with large cross-sections', manuscript.

Forni, M., M. Hallin, M. Lippi, and L. Reichlin (2000). 'The generalized factor model: Identification and estimation', *Review of Economics and Statistics*, 82(4), 540–54.

Forni, M., M. Hallin, M. Lippi and L. Reichlin (2005b). 'The generalized factor model: One-sided estimation and forecasting', *Journal of the American Statistical Association*, 100, 830–40.

Forni, M. and L. Reichlin (2001). 'Federal policies and local economies: Europe and the US', *European Economic Review*, 45, 109–34.

Frankel, J. and A.K. Rose (2002). 'An estimate of the effect of common currencies on trade and income', *The Quarterly Journal of Economics*, 117(2), 437–66.

Heinz, F.F. and M. Ward-Warmedinger (2006), 'Cross-border labour mobility within an enlarged EU', ECB Occasional Paper Series No. 52, October.

Honohan, P. and P.R. Lane (2003), 'Divergent inflation rates in EMU', *Economic Policy*, 18, 357–94.

Jimeno, J.F. and S. Bentolila (1998). 'Regional unemployment persistence (Spain, 1976–1994)', *Labour Economics*, 5, 25–51.

Kapetanios, G. and M. Marcellino (2004). 'A comparison of estimation methods for dynamic factor models of large dimension', mimeo, Queen Mary.

Kose, M.A., C. Otrok and C.H. Whiteman (2003). 'International business cycles: World, region and country-specific factors', *American Economic Review*, 93(4), 1216–39.

Krugman, P. (1993). 'Lessons of Massachusetts for EMU', in F. Torres and F. Giavazzi (eds.), *Adjustment and Growth in the European Monetary Union*, Cambridge University Press, Cambridge, UK, pp. 241–61, as reprinted in De Grauwe (2001), *The Political Economy of Monetary Union*, Edward Publishing Limited, Cheltenham.

Krugman, P. and A.J. Venables (1996). 'Integration, specialization, and adjustment', *European Economic Review*, 40, 959–67.

Layard, R., S. Nickell and R. Jackman (2005). *Unemployment. Macroeconomic Performance and the Labour Market*, 2nd edn, Oxford University Press, Oxford.

Overman, H. and D. Puga (2002). 'Unemployment clusters across Europe's regions and countries', *Economic Policy*, 117–47.

Quah, D.T. (1996). 'Regional convergence clusters across Europe', *European Economic Review*, 40, 951–58.

Rogers, J. (2007). 'Monetary union, price level convergence, and inflation: How close is Europe to the USA?', *Journal of Monetary Economics*, 54(3), 785–96.

Rose, A. and C. Engel (2002), 'Currency unions and international integration', *Journal of Money, Credit, and Banking*, 34(4), 1067–89.

Samuelson, P.A. (1964) 'Theoretical notes on trade problems', *Review of Economics and Statistics* 46, 145–54.

Stock, J.H. and M.W. Watson (2002a). 'Forecasting using principal components from a large number of predictors', *Journal of the American Statistical Association*, 97, 1167–79.

— (2002b). 'Macroeconomic forecasting using diffusion indices', *Journal of Business and Economic Statistics*, 20(2), 147–62.

Woodford, M. (2003). *Interest and Prices: Foundations of a Theory of Monetary Policy*, Princeton University Press, Princeton, NJ.

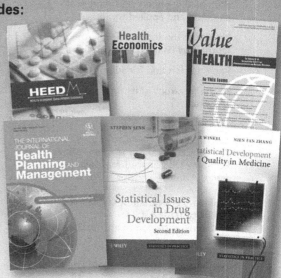

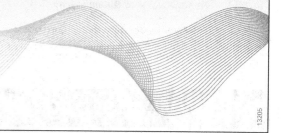

The ECONOMIC JOURNAL

THE JOURNAL OF THE ECONOMIC SOCIETY

- High quality papers on theoretical, empirical and applied topics

- Ranked in the top 5 general economics journals by ISI in 2007 and 2006

- Rapid turnaround for submitting authors

- At the forefront of its field for over 115 years

HIGHLIGHTS IN 2009

- **The Effects of Labour Market Policies in an Economy with an Informal Sector**
  James Albrecht, Lucas Navarro & Susan Vroman

- **Monetary Policy, Endogenous Inattention, and the Volatility Trade-off**
  William Branch, John Carlson, George Evans & Bruce McGough

- **Heritage and Agglomeration: The Akron Tire Cluster Revisited**
  Guido Buenstorf & Steven Klepper

- **Exchange and Specialisation as a Discovery Process**
  Sean Crockett, Vernon L. Smith & Bart J. Wilson

- **Measuring Financial Asset Return and Volatility Spillovers, with Application to Global Equity Markets**
  Francis X. Diebold & Kamil Yilmaz

- **The Empirics of International Currencies: Historical Evidence**
  Marc Flandreau & Clemens Jobst

Editors

Antonio Ciccone,
Universitat Pompeu Fabra

Steve Machin, (Features Editor)
University College London

David Myatt
University of Oxford

Jörn-Steffen Pischke,
London School of Economics

Andrew Scott, (Managing Editor)
London Business School

WILEY-BLACKWELL

www.res.org.uk/economicjournal